THE MAYFLOWER DESCENDANT

A Quarterly Magazine of
Pilgrim Genealogy and History

Volume I
1899

Massachusetts Society
of
Mayflower Descendants

HERITAGE BOOKS
2008

HERITAGE BOOKS
AN IMPRINT OF HERITAGE BOOKS, INC.

Books, CDs, and more—Worldwide

For our listing of thousands of titles see our website at
www.HeritageBooks.com

A Facsimile Reprint
Published 2008 by
HERITAGE BOOKS, INC.
Publishing Division
100 Railroad Ave. #104
Westminster, Maryland 21157

Originally published by the
Massachusetts Society of Mayflower Descendants
Boston, Massachusetts
1899

Editor: *George Ernest Bowman*
623 Tremont Building, Boston

Committee on Publication:
Morton Dexter   Winslow Warren
Charles Augustus Hopkins   Frederick Wesley Parker
George Ernest Bowman

— Publisher's Notice —
In reprints such as this, it is often not possible to remove blemishes from the original. We feel the contents of this book warrant its reissue despite these blemishes and hope you will agree and read it with pleasure.

International Standard Book Numbers
Paperbound: 978-0-7884-4856-0
Clothbound: 978-0-7884-0053-7

INDEX OF SUBJECTS.

Adams, John, Inventory of, 157
Allyn, Thomas and Winnefred, Deed of, 139
Ancestors of the Pilgrims, 61
Anne, The, 62, 149, 151, 153, 229
Answer to Cobb Query, 256

Bassett, William, Deed of, 96
Beachampe, John, Estate of, 215-217
    Letter of, 218
Bible Records, Photographs of, 34, 62, 89
Births, Marriages and Deaths:
  Middleborough, Mass., 219
  Plymouth, 139, 206
  Plympton, Mass., 174, 245
  Scituate, Mass., 42, 106, 164, 233
Book Notes, 64, 128, 192
Bradford's History of Plimoth Plantation, 126
Bradford Meerstead, 191, 255
Bradford's Passenger List, The Date of, 161
Brewster Book, 1, 71, 168, 193
Brewster, widow, Deed of, 137
Brooks—Winslow Query, 192
Brown—Moses Query, 64
Brown, Peter, Inventory of, 79
Buck—Cushman Query, 192

Cattle, Division of, in 1627, 148
Chandler Query, 128
Cobb, Answer to Query, 256
Cobb—Standish Query, 128
Colonial Research Fund, 254
Committees Appointed, 48, 121, 189
Compact, The Mayflower, 77
Connecticut Society, 53, 122, 187, 251
Coombs—Cushman Query, 255
Corwin, Elizabeth (Winslow) (Brooks), 238
Cushman Query, 255
Cushman—Buck Query, 192
Cushman—Coombs Query, 255

Deeds, Grantors and Grantees:
  Allyn, Thomas and Winnefred, 139
  Basset, William, 96
  Beachampe, John, 215-217
  Brewster, widow, 137
  Chambers, Thomas, 95
  Churchill, John, 134
  Coleman, Joseph, 133
  Collamore, Peter, 91
  Eaton, Samuel, 137
  Foster, Richard, 98
  Fuller, Matthew, 137
    Samuel, 137
    Samuel and Jane, 91
  Howell, Thomas, estate of, 213
  Howland, Henry, 97
  Little, Thomas and Ann, 98
  Masterson, Nathaniel, 134, 136
  Merrick, William, 135
  Mitchell, Experience, 97, 214
  Morton, Nathaniel, 214
  Partridge, George, 135
    Ralph, 96
  Pope, Thomas, 132
  Reyner, John, 96, 214
  Richards, William, 93, 95
  Robinson, Thomas and Silence, 93
  Shaw, Joseph, 93, 95
  Shreeve, Thomas and Martha, 214
  Smith, Ralph and Mary, 136

Deeds cont'd. } Waterman, Robert, 213
  Weston, Edmund, executor, 213
  White, Gowin, 95
    Peregrine, 96
  Winter, Christopher, 133
    John, 136
Descendant of 22 Mayflower Passengers, 63
Diary of Jabez Fitch, Jr., 36, 100, 178, 240
District of Columbia Society, 48, 60, 124, 189, 253
Division of Cattle in 1627, 148
Division of Land, 227
Donations to Libraries, 49, 54, 58, 61, 114, 123, 183, 189, 248, 251-253

Eaton, Francis, Inventory of, 197
  Query, 128
  Samuel, Deed of, 137

Fallowell, Jonathan, Indenture of, 131
Foreign Research Fund, 125, 190, 255
Fortune, The, 2, 62, 89
Fuller, Query, 63
  Samuel, Will of, 24
  Samuel and Jane, Deed of, 91

Godbertson, Godbert, Inventory of, 154

Harding, Martha, Inventory of, 82
Hartford Bible, 126
Hopkins, Gyles, Will of, 110
Howell, Thomas, estate of, Deed of, 213
Howland, Henry, Deed of, 97

Illinois Society, 48, 57, 123, 187, 252
Illustrations:
  Brewster Book, facing pp. 1, 193
  Paul Prince Bible, facing p. 34
  John Taylor Bible, facing p. 89
  Peregrine White's Will, facing p. 129
  Mary (Chilton) Winslow's Will, facing p. 65
Indentures:
  Fallowell, Jonathan, 131
  Soule, Mary, 214
Inventories, see Wills and Inventories

Jacob, The, 149, 150, 152

Lanckford, Richard, Inventory of, 83
Little, Thomas and Ann, Deed of, 98
Little James, The, 62

Massachusetts Society, 4, 5, 37, 47, 61-63, 89, 113, 124, 125, 182, 191, 248, 254
Masterson, Nathaniel, Deeds of, 134, 136
Mayflower, The, 2, 20, 62
  Ascendants, 126
  Compact, 77
  Genealogies, 124, 191, 254
  Passengers, Bradford's List of, 9
  Relics, 127
Members elected, 50, 52, 55, 56, 58, 60, 61, 115, 121-124, 183, 186-189, 249, 251-253
Merrick, William, Deed of, 135
Middleborough, Mass., Births, Marriages and Deaths, 219
Morton, Nathaniel, Deed of, 214
Moses—Brown Query, 64
Mullins, William, Will of, 230

iii

Index of Subjects.

New York Society, 51, 121, 186, 251

Officers elected, 48, 51, 54, 56, 57, 59, 60, 123
Ohio Society, 48, 59, 123, 188, 253
Old Style and New Style Dating, 17

Paul Prince Bible, 34
Pedigree Papers, Preparation of, 125
Pennsylvania Society, 56, 122, 187, 252
Pilgrim Anniversaries, 86
Pilgrim Notes and Queries, 61, 124, 190, 254
Plymouth Births, Marriages and Deaths, 139, 206
Plymouth Colony Deeds, 91, 131, 213
Plymouth Colony Wills and Inventories, 23, 79, 154, 197
Plympton, Mass., Early Records of, 174, 245
Preston, Conn., 255

Queries:
  Brooks—Winslow, 192
  Brown—Moses, 64
  Buck—Cushman, 192
  Chandler, 128
  Cobb—Standish, 128
  Coombs—Cushman, 255
  Cushman, 255
  Cushman—Buck, 192
  Cushman—Coombs, 255
  Eaton, 128
  Fuller, 63
  Fuller—Sirkman, 63
  Moses—Brown, 64
  Ramsdell, 64
  Reed—Thomson, 192
  Richmond—Rogers, 192
  Rogers—Richmond, 192
  Sirkman—Fuller, 63
  Soule, 64
  Standish—Cobb, 128
  Thomson—Reed, 192
  Walker—Warren, 256
  Warren, 128
  Warren—Walker, 256
  Winslow—Brooks, 192

Ramsdell Query, 64

Reed—Thomson Query, 192
Reports from State Societies, 47, 113, 182, 248
Richmond—Rogers Query, 192
Ring, Mary, Will of, 29
  Inventory of, 31
Rogers—Richmond Query, 192

Scituate, Mass., Births, Marriages and Deaths, 42, 106, 164, 233
Sirkman—Fuller Query, 63
Soule, Mary, Indenture of, 214
  Query, 64
Standish—Cobb Query, 128
Starr, Hannah (Brewster), 224
Supplemental Lines Filed, 51, 53, 55, 59, 117, 123, 185, 187, 188, 190, 250, 252, 253

Taylor Bible, The John, 89
Thomson—Reed Query, 192
Thorp, John, Inventory of, 158

Virginia Company, 78

Walker—Warren Query, 256
Warren Query, 128
Warren—Walker Query, 256
White, Peregrine, Will of, 129
Wills and Inventories:
  Adams, John, 157
  Brown, Peter, 79
  Eaton, Francis, 197
  Fuller, Samuel, 24
  Godbertson, Godbert, 154
  Harding, Martha, 82
  Hopkins, Gyles, 110
  Lanckford, Richard, 83
  Mullins, William, 230
  Ring, Mary, 29
  Thorp, John, 158
  White, Peregrine, 129
  Winslow, Mary (Chilton), 65
  Wright, William, 200
Winslow—Brooks Query, 192
Winslow, Mary (Chilton), Will of, 65
  Inventory of, 69
Wright, William, Will of, 200
  Inventory of, 203

1627 1695
1627

Johnathan Brewster was borne at Scrooby in Nottinghamshire the 12th of August 1593

Mary Brewster the wyfe of William Brewster dyed at Plymouth in New England the 17th of Aprill 1627

William Brewster dyed at Plymouth in New England the 10th of Aprill 1644

William Brewster the sonne of Johnathan Brewster borne at Plymouth in New England the 9th of March 1625

Mary Brewster the daughter of Johnathan borne at Plymouth the 16th of Aprill 1627

Johnathan the sonne of Johnathan Brewster borne at Plymouth 17th July 1629

Ruth the daughter of Johnathan borne at Jones River the 3rd of October 1631

The Mayflower Descendant

THE BREWSTER BOOK.

By George Ernest Bowman.

In the summer of 1896 my attention was called to a manuscript in the Boston Public Library, which was said to be a copy of family records entered in " The Brewster Book." An examination of this copy convinced me that, if these were genuine contemporary records, the book was of inestimable value to the student of Pilgrim genealogy and history, and I at once began a search for the original. In March, 1897, I learned that the owner was Mr. Cordilla Walker Fitch, of Morrisville, Vt., and addressed to him a request for permission to make a critical study of the book. A most courteous reply was returned, and in a few days the book was in my care.

It took but a short time to decide that the records were contemporary entries, and that much would be added to our knowledge of the Brewster family; and a great deal of time has been spent in transcribing and studying the entries, all of which will be printed in this magazine, with copious notes.

"The Brewster Book" was a " wast " or blank book of at least 368 pages, strongly bound in dark leather, $7\frac{3}{4}$ inches tall and 6 inches wide. Both covers are detached, but are with the book. Of the original 184 leaves there remain only 122, and one of these is loose, but by good fortune it immediately precedes the first page of what remains. Another loose leaf disappeared but a few years ago.

Six leaves at the beginning and four at the end are missing, and fifty-two have been cut or torn from the body of the book. As paper was scarce in the early days, it is probable that many of these leaves were used for writing letters. Confirmation of this theory is found in a letter to Daniel Wetherell, written on a blank leaf by his brother-in-law, Benjamin [3] Brewster (Jonathan,[2] William[1]). It would be interesting to know why this letter was not cut out and forwarded to Wetherell.

For convenience of reference, the 122 leaves have been numbered as pages 1 to 244 inclusive. Of these pages, 201 contain entries, and 43 are blank. Not one leaf remains whole, the two pages presented in the frontispiece showing about their average condition. The book has been subjected to the action of some liquid, possibly salt water, and the parts affected have become extremely brittle, resulting in a gradual disintegration, which is especially marked at the beginning and the end, a few leaves in the middle being nearly complete.

That this damage occurred before the family records were begun is clearly shown by the fact that, with rare exceptions, these entries do not extend over the badly injured part of the page, and nearly every record is perfect. On the other hand, of the earlier entries not one is complete.

The original ownership of the book is still a matter of doubt, but the earlier entries show conclusively that it belonged to some person interested in colonizing or trading in America, possibly to one of the adventurers.

The first sixty pages contain copies of a commission to Capt. John Mason, and of a license to Thomas Weston; an abstract of the patent of November, 1620; directions for transporting passengers to New England; lists of articles necessary for fitting out a fishing vessel, with the cost of the various items; and extracts from letters sent from New England and from Jamestown, Va. One of these letters was sent back in the *Fortune* in December, 1621, and the fact that all are said to be "from" New England and Virginia is evidence that the copies were made while the book was still in England. Consequently it could not have come in the *Mayflower*.

None of the handwriting has been identified as that of

Elder William Brewster, but there are entries which seem to prove that at the time of his death the book was a part of his estate.

On the fifth of June, 1644, the General Court appointed Jonathan and Love Brewster administrators of their father's estate, and on the eighteenth of the same month Jonathan sold to John Bemon a number of books which had been a part of the Elder's library. This and other sales are recorded in the handwriting of Jonathan on pages 61, 62 and 63, immediately following the entries of the original owner. As these sales are the earliest entries made by Jonathan, it is probable that the book had come into his possession at his father's death.

In the Proceedings of the Massachusetts Historical Society, 2d Series, Vol. V, pp. 37–85, will be found a paper prepared by Rev. Henry M. Dexter, D.D., in which he presents the results of his labors in identifying the books so briefly mentioned in the inventory * of Elder Brewster's library. With the help of this paper the majority of the books sold by Jonathan are shown to have been the property of his father.

Near the end of the book, on pages 217 to 237, both inclusive, is an extract from Campanella's "De Monarchia Hispanica Discursus," the handwriting closely resembling that of the entries on the first sixty pages.

After the marriage of his daughter Mary to John Turner, Senior, the importance of a record of his family seems to have occurred to Jonathan Brewster; and he took the book, turned it upside down, and began such a record on page 216, opposite the extract from Campanella. The half-tone frontispiece shows these two pages (217 and 216) facing each other.

After entering the birth of his daughter Ruth, Jonathan turned over the leaf to continue the record on the next page, and was doubtless surprised to find that he had been anticipated. On page 215 appeared several childish attempts at drawing pictures of horses, and in one corner the entry, "This horse may be rid With out bridel or saddel I have

* This inventory will be printed in an early issue of this magazine.

taugh him to ambel." On the opposite page (214) was another horse, drawn as large as the space would permit, and the inscription, "This was picketore Drone by Wilyem Bruster." These two entries are by different persons, and the second is written with a much coarser quill and blacker ink.

Turning over another leaf, Jonathan completed his record on pages 213 and 212, his last entry being made soon after October, 1651. Since that date the book has passed through many hands before coming into the possession of Mr. Fitch, who has recently become a member of the Society of Mayflower Descendants in Massachusetts. It is worthy of special note, that with the exception of the dates of the death of his great-grandfather, Jabez Fitch, Jr., and the birth and death of his grandmother, every date in Mr. Fitch's pedigree paper, down to and including the birth of his father, was taken from "The Brewster Book." And still more remarkable is the fact that, excepting the three dates noted and the death of his grandfather, all of the entries were made by three persons — Jonathan Brewster, his son Benjamin, and Jabez Fitch, Jr., a great-grandson of Benjamin. Jonathan recorded his own birth (which occurred in 1593), his marriage, and the birth of his son Benjamin. Benjamin recorded his own marriage, the birth of his daughter Mary, her marriage to Samuel Fitch, and the birth of their son Jabez Fitch, Sr. Jabez Fitch, Jr., recorded the marriage of his father, his own birth and marriage, the birth and marriage of his son Cordilla, and the birth in 1798 of his grandson Jabez Deming Fitch, who was the father of the present owner.

Since the time when Jonathan Brewster owned the book, the entries have been of many kinds and by many hands. Some are written with the book right side up, some with it reversed, and others with it held sideways.

In printing the records, the use of capitals, the forms of spelling, and the punctuation of the original have been followed with great care, and the position of the entries, whether right side up or reversed, has been noted.

A number of photographs of the book, each showing two

The Brewster Book. 5

pages, and of the exact size of the original, are for sale by the Massachusetts Society.* The proceeds are to be used to continue the work until every page has been photographed. The leaves will then be treated by the Emery Process, to prevent further disintegration.

As the various family records are of the most importance at this time, they will follow the entries of Jonathan Brewster here presented.

(p. 61.)
Sold to John Bemon in boo(*worn*)
18th of June . 1644

it : Syons plea	0 . 4 . 0 .
it : 2 . Sweds intellegr	0 . 4 . 0 .
it : 1 . remonstrance of King Jaes	0 . 2 . 8 †
it : Taylor : tryall	0 . 1 . 0
it : donam reply agist whitgift	0 . 3 . 6 .
it : 1 . booke : of 4 . serms	0 . 2 . 0 .
it : ministers of lincolne reply	0 . 2 . 0 .
it : 1 . other boke	0 . 2 . 6 .
it : 1 . littell boke	0 . 1 . 0
	1 . 2 . 8

wherof he is to paye
Jones : 12s : to sett of
for my 2 . sones teaching to handle
armes :

"John Beamont" is found in the list, made in August, 1643, of "The Names of all the Males that are able to beare Armes from xvi. Yeares old to 60 Yeares....." He is credited to Scituate.

In the same list "Ralph Joanes" is credited to Plymouth. *Plym. Col. Records (Printed)* VIII : 187, 191.

"Syons plea" is No. 216 in Dr. Dexter's article; "2 . Sweds intellegr" is doubtless Nos. 193 and 209; "ministers of lincolne reply" is No. 195. The other items I have been unable to positively identify.

* See advertising pages.

† Only part of the figure 8 remains, but the total of 1.2.8 shows what must have been written.

(p. 62.)

	s.
(*worn*)isdall oweth me this 28th	
(*worn*)e for bokes : 1644	
(*worn*)comen : 1 . Corin —	4 . 0
(*worn*)g on Hebrews —	3 . 0
(*worn and illegible*) Sermons —	2 . 6 .
	9 . 6

The purchaser in the preceding entry must have been John Tisdale, yeoman, whose name first appears on the Plymouth Colony Records under date of 7 June, 1636. He was granted land at Duxbury on 2 October, 1637. *Plym. Col. Records* (*Printed*) I : 41, 42, 66.

The first book is the one numbered 35 by Dr. Dexter. The second is No. 204.

(*worn*)nd Chandeler had of me the
(*worn*) of June . 1644 . in bookes.

The preceding entry must refer to Edmund Chandler, whose name appears in the first list of freemen, 1633. *Plym. Col. Records* (*Printed*) I : 4.

(p. 63.)

goodman washbone

cases of Conscience —	2 . 6 .
dod Comadents .	3 . 0
Calvin Joshuay —	1 . 6 .
Chistians dayly walke .	1 . 0 .
Rogers esy : 5 —	2 . 6
	10 6 .
Receaved of him, — for haye : —	10 . 0 .
(*illegible*) 1 : bush . ½ . —	4 . 6

soe I owe : 4s :

"goodman washbone" was probably John Washburn, Senior, of Duxbury. "cases of Conscience" is No. 364 in Dr. Dexter's article; "dod Comadents" is either No. 121, No. 176, or No. 208 (three copies of the same book); "Calvin Joshuay," No. 54; "Chistians dayly walke," No. 373; "Rogers esy : 5," No. 287.

(p. 216, *upside down*.)
Johnnathan Brewster was borne
at Scroby in Nottinghamshyre.
the 12th of August 1593 . yeaes

Mary Brewster the wyfe of william
Brewster dyed at Plymouth in new
England the 17th of Aprill 1627 :

William Brewster dyed at Plymouth
in New England the 10th of Aprill
1644.

William Brewster the sonn of Joh(*worn*)
nathan Brewster borne at Plymou(*worn*)
in New England the 9th of March
1625 :

Mary Brewster the daughter of
Johnnathan borne at Plymouth the
16th of Aprill 1627 :

Johnnathan the sonn of Johnnathan
Brewster borne at Plymouth
17th July . 1629.

Ruth the daughter of Johnnathan
borne at Jones River the 3 . of
October 1631.

(p. 213, *upside down*.)
Beniamin Brewster the sonn of
Johnnathan Brewster borne at
Duxborow the 17 . of november
1633.

Elizabeth the daughter of Johnnathan
Brewster borne at Duxborow, the
first of May : 1637.

Grace . the daughter of Johnnathan
borne at Duxborow the first of
November . 1639.

Hanna . the daughter of Johnnathan
borne at Duxborow, the 3ᵈ of
November 1641.

(The following entry was made by Jabez Fitch, Jr., born 1737, great-grandson of Benjamin.)

The above Named Benjamin Brewster died
in Norwich yᵉ 14ᵗʰ of Sept : 1710 & was
Buried on Brewster Plain

(p. 212, *upside down.*)

Johnnathan Brewster marryed
Lucretia Oldam . of Darby .
the 10ᵗʰ Aprill . 1624.
who had children :

{ William
  Mary
  Johnnathan
  Ruth

{ Beniamin
  Elizabeth
  Grace
  Hanna

Mary Brewster marryed John
Turner of Situate the Elder
the 10ᵗʰ November . 1645

With the exception of the death of Benjamin Brewster, on page 213, the entries on pages 216, 213, and 212 to this point were made by Jonathan Brewster, all at one time and with the same ink. The next two entries were also made by Jonathan, but with a different ink and at a later date.

Ruth Brewster maryed to Joh(*worn*)
Pickett the 14ᵗʰ of March
1651 :

William Brewster maryed
Mary Peame of London the
15ᵗʰ October 1651

(To be continued.)

GOVERNOR BRADFORD'S LIST OF THE MAY-FLOWER PASSENGERS.

The names of those which came over first, in ye year .1620. and were (by the blesing of God) the first beginers, and (in a sort) the foundation, of all the plantations, and Colonies, in New England. (And their families.)

.8. & .2. m^r John Carver. Kathrine his wife. Desire Minter; man-servants John Howland Roger Wilder. William Latham, a boy. & a maid servant. & a child y^t was put to him called, Jasper More

.6. m^r William Brewster. Mary his wife, with .2. sons, whose names were Love, & Wrasling. and a boy was put to him called Richard More; and another of his brothers the rest of his childeren were left behind & came over afterwards.

.5. m^r Edward Winslow Elizabeth his wife, & 2. men servants, caled Georg Sowle, and Elias Story; also a litle girle was put to him caled Ellen, the sister of Richard More.

.2 William Bradford, and Dorathy his wife, having but one child, a sone left behind, who came afterward.

.6. m^r Isaack Allerton, and Mary. his wife; with .3. children Bartholmew Remember, & Mary. and a servant boy, John Hooke.

.2. m^r Samuell fuller; and a servant, caled William Butten. His wife was behind & a child, which came afterwards.

.2. John Crakston and his sone John Crakston

.2. Captin Myles Standish and Rose, his wife

.4. m^r Christpher Martin, and his wife; and .2. servants, Salamon prower, and John Langemore

.5. m^r William Mullines, and his wife; and .2. children Joseph, & priscila; and a servant Robart Carter.

.6. m^r William White, and Susana his wife ; and one sone caled resolved, and one borne a ship-bord caled perigriene ; & .2. servants, named William Holbeck, & Edward Thomson

.8. m^r Steven Hopkins, & Elizabeth his wife ; and .2. children, caled Giles, and Constanta a doughter, both by a former wife. And .2. more by this wife, caled Damaris, & Oceanus, the last was borne at sea. And .2. servants, called Edward Doty, and Edward Litster.

.1. m^r Richard Warren, but his wife and children were lefte behind and came afterwards

4 John Billinton, and Elen his wife : and .2. sones John, & Francis.

.4. Edward Tillie, and Ann his wife : and .2. childeren that were their cossens ; Henery Samson, and Humillity Coper

.3. John Tillie, and his wife ; and Eelizabeth their doughter

.2. Francis Cooke, and his sone John ; But his wife & other children came afterwards

.2. Thomas Rogers, and Joseph his sone ; his other children came afterwards.

.2. Thomas Tinker, and his wife, and a Sone

2. John Rigdale ; and Alice his wife.

3. James Chilton, and his wife, and Mary their dougter ; they had another doughter y^t was maried came afterward.

.3. Edward fuller, and his wife ; and Samuell their sonne.

.3 John Turner, and .2. sones ; he had a doughter came some years after to Salem, wher she is now living.

.3. Francis Eaton. and Sarah his wife, and Samuell their sone, a yong child

.10. Moyses fletcher, John Goodman, Thomas Williams, Digerie Preist, Edmond Margeson, Peter Browne, Richard Britterige, Richard Clarke, Richard Gardenar, Gilbart Winslow

Bradford's List of Mayflower Passengers. 11

1. John Alden was hired for a cooper, at South-Hampton wher the ship victuled; and being a hopefull yong man was much desired, but left to his owne liking to go, or stay when he came here, but he stayed, and maryed here.

2. John Allerton, and Thomas Enlish were both hired, the later to goe m^r of a shalop here. and ye other was reputed as one of ye company, but was to go back (being a seaman) for the help of others behind. But they both dyed here, before the shipe returned.

2. Ther were allso other .2. seamen hired to stay a year here in the country, William Trevore; and one Ely. But when their time was out they both returned.

These bening aboute a hundred sowls came over in this first ship; and began this worke, which god of his goodnes hath hithertoo blesed; let his holy name have ye praise.

And seeing it hath pleased him to give me to see .30. years compleated, since these beginings. And that the great works of his providence are to be observed. I have thought it not unworthy my paines, to take a veiw of the decreasings, & Increasings of these persons, and such changs as hath pased over them, & theirs, in this thirty years. It may be of some use to such as come after; but however I shall rest in my owne benefite.

I will therefore take them in order as they lye.

15. m^r Carver and his wife, dyed the first year, he in ye spring, she in ye somer; also his man Roger, and ye litle boy Jasper, dyed before either of them, of ye commone Infection. Desire Minter, returned to her freind & proved not very well, and dyed in England. His servant boy Latham after more then .20. years stay in the country went into England; and from thence to the Bahamy Ilands in ye west Indees; and ther with some others was stavred for want of food. His maid servant maried, & dyed a year or tow after here in this place. His servant John Howland maried the daughter of John Tillie, Elizabeth, and they are both now living; and have .10. children now all living and their eldest dough-

ter hath .4. children And ther .2. dougter, one, all living and other of their Children mariagable. so .15. are come of them.

m^r Brewster lived to very old age; about .80. years he was when he dyed, having lived some .23. or .24. years here in ye countrie. & though his wife dyed long before, yet she dyed aged. His sone Wrastle dyed a yonge man unmaried; his sone Love, lived till this year .1650. and 4. dyed, & left .4. children, now living. His doughters which came over after him, are dead but have left sundry children alive; his eldst sone is still liveing, 2. and hath .9. or .10. children, one maried. who hath a child, or .2.

Richard More, his brother dyed the first winter; but he 4. is maried, and hath .4. or .5. children, all living.

m^r Ed: Winslow, his wife dyed the first winter; and he 2. maried with the widow of m^r White, and hath .2. children living by her marigable, besids sundry that are dead. one of his servants dyed, as also the litle girle soone after the ships arivall. But his man Georg .8 Sowle, is still living, and hath .8. children.

William Bradford, his wife dyed soone after their arivall; 4 and he maried againe; and hath .4. children, .3: wherof are maried.
who dyed 9 of May, 1658.

m^r Allerton his wife dyed with the first, and his servant John Hooke. his sone Bartle is maried in England but I know not how many children he hath. His doughter remember is maried at Salem & hath .3. or .4 children .8. living. And his doughter mary is maried here, & hath .4. children. Him selfe maried againe with ye dougter of m^r Brewster, & hath one sone living by here but she

---

*This note and that giving the date of Captain Standish's death are in the same handwriting.

Prince's note in his own copy of the New England Memorial (see p. 452 of Bradford's History, Ed. 1856) shows that these two entries must have been made before he received the manuscript. In neither entry is the year correctly stated. Governor Bradford died 9 May, 1657, and Captain Standish 3 October, 1656.

Bradford's List of Mayflower Passengers. 13

is long since dead. And he is maried againe, and hath left this place long agoe. So I account his Increase to be :8: besids his sons in England.

.2. m^r ffuller, his servant dyed at sea; and after his wife came over, he had tow children by her; which are living and growne up to years. but he dyed some .15. years agoe.

John Crakston dyed in the first mortality; and about some .5. or 6. years after his sone dyed, having lost him selfe in ye wodes, his feet became frosen, which put him into a feavor, of which he dyed.

.4. Captain Standish his wife dyed in the first sicknes; and he maried againe, and hath .4. sones liveing, and some are dead.
who dyed .3. of Octob. 1655.*

m^r Martin, he, and all his, dyed in the first Infection; not long after the arivall.

.15. m^r Molines, and his wife, his sone, & his servant dyed the first winter. Only his dougter priscila survied, and maried with John Alden, who are both living, and have .11. children. And their eldest daughter is maried & hath five children.
See N. E. Memorial, p. 22.†

.7. m^r White, and his .2. servants dyed soone after ther landing. His wife maried with m^r Winslow (as is before noted) His .2. sons are maried, and resolved hath .5. children; perigrine tow, all living. So their Increase are :7

.5. m^r Hopkins, and his wife are now both dead; but they lived above .20. years in this place, and had one sone, and .4. doughters borne here. Ther sone became a seaman, & dyed at Barbadoes, one daughter dyed here. and .2. are maried. one of them hath .2. children, and one is yet to mary. So their Increase, which still survive, are
4. .5. But his sone Giles is maried, and hath .4. children.

---

* See footnote under William Bradford, preceding.
† This entry is in a different hand.

.12. his daughter Constanta, is also maried, and hath .12. children all of them living, and one of them maried.

4 m^r Richard Warren lived some .4. or .5. years, and had his wife come over to him, by whom he had .2. sons before dyed; and one of them is maryed, and hath .2. children So his Increase is .4. but he had .5. doughters more came over with his wife, who are all maried, & living & have many children.

.8. John Billinton after he had bene here .10. yers, was executed, for killing a man; and his eldest sone dyed before him; but his .2. sone is alive, and maried, & hath .8. children

.7. Edward Tillie, and his wife both dyed soon after their arivall; and the girle Humility their cousen, was sent for into Ento England, and dyed ther. But the youth Henery Samson, is still liveing, and is maried, & hath .7. children.

John Tillie, and his wife both dyed, a litle after they came ashore; and their daughter Elizabeth maried with John Howland and hath Isue as is before noted.

.8.
.4. Francis Cooke * is still living, a very olde man, and hath seene his childrens, children, have children: after his wife came over. (with other of his children) he hath .3. still living by her, all maried, and have .5. children so their encrease is .8. And his sone John which came over with him, is maried, and hath .4. chilldren living.

.6. Thomas Rogers dyed in the first sicknes, but his sone Joseph is still living, and is maried, and hath .6. children. The rest of Thomas Rogers came over, & are maried, & have many children.

Thomas Tinker, and his wife, and sone, all dyed in the first sicknes.

And so did John Rigdale, and his wife.

James Chilton, and his wife also dyed in the first Infec-

---

* In the margin, in a different hand, is written " dyed 7 of April 1663 above 80."

.10. tion. but their daughter mary, is still living and hath .9. children ; and one daughter is maried, & hath a child ; so their Increase is .10.

4 Edward ffuller, and his wife dyed soon after they came ashore ; but their sone Samuell is living, & maried, and hath .4. children. or more.

John Turner, and his .2. sones all dyed in the first siknes. But he hath a daugter still living, at Salem, well maried, and approved of.

4 Francis Eeaton, his first wife dyed in the generall sicknes; and he maried againe, & his .2. wife dyed, & he maried the .3. and had by her .3. children. one of them is maried, & hath a child ; the other are living, but one of them is an Ideote. He dyed about .16. years agoe.

.1. his sone Samuell, who came over a sucking child is allso maried, & hath a child.

Moyses fletcher Thomas Williams Digerie preist John Goodman Edmond Margeson Richard Britterige Richard Clarke All these dyed sone after their arivall. in the Generall sicknes that befell. But Digerie preist had his wife & children sent hither afterwards she being m^r Allertons sister. But the rest left no posteritie here.

Richard Gardinar, became a seaman, and dyed in England, or at sea.

Gilbert Winslow after diverse years aboad here, returned into England and dyed ther.

6 Peter Browne maried twise, by his first wife he had .2. children, who are living, & both of them maried, and the one of them hath .2. children. by his second wife, he had .2. more ; he dyed about 16 years since

Thomas English ; and John Allerton, dyed in the generall siknes.

John Alden maried with priscila, m^r Mollines his doughter, and had Isue by her as is before related.

Edward Doty, & Edward Litster the servants of m^r Hopkins. Litster After he was at liberty, went to Virginia, & ther dyed. But Edward Doty by a second wife hath .7. children and both he and they are living

Of these 100 persons which came first over, in this first ship together; the greater halfe dyed in the generall mortality; and most of them in .2. or three monthes time. And for those which survied though some were ancient & past procreation; & others left ye place and cuntrie. yet of those few remaining are sprunge up above .160. persons; in this .30. years. And are now living in this presente year .1650. besids many of their children which are dead and come not within this account.

And of the old stock, (of one, & other) ther are yet living this present year .1650. nere .30. persons. Let the Lord have ye praise; who is the High preserver of men.

Twelfe persons liveing of the old Stock this present yeare 1679.

Two persons liveing that come over in the first Shipe 1620 this present yeare 1690. Resolved White and Mary Chusman, the Daughter of m^r Alderton

and John Cooke the Son of frances Cooke that Came in the first ship is still liveing this present yeare 1694

& Mary Cushman. is still liveing this present yeare 1698

The last four entries, made many years after Governor Bradford closed his record, were written by two different persons.

It is impossible to determine the exact date of the first entry, but the writer overlooked at least two "of the old Stock." The following list contains the names of *fifteen* who were alive at the beginning of the year 1679:—

Peregrine White, died 1704; Mary (Allerton) Cushman, died 1699; John Cooke, died 1695; Resolved White, died between 1690 and 1694; Richard More, died 1690 or later; Gyles Hopkins, died 1690; Elizabeth (Tilley) Howland, died 1687; John Alden, died 1687; Francis Billington, died about 1686; Henry Samson, died 1684; Samuel Eaton, died 1684; Samuel Fuller, 2d, died 1683; Susanna (Fuller) (White) Winslow, died 1680; George Soule, died 1680; Mary (Chilton) Winslow, died 1679. The last named died early in 1679, perhaps before the entry was made.

Bradford wrote that there were "nere 30 persons" living in 1650, but he named only twenty-eight — those alive in 1679, and the following thirteen : Joseph Rogers, died 1678; Constance (Hopkins) Snow, died 1677; John Howland, died 1673; Damaris (Hopkins) Cooke, died between 1666 and 1669; Francis Cooke, died 1663; Isaac Allerton, died 1659; William Bradford, died 1657; Myles Standish, died 1656; Edward Doty, died 1655; Edward Winslow, died 1655; Remember (Allerton) Maverick, died about 1652; also Priscilla (Mullins) Alden and Bartholomew Allerton, both of whom Bradford mentions as living in 1650, but the years of their decease cannot be stated with any approach to accuracy.

OLD STYLE AND NEW STYLE DATING.

Julian and Gregorian Calendars.

By F. Apthorp Foster.

If an apology were needed for trying, with an attempt at succinctness, to treat of the calendar that our ancestors used when they first came to this country, and of the one that we now employ, which, though having had birth in 1582, was not adopted by Great Britain and her dependencies until 1752, such an apology were more than justified by the prevailing ignorance of the subject on the part of the average person. Some know that once upon a time something was done to the calendar, but so long ago as not to be worth troubling themselves about; some religiously copy double years or "O. S." and "N. S." after dates with only a vague idea of their meaning; while others, the greatest number, unfortunately, know nothing about the matter.

It is in the hope of throwing a little light on what is regarded as a puzzling subject by those who encounter it for the first time, that the following has been written. It makes no claim to originality, but is based on such trustworthy authorities as were found.*

As the calendar now in use was preceded by the Julian calendar, and that in turn by others, it may be of interest briefly to trace their succession.

To Romulus is given the credit of having, during his reign, divided the year into ten months with a total of 304 days. His successor, Numa, made changes in this method of reckoning for purposes of greater accuracy; but even so, in 452 B.C. the year had only been given 355 days, or a deficiency of a fraction over 10 days according to the solar

---

* For those who care to pursue the subject further the following list of books will be found useful: Saint-Allais, *L'Art de vérifier les dâtes*, Paris, 1818; Nicolas, *Chronology of History*, London, 1833; Bond, *Handy-Book of Rules and Tables for Verifying Dates with the Christian Era*, London, 1869; *Encyclopædia Britannica*, ed. 9, IV.

reckoning. Further corrections were subsequently made and the year increased to 366¼ days, or an excess of (approximately) one day per year. This error was rectified and the number of days put at 365¼. The right to alter the calendar for purposes of correction was placed in the hands of the Roman pontiffs, who so misused their power for political ends that in the time of Cæsar the vernal equinox, according to the calendar, differed from the true astronomical time by three months, and appeared in the summer.

JULIAN CALENDAR, OR OLD STYLE.

The necessity of some action to eliminate these discrepancies had become so great that Cæsar, as Pontifex Maximus, in his third consulate, inserted in the calendar two intercalary months, with a total of sixty-seven days, between November and December, and gave an additional twenty-three days to February, which, added to the 355 days of the year as previously reckoned, made a total of 445 days and brought about uniformity between the calendar and actual time, so that the vernal equinox was restored to March 25.

To form a calendar which should more nearly approximate correctness, Cæsar, with the aid of Sosigenes, a famous Egyptian scholar, based his calculations upon a (mean) solar year of 365¼ days. For purposes of intercalation a day was added every fourth year to the month of February. Such years were known as bissextile.* This new calendar went into effect in the year 45 B.C.†

* From *bissextus* = twice six. "This extra day was provided for by reckoning twice the sixth day before the calends (or first) of March, . . . the 'sixth' (or first sixth) day proper thus corresponding to February 25, according to our reckoning, and the extra 'sixth,' or 'second sixth,' to our February 24. Since 1662, when the Anglican liturgy was revised, the twenty-ninth day of February has been more conveniently regarded as the intercalated day in all English-speaking countries. In the ecclesiastical calendars of the countries of continental Europe, however, the twenty-fourth day of February is still reckoned as the bissextus or intercalary day." — *Century Dictionary.*

† The Roman year began in March, the months following in their present order, though February had at one time preceded January. March, May, July, September, November, and January had each thirty-one days: the remaining months had each thirty days with the exception of February, which in common years had twenty-nine days, and every fourth year thirty days. The lack of system in the number of days in the months as we now know them is interesting. July (previously *Quintilis*) was named after Cæsar; August (previously *Sextilis*) was called after Augustus, and to gratify the inordinate vanity of this sovereign by giving his month as many days as Cæsar's —

Old Style and New Style Dating.

GREGORIAN CALENDAR, OR NEW STYLE.

In March, 1582, Pope Gregory XIII, having found the principal Catholic countries ready to adopt his views, issued a brief abolishing the Julian calendar and substituting in its place the one since generally known by his name, the author of which was one Aloysius Lilius, or Lilio Ghiraldi, a Neapolitan astronomer and physician. In order to bring the vernal equinox to March 21, as it was at the time of the Council of Nice, in 325 — for it had now retrograded to March 11 — the Pope directed that the 5th of October be reckoned the 15th, and that in future the year begin on January 1st. For purposes of intercalation, such years as were evenly divisible by four (for example, 1604, 1728, 1896, etc.), and such centesimal years as were evenly divisible by 400 (for example, 1600, 2000, etc.), were to be considered bissextile or leap years, and an extra day was to be added to February. In other, or common, years February was to have twenty-eight days.*

The new style of reckoning was promptly adopted by most Catholic countries, some coincidently with Rome, others later.†

In the cities of the Protestant Netherlands,‡ *e. g.* Rotterdam, Amsterdam, Leyden, Delft, Harlaem, and The Hague, Old style ended on Friday, December 21, 1582, and New Style began on Saturday, December 22 (January 1), 1582–3.

England, however, adhered for 170 years to the Old Style, with a pertinacity due to prejudice in favor of ancient practice against which reason and convenience seemed to have

---

thirty-one — February was robbed of a day. To avoid three consecutive months of thirty-one days each, September and November were reduced to thirty days and October and December were each given an extra day.

* " The Gregorian calendar gives ninety-seven intercalations in 400 years, or, reduced to days, hours, etc., an excess of twenty-six seconds a year over solar time, or one day in 3,323 years. To correct this slight error, it has been suggested that the year 4000 and its multiples be considered common years." — *Encyclopædia Britannica.*

† See especially Bond's *Handy-Book* for full tables.

‡ " By Edict or Plakaet of 10 December, 1582 (entered in the Great Plakaet boek, I, 395, in the Record Office of the Hague), introduction of the New Style was fixed for the fifteenth of December, 1582; but afterwards settled by a resolution of the States of Holland, to begin on the first of January, 1583." — Bond, *op. cit.*

no weight. It was not until 1751 that the correction of the calendar was introduced by Act of Parliament (24 Geo. II, ch. 23).* It was enacted that throughout all his majesty's dominions the 1st of January, 1752, should be reckoned the first day of the year, and to correct the error of eleven days, the 3rd of September should be reckoned the 14th.

Many mistakes have been made in reducing Old Style to New Style from a misapprehension of the number of days' difference between the two. Thus the 22nd of November, 1620, N. S., has been erroneously adopted, *instead* of the 21st, for the date of the Signing of the Compact on the *Mayflower*, and the Landing of the Pilgrims has been placed (equally erroneously) on the 22nd of December, 1620, N. S., *instead* of the 21st. This mistake seems due to the idea that as eleven days were needed to reduce Old Style to New Style when the calendar was corrected in 1752, therefore eleven is the magic number to be used in all such cases, no matter what the century concerned is.

The following table shows the correct number of days to be applied to change Old Style to New Style: —

From March 1, 1399, to February 29, 1499, inclusive, add 9 days.
,, ,, ,, 1499, ,, ,, ,, 1599, ,, ,, 10 ,,
,, ,, ,, 1599, ,, ,, ,, 1699, ,, ,, 10 ,, †
,, ,, ,, 1699, ,, September 2, 1752, ,, ,, 11 ,,

Russia and the Greek Church still hold to the Julian calendar, and according to our reckoning are now twelve days behind time.

* A similar attempt was made March 16, 27 Eliz., 1584-5; but after a second reading in the House of Commons it was lost sight of. (For this and the preceding, see Nicolas, *Chronology of History*, 34.)

† The lack of retrogression here is due to the fact that 1599-1600 was a leap year in both styles. The table which follows is arranged to show where the gain of a day comes in on March 1, in such years as were leap years, O. S., and common years, N. S.: —

FEBRUARY – MARCH, 1699-1700.

	Mon.	Tues.	Wed.	Thur.	Fri.	Sat.	Sun.	Mon.	Tues.	Wed.	Thur.	Fri.	Sat.	Sun.	Mon.
O. S.	18	19	20	21	22	23	24	25	26	27	28	29	1	2	3
Add days	10	10	10	10	10	10	10	10	10	10	10	10	11	11	11
N. S.	28	1	2	3	4	5	6	7	8	9	10	11	12	13	14	etc.

COMMENCEMENT OF THE YEAR.

In England the year commenced as follows previous to the adoption of the New Style, 1752, when January 1 was made the legal date:—

Seventh to thirteenth centuries, on Christmas Day.
Twelfth century, by the Church, on March 25.
Fourteenth century, by civilians, on March 25.

In Holland and the Low Countries the year commenced as follows:—

Some provinces of the Low Countries, for example, Gueldres, Friesland, and Utrecht (since 1333), at Christmas.
Utrecht, previous to 1333, on March 25.
Delft, Dort, Brabant, on Good Friday.
Holland, Flanders, and Hainault, on Easter day.*

Two forms have generally existed in England for the commencement of the year, namely, (1) that which began on anuary 1 and was known as the *historical* year; (2) that which began on March 25 and was known as the *civil, legal,* and *ecclesiastical* year.

This double system has been the cause of much confusion, for some writers have used one form and some the other, yet both were equally correct from different points of view. To lessen the confusion and to avoid mistakes, it became the general custom to double-date, that is, to give both the legal, or civil, and historical years; for example:—

$$26 \text{ January, } 163\tfrac{1}{2} \begin{cases} \text{Civil and legal year,} \\ \text{Historical year;} \end{cases}$$

or, as it is often seen, 163½ or 1631–2, according to the fancy of the writer.†

---

*This "style notaries adopted in their acts; but to avoid mistakes, they were compelled to add, 'according to the style of the court,' or 'before Easter,' or 'more Gallicano.' In 1575 the duke of Requesens, governor of the Low Countries, ordered the year to commence on the first of January. The States of Holland had long before adopted this calculation [?], and endeavoured, as early as 1532, to bring it into general use."— Nicolas, *op. cit.*, 44, 45.

†Where Old and New Styles are designated at the same time the following methods are employed:—

January$\frac{1}{11}$ 1631–2, or January 1 (11), 1631–2, or $\frac{\text{February 26, 1699}}{\text{March 8, 1700}}$.

It was customary also to number the months and days of the week.* It should be borne in mind that in Old Style the order of the months was:—

1. March,	5. July,	9. November,
2. April,	6. August,	10. December,
3. May,	7. September,	11. January,
4. June,	8. October,	12. February.

It was usual to place the day of the month first, then the month, and lastly the year, but examples can easily be found which begin with the month. The following have been taken at random: 26—2 mo—46, ye 14 11 82, (18) (12) 1648, 6th mo. 18, 1663. A numerical abbreviation of the month is sometimes seen, as, for instance, 7^{ber}, 8^{ber}, 9^{ber}, 10^{ber}, for September, October, November, and December.

Where a single date is "given as the first month in the seventeenth century, without any surrounding entries to show the chronological position, it will almost always be safe to double-date it"; † for example, if the entry reads 13 day 1 mo. 1658, add the historical year thus, 1658[-9].

CONCLUSION.

Many persons prefer (quite properly) not to trust to *copies* of records as final if they can consult the originals for their information. To these persons I would take the liberty of offering the following suggestions:—

1. "In making notes and citing references, the rule is absolute that every extract which is in the words of the author should be set off by quotation marks; and that all omissions within such a quoted extract should be shown by points or stars (. . . * * *)." ‡

2. When making abstracts, preserve as far as possible the spelling and form of the original.

*The Latin names for the days of the week are: Dies Saturni, Saturday; Dies Solis, Sunday; Dies Lunæ, Monday; Dies Martis, Tuesday; Dies Mercurii, Wednesday; Dies Jovis, Thursday; Dies Veneris, Friday.

†Letter of W. H. Whitmore in Boston Record Commissioners' Report, No. 28, p. vii.

‡ Hart, *American History Told by Contemporaries*, I, 17.

3. Always copy dates in your notes as they are found. In this way you know how the record actually reads, whereas if you reduce Old Style to New Style, or take other liberties with dates, you make the original record responsible for your own interpolations.

4. If you add anything to a date for future guidance, as a result of investigation, or if within a quoted extract you insert words of your own, do not fail to use brackets [ ].

5. Do not jump at the conclusion that because 8. 9. 56 in one record means 8th day 9th mo. 56, that it means the same in another. It may just as well mean 8th mo. 9th day 56. The methods and peculiarities of each author or of each clerk's system of entries must be the only guide for your opinions.

PLYMOUTH COLONY WILLS AND INVENTORIES.

Literally transcribed from the Original Records at Plymouth, Mass.,

BY GEORGE ERNEST BOWMAN.

The first volume contains 252 pages, numbered as 126 folios. A note on the fly-leaf states that "This volume was interleaved and new bound at the expense of the Government of Massachusetts, and under the direction of the Rev[d] James Freeman, D. D., Samuel Davis and Benjamin R. Nichols, Esq[s] their Committee, Anno Domini 1818."

On the first page of the original is written in a comparatively modern hand:

From 1633 — to 1654 —
Vide — Tab — Folio — 24

On the second page is written:

New Plimouths : Registry of Wills
and Inventorys from the year 1633
to the year 1654:
See Alphabetical Table — Folio — 24 (*same hand as on p.* 1)

The first entry on the second page was evidently made soon after the volume was completed.

Plymouth Colony Wills and Inventories.

The third page is the original title page, and has, in a bold hand, the following entry:

> New Plymouth
> A Register of the Wills and
> Testaments of the deaceased wth
> a true Coppy of the Inventories of
> their goods and Chattels as they
> were presented in publick Court
> uppon Oath.
> Anno Dom. 1633.
> As also the Inventories of the goods of
> such as died without wills.
>
> Likwise the depositions of witnesses (*in a different hand*).
>
> See ye Table — Folio — 24 — (*same hand as on p.* 1)

The fourth page is blank, and with the next leaf begins the numbering by folios. This is indicated in these printed pages by numerals enclosed in brackets and inserted before the first word of each folio.

[1] NEW PLYMOUTH WYNSLOW GOVN^R.
1633.

> A true Coppy of the last will & Testm of Samuell ffuller the elder as it was proved in publick Court the 28th of Oct in the ninth yeare of the raigne of our Soveraigne Lord Charles by the grace of God King of Engl. Scotl. ffr. & Irel. Defender of the ffaith &c.

I Samuel ffuller thelder being sick & weake but by the mercie of God in prfect memory ordaine this my last will & Testm^t. And first of all I bequeath my soule to God & my body to the earth untill the resureccon Item I doe bequeath the educacon of my children to my Brother Will Wright & his wife, onely that my daughter Mercy be & remaine wth goodwife Wallen so long as she will keepe her at a reasonable charge. But if it shall please God to recover my wife out of her weake estate of sicknes then my children to be wth her or disposed by her. Also whereas there is a childe comitted to my charge called Sarah Converse, my wife dying as afore I desire my Brother Wright may have the bringing up of her. And if he refuse then I comend her to my loving neighbour & brother in Christ Thomas Prence desiring that whosoever of them receive her pforme the duty of a step ffather unto her & bring her up in the ffeare of God as their owne wch was a charge laid upon me pr her sick ffather when he freely bestowed her upon me & wch I require of them. Item whereas Eliz. Cowles was comitted to my educacon by her ffather & Mother still living at Charles Towne, my will is that she be conveniently apprelled & returne to her ffather or mother or either of them. And for George ffoster being placed wth me upon the same termes by his prents still living at Sagos my will is that he be restored to his Mother likewise. Item I give unto Samuell my son my howse & lands at the Smeltriver to him & his heires for ever. Item (*worn*) will is that my howse & garden at towne be sold & all my moveables there & at the Smeltriver (except my Cattle) togeather wth the prnt Croppe of Corne there standing by my Overseers heereafter to be menconed. except such as they shall thinke meet in the prnt educacon of my two children Samuell & Mercy my debts being first pd out of them, the overplus to be disposed of towards the encrease of my stock of Cattle for their good at the discretion of my overseers. Item I give two Acres of land that fell unto me by lott on the Sow^th side the Towne adjoyning to the Acres of m^r Isaack Allerton to Samuell my son. Also two other Acres of land wch were given me by Edward Bircher scituate & being at Strawberry hill if m^r Roger Williams refuse to accept of them as formerly he hath done. Also one oth^r Acre by m^r Heeks his Acres neer the Reed pond, All wch I give to the said Samuell & his heires for ever. It. my will is that my Cozen Samuell goe freely away wth his Stock of Cattle & Swine w^thout any further recconing wch swine are the halfe of six sowes Six hogges one boare & fowr shotes Also one Cow & one heyfer. Item my will is that not onely the other halfe afore menconed but also all other mine owne propr stock of Swine be sold wth other my moveables for the use before expressed except my best hogg wch I would have killed this winter for the prnt comfort of my children. It. whereas I have disposed of my children to my Brother Will. Wright & Prisilla his wife my will is that in case my wife die he enter upon my howse & land at the Smelt River, & also my Cattle not disposed on together wth my two serv^ts Thomas Symons & Robt Cowles for the Remainder of their several termes to be employed for the good of my children he being allowed for their charg vizt. my childrens what my Overseers shall thinke meet. But if in case my said brother Will Wright or Prisilla his wife die then my said Children Samuell & Mercy together wth the said joynt charge comitted to the said Will & Prisilla be void except my Overseers [2] or the survivor of them shall think meet. To whos(*worn*) godly care in such case I leave them to be disposed of else where as the Law shall direct them. By cattle not disposed on o to be employed for the good of my children I meane three Cowes & two steere calves Six old ewes & two ewe lambs two old wethers & three wether lambs together wth such overplus upon the sale of my goods before expressed as my Overseers shall adde heereunto. It. I give out of this stock of Cattle the first Cow calfe that my Browne Cow shall have to the Church of God at Plymouth to be employed by the Deacon or Deacons of the said Church for the good of the said Church at the oversight of the ruling Elders. Item I give to my sister Alice Bradford twelve shillings to buy her a paire of gloves. Item whatsoever is due unto me from Capt Standish I give unto his Children. It. that a pr of gloves of 5sh be bestowed on m^r Joh. Wynthrop Govr of the Massachusets. It. I give unto my Brother Wright aforesaid one cloath suit not yet fully finished lying in my trunk at Towne wch I give notw^thstanding my wife survive. It. whereas Capt John Endecott oweth me two pownds of Beaver I give it to his sonne. It. my will is that when my children come to age of discretion that my Overseers make a full valuacon of that Stock of Cattle & thencrease thereof, & that it be equally devided between my children. And if any die in the meane time the whole to goe to the survivor or survivors. It. my will is that they be ruled by my Overseers in marriage. Also I would have them enjoy that smale porcon the Lord shall give them when my Overseers thinke them to be of fit discretion & not at any set time or appointm^t of yeares. It. whereas my will is that my Overseers shall let out that stock of Cattle wch shall be bought wth the Overplus of my goods to halves to such as shall be as well carefull as honest men. My will is that my brother Wright have the refusall of them. It. I give unto John Jenny & Joh. Wynslow each of them a paire of gloves of five shillings. It. I give unto m^{rs} Heeks the full sum of twenty shillings. It. I give to old m^r William Brewster my best hat & band wch I h(*worn*) never wore. Item my will is that if my children die that then my stock be thus distributed. ffirst that what care or paines or charge hath been by any about my children be fully recompensed. Next at the discretion of the Overseers I thus bequeath the rest vizt so as it may redownd to the Governing Elder or Elders of this Church at Plymouth aforesaid & towards the helping of such psons as are members of the same & are (*illegible*)* as my Overseers shall thinke meet. It. I give to Rebecca Prence 2sh 6d to buy her a paire of gloves It. my will is that in case my sonne Samuell & other my children die before such time as they are fitt to enter upon my land for inheritance that then my kinsman Sam. ffuller now in the howse wth me enjoy w^{t}soever lands I am now possessed of except my dwelling howse at town or whatsoever shall be due to me or them. It. I give to him my Rufflet Cloake & my stuffe sute I now weare It. I institute my son Samuell my Executor. and because he is young & tender I enjoyne him to be wholly ordered by Edw Wynslow m^r Wil Bradford & m^r Tho. Prence whom I make his Overseers & the Overseers of this my last will & Testm^t. so often menconed before in the same. And for their paines I give to each of them twenty shillings apeece. It. I give to Mercy my daughter one Bible wth a black Cover wth Bezaes notes. It. I give all the rest of my bookes to my sonne Samuell wch I desire my Brother Wright

---

* In the record this word is composed of the five letters "ident," preceded by two characters which could not be deciphered.

Will safely preserve for him. It my will is that when my daughter Mercy is fitt to goe to scole that m^rs Heeks may teach her as well as my sonne. It. whatsoever m^r Roger Williams is indebted to me upon my booke for phisick I freely give him. Last of all whereas my wife is sick & weake I have disposed of my children to others my will is if she recover that she have the educacon of them, & that the other gifts & legacies I have given may be pformed And if in case any of my Overseers or all of them [3] die before my children be judged by them of age of discretion then my desire is they will before such time when they dispose of their owne affaires depute some other of the Church to pforme this duty of care & love towards my children, wch I allow & binde my children to obedience to them as before. In witnes that this is my last will & Test I have set to my hand & seale the 30th of July Anno 1633.

            Samuell ffuller

Memorand that whereas the widow
Ring comitted the Oversight of her sonne
Andrew to me at her death, my will is that
m^r Tho Prence one of my Overseers
take the charge of him & see that he be
brought up in the ffeare of the Lord
& See that he sustaine no wrong by any.

    Witnesses heerunto
    Robt Heeks
    John Wynslow.

See his Inventory, Fol. 22. (*This line is in a different hand.*)

> A note of such debts as Sam ffuller acknowledged upon his death bed, at the making of the foresaid will.

I owe to the Acco of Company in the Massachusets six or ten shillings if ffr Johnson of Salem have not pd it.
It. I owe m^r Joh Winthrop one hogsh of Corne for lines I bought of him, but doubt whether pd or not. If he demand it, pay it.

It. I owe him for a Sow of leade except X sh wch I have pd as appeareth pr receipt

It. whereas Henry Wood demands an old debt due at Leyden I desire that w^tsoever he demand as due debt be pd by my overseers he dealing faithfully.

It. whereas I have an herball belonging to Joh. Chew of Plymouth in old Engl. I desire when the price is known he may be pd.

Also whereas there is an Acco between Joh Jenny Manasseh Kempton & myselfe where in we are all debtors to Joh. Cheew my desire is my pt may be pd.

[4] NEW PLYMOUTH   WYNSLOW GOV^R.
    1633

A Coppy of the will & Test of Mary Ring widow who dyed the 15th or 19th of July 1631. the will being proved in publick Court the 28th of Oct. in the ninth yeare of the raigne of our Sov. Lord Charles &c.

I Mary Ring being sick in body but in prfect memory thanks be to God, doe make this my last will & Test. in manner & forme as followeth. ffirst I bequeath my sowl to God that gave it me & my body to the earth from whence it was taken. Next my will is that such goods as God hath given I give also. I give unto Andrew my sonne all my brasse and pewter. I give unto my son Andrew my new bed & bolster wth the ffether (worn) to put in it wch I have ready Item I give to my son andrew two white blankets, one red blanket wth the best Coverlet wch lieth upon my bed & the curtaines It. I give unto my sonne Andrew three pre of my best sheets & two paire of my best pillow beeres. It. I give also to him one dyapr tablecloath & one dyapr towell & halfe a dozen of napkins. It. I give unto him all my wollen cloath unmade except one peece of red wch my will is that my daughter Susan shall have as much as will make a bearing Cloath and the remainer I give unto Stephen Deanes childe It. I give unto my sonne Andrew my bolster next the best. It. I give unto him my truncke

& my box & my Cubbert. It. I give unto him all my cattle. It. I give unto him halfe the Corne wch groweth in the yard where I dwell, And the other halfe I give unto Stephen Deane. It the rest of my Corne in other placs I give to Andrew my sonne. It. I give to Steph. Deane my (*illegible*)* to make him a Cloake. It. Timber y^t I lent to m^r Wynslow that Cost me a pownd of Beaver. besise a peece more that they had of me. It. I give to my son Andrew all my shares of land that is due to me or shall be. I give to my sonne Andrew all my tooles. It. the money that is due to me from the Governour forty shillings As also the forty shillings of Comodities I am to have out of Englan (worn) I give unto him also except the green Say wch I give unto Stephen Deanes childe to make her a Coat. It. one peece of new Linnen I give unto my sonn Andrew. It. I give unto my daughter Susan Clarke my bed I lay upon wth my gray Coverlet & the teeks of the two pillows: but the ffethers I give unto my son Andrew. It. one Ruffe I had of goodman Gyles I give to my daughter Eliz. Deane. All the rest of my things not menconed I give unto my daughters to be equally devided between them. I give unto my son And all my bookes my two pr of potthooks & my tramell, one cowrse sheet to put his bed in, & all the money that is due to me from goodman Gyles. And my will is that he shall have the peece of black stuffe. The goods I give my two daughters are all my wearing cloathes, all my wearing linnen. It. I give unto m^rs Warren one woodden cupp wth a foote as a token of my love. It. my will is that the Cattle I give my sonne be kept to halfes for him by Stephen Deane, or at the discretion of my Overseers to take order for them for the good of the childe. It. I give to Andrew my sonne all my handkerchers buttoned or unbuttoned. It. I give to Andrew one silver whissell It. I give hi one course kercher & one fine kercher. It. my will is that Andrew my son be left wth my son Stephen Deane; And doe require of my son Deane to help him forward in the knowledge & feare of God, not to oppresse him by any burthens but to tender him as he will

---

* In the record this word is composed of the five letters "enock," preceded by an undecipherable character.

answere to God. My Overseers of my will I institute & make my loving ffriends Samuell ffuller & Thomas Blossom. whom I entreate to see this my will pformed according to the true intent of the same. And my will is that my son Andrew have recourse unto these two my loving friends for councell & advice & to be ruled by them in anything they shall see good & convenient for him. Also my will & desire is that my Overseers see that those goods wch I have given unto my sonne Andrew be carefully preserved for him, untill such time as they shall [5] judge it meet to put them into his own hands. My will also is that if my Overseers shall see it meet to dispose of my sonne Andrew otherwise then wth his Brother Deane That then my son Deane shall be willing to consent unto it, & they to dispose of him, provided it be alwaies wth the good will of my sonne Andrew. I give unto Andrew a linnen Capp wch was his ffathers, buttons for his handkercher unbuttoned I leave for him. My will is that Andrew my sonne shall pay all my debts & chargs about my buriall. In witnes whereof I set my hand before witnes

Witnesses   Mary Ring
Samuell ffuller
Thomas Blossom.

An Inventory of the goods of Mary Ring deceased as it was presented wth the will of the said Mary by Tho Prence whom Samuell ffuller requested to pforme his charge & trust comitted in behalfe of the said Andrew & the sd Thomas acknowledgeth to accept in publick Court the Overseers of the will being both deceased & the childe young.

Inpr one peece of black grogerum	00 12 00
it one peece of gray kersey 2 yrds	00 04 00
it one peece of red moll 1 yrd	00 01 06
it one peece black Say	00 01 00
it 1 peece blew Moll	00 08 00
it 1 peece of blew cloath 3 yrds 1 naile	00 06 03
it 1 peece blew Cloath	00 01 00

it 1 peece of blew cloath	00 01 0(*)
it 1 Gowne of Stuffe	00 12 (*)
it 1 black Say kertle	00 12 00
it 1 Red petticote	00 16 00
it 1 violet Coloured petticoate	00 05 00
it 1 Dutch Yock	00 10 00
it 1 pr of sleeves called a buffe	00 01 02
it 1 violet coloured Wastcoate	00 08 00
it 1 Wastcoat mingled coloured	00 03 00
it 1 violet coloured wastcoate	00 01 06
it 1 black Say apron	00 07 00
it 1 huke	01 04 00
it 1 hatt	00 05 00
it 1 old hat	00 00 04
it 1 murrey apron	00 00 05
it 1 pr white Irish stockins	00 01 06
it 1 pr blew stockins	
it 1 stomacher for a gowne	00 00 02
it 1 mingled coloured petticoate	00 05 00
it 1 old Coate unbound	00 01 00
it 5 pr of sheets	02 00 00
it 1 peece of new linnen	00 03 00
it 2 doz. tablenapkins	00 04 00
it 2 little peeces of branched taffaty	00 00 08
it 7 Smocks	00 14 00
it 1 Diapr Tablecloath	00 05 00
it 3 blew Aprons	00 03 00
it 2 white aprons	00 04 00
it 1 peece to make a case for a bolster	00 02 00
it 2 fine pillow beeres	00 06 00
it 3 fine kerchiefes	00 08 00
it 1 Cowrse kercher	00 01 06
it 2 little pillow beeres	00 00 08
it 1 border for a bearing cloath	00 02 00
it 3 white stomachers	00 01 04
it 1 halfe sheet	00 03 00
it 1 white wastcoate	00 02 04
[6] it 1 peece linnen to make a kercher	00 03 04

* Worn.

it 1 little band for a childe	00 00 06	
it 1 ruffe bought of Edm. Gyles	00 06 00	
it More 5 Ruffes	00 04 00	
it 3 linnen Capps	00 00 09	
it 1 ffetherbed & bolster	02 10 00	
it 1 fflock bed & an old bolster	01 03 00	
it 3 pillowes of ffethers	00 12 00	
it 1 flock bolster	00 06 00	
it 3 blankets	00 12 00	
it 2 Curtaines	00 04 00	
it 2 Coverlets	00 12 00	
it 1 pillowbeer full of ffethers	00 03 00	
it 3 brasse potts	01 02 00	
it 2 kettles	00 07 00	
it 2 Skellets	00 05 05	
it 1 Scumer	00 00 04	
it 1 lamp & Candlestick	00 01 06	
it 1 warming panne	00 04 00	
it 1 Chafing dish	00 01 06	
it 1 ffrying panne	00 01 06	
it 1 old brasse kettle	00 00 10	
it 1 Canne	00 00 04	
1 pr of Bellowes	00 01 04	
1 doz. of trenchers	00 00 06	
it 1 erthen platter	00 00 03	
it 2 Sives	00 01 06	
it 1 Grydiron	00 01 00	
it 1 fire Iron	00 01 00	
it 2 pr of pothooks	00 01 00	
it 1 Tramell	00 01 04	
it 1 slice		
it 1 spitt	00 00 08	
it 2 pr of shoes	00 02 00	
it 1 peece of lether	00 01 00	
it 4 platters of pewter	00 08 (*)	
it 1 fruit dish	00 00 (*)	
it 2 Basons	00 03 00	
it 3 Sawsers & a saltseller	00 01 06	

* Worn.

it 3 Cupps & a quart pot	00 03 00
it 2 trayes & a bowle & a wodden platter	00 01 06
it 3 payles 1 Cupboard & a box	00 12 00
it 1 Chest & 1 trunck	00 10 00
it 3 porrengers 1 pewter bottle 1 ladle	00 02 00
it 1 Chamberpott & one glasse bottle	00 02 10
it 1 hogsh. & 2 Tubbs	00 04 00
it 1 chaire & a chopping knife	00 02 00
it 1 bible 1 dod. 1 plea for Infants 1 ruine of Rome	
it 1 Troubler of the Church of Amsterdam. 1 Garland of vertuous dames 1 psalmebooke 1 pennery 1 pr hings	00 04 00
1 fishing line	00 00 08
it 1 Iron forke 1 tin grate 1 silver whistle	00 02 00
it 1 hatchet 1 hamer 2 plaines 2 sawes 1 chisell	00 03 00
it 1 peece of redd 2 yrds	00 07 00
it Beaver 13 oz.	00 04 10
it Due from the Gov	02 00 00
it To come out of Engl	02 00 00
it Bever due from m^r Wynslow	00 06 00
it Due from Goodman Gyles in money	
it Corne upon the ground	

(*To be continued.*)

THE PAUL PRINCE BIBLE.

Communicated by MRS. ELLA G. S. PEASE, of Boston.

This Bible, once the property of Paul[4] Prince (Benjamin,[3] Thomas,[2] Elder John[1]), of North Yarmouth, Me., and containing the record of births of his children, was printed in Edinburgh, in 1791, by Mark and Charles Kerr. The pages reproduced here are between the Old and New Testaments, facing each other, and contain the following entries:

Paul Prince and Hannah his wife were married (*worn*) Anno Domini 1743.

Paul Prince Born at Duxbury May 14th 1720.

Hannah his wife Born at Hingham May 8th 1722.

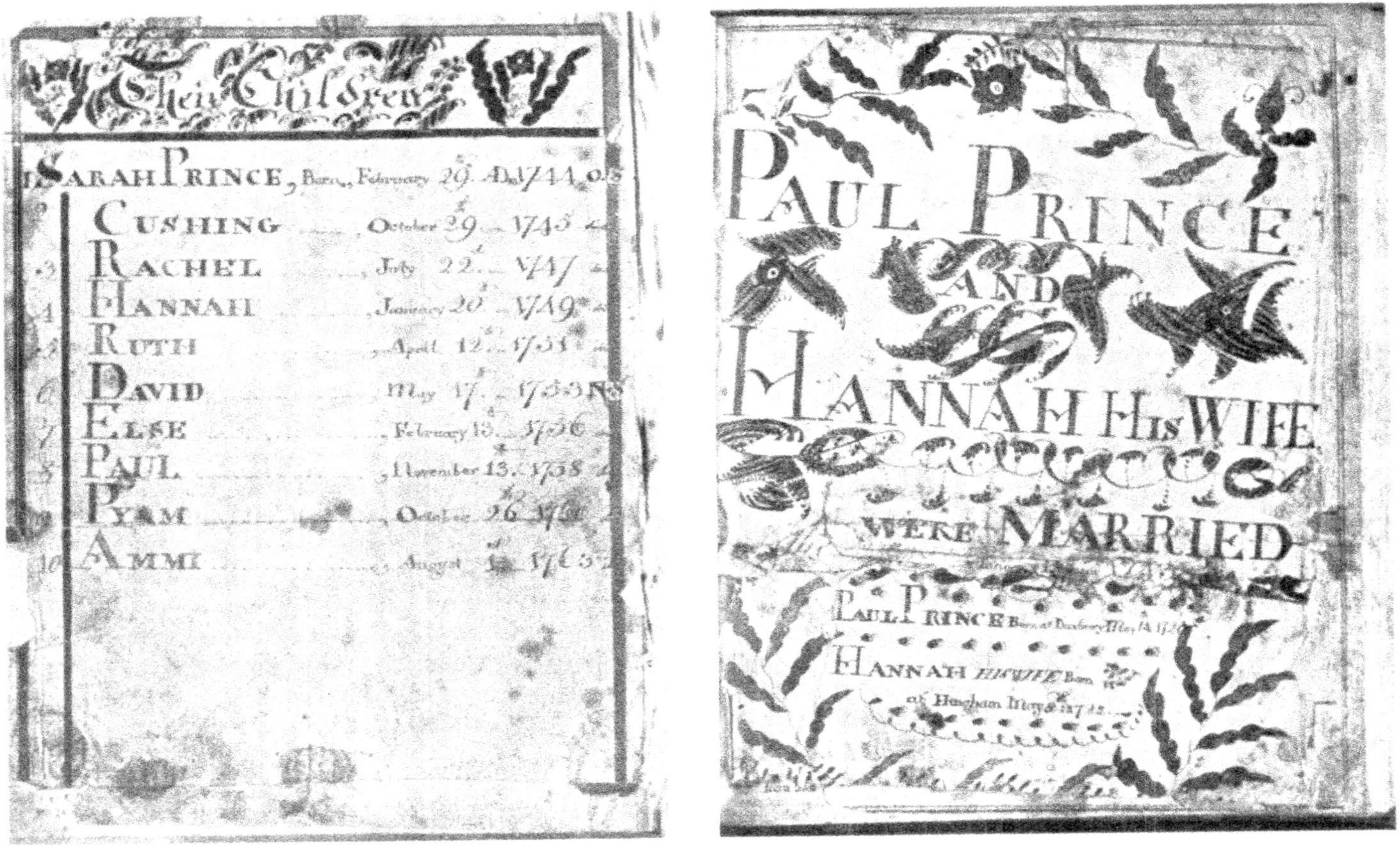

PAUL PRINCE AND HANNAH HIS WIFE WERE MARRIED

PAUL PRINCE Born at Rochester Mass. 1717
HANNAH HEWITT Born at Rochester May 6 1724

Their Children

Sarah Prince	Born February 20	Anno	1744/5
1. Cushing	October 29		1745
2. Rachel	July 22		1747
3. Hannah	January 20		1749
4. Ruth	April 12		1751
5. David	May 17		1753
6. Else	February 13		1756
7. Paul	November 13		1758
8. Pyam	October 26		1760
9. Ammi	August		1763

The Paul Prince Bible.

THEIR CHILDREN:

1. Sarah Prince, Born, February 29th A. D. 1744 O. S.
2. Cushing October 29th 1745 ibid.
3. Rachel July 22d 1747 ibid.
4. Hannah January 20th 1749 ibid.
5. Ruth April 12th 1751 ibid.
6. David May 17th 1753 N. S.
7. Else February 13th 1756 ibid.
8. Paul November 13th 1758 ibid.
9. Pyam October 26th 1760 ibid.
10. Ammi August 1st 1763 ibid.

The lines were drawn with a pen, and filled in with some brown wash, probably sepia. A slip of paper in the book, signed "J. B. Sweetser, 1870,"* says: "Written with a wild goose quill about 100 years ago by Nicholas Hughes, who was of Irish birth and taught school in North Yarmouth." On the back of the leaf containing the marriage of Paul and Hannah is written, "The property of Rachel Weeks."

Paul Prince, the son of Benjamin and Abiel (Nelson) Prince, removed to North Yarmouth with his father in 1727. He married there, September 8, 1743, Hannah, daughter of David and Rachel (Lewis) Cushing, who died February 6, 1814. Paul died November 25, 1809, and both are buried in Cumberland graveyard. After his marriage he lived in the blockhouse with Solomon Loring (who had married Alice, the elder sister of Hannah), until after the birth of his children, Sarah and Cushing, when he built a house in that part of North Yarmouth now Cumberland, and resided there until his death. He was a man of character and ability, respected and valued by the community, and interested in all public as well as private affairs.

Paul Prince's grandfather, Thomas Prince, married Ruth, daughter of John[2] Turner the elder (Humphrey[1]), of Scituate, by his wife Mary[3] Brewster (Jonathan,[2] Elder William[1]).†

The children of Paul and Hannah all lived to rear families,

---

* The youngest son of Prince Sweetser and grandson of Rachel, who spent her last years in his house.

† See article on "The Brewster Book" in this number.

Paul, Jr., who died in 1804, at the age of 46, being the first to break the family ties; David, the last, in 1849, aged 96. Sarah, the eldest daughter, married Eliphalet Greeley; Cushing married Hannah Blanchard; Rachel and Else married brothers, Salathiel and William Sweetser (John,[4] Benjamin,[3] Benjamin,[2] Seth[1]), and, Salathiel dying, Rachel married 2d Nathaniel Weeks; Hannah married Thomas[5] Prince (Joseph,[4] Joseph,[3] Isaac,[2] Elder John[1]); Ruth married Onesiphorous Fisher; David married Elizabeth Oakes; Paul married Sarah Southworth; Pyam married Martha Leach Drinkwater; and Ammi married Desire Sylvester.

Rachel, to whom the Bible descended, had, by her marriage with Salathiel Sweetser, four sons, Mrs. Mary C. S. Quincy and Mrs. Ella G. S. Pease, of this society, being granddaughters of her second son, Prince, through his third son and eighth child William. Mr. Andrew Gray Weeks, also of this society, who is the present possessor of the Bible, is the son of Ezra Weeks, the youngest son of Rachel, by her second husband, Nathaniel Weeks. Both Mrs. Quincy and Mr. Weeks remember the affection of the little grandmother for the Bible, and her pleasure in showing it to them.

THE DIARY OF JABEZ FITCH, JR.

Communicated by FREDERICK WESLEY PARKER.

Jabez Fitch, Jr., of Norwich, Conn., was born 15 February, 1737 (O. S.), as recorded by himself in the Brewster Book. In April, 1756, he enlisted for service against the French and Indians, and about this time began his diary, written in little sixteen-page blank books, made by himself, the leaves being fastened by hand-made pins.

The first book, although written in 1756, records events beginning with 1749, and the diary was kept up until a few days before the author's death, at Hyde Park, Vt., 29 February, 1812, but much of it has been lost.

The diary is now the property of a great grandson of Jabez

Fitch, Jr., Mr. Cordilla W. Fitch, who has deposited it with the Massachusetts Society of Mayflower Descendants.

An exact copy of the first book follows : —

1749 In the Foll of ye Year I Had a Long Fit of Sickness — About this time ye Second bridg Was Raisd at ye Landing — the winter Following I Went to Scool to Brother Elisha to Larn Rethmatick

1750 Somtime In Jany Elijah Brewster Was Married — In February Uncel Pelatiah Fitch Died — ye 6th of March Brother Elisha Was Married — This winter and Spring there was Several Remarkable Lights in ye Air Seen the Latter Part of ye Sumer Following Sister Lurene Had a Long Fit of Sickness — In Septr there Was a Remarkable Nois Hered in ye air — ye Third Bridg was Raisd at ye Landing this Foll — In Decr Mr Spicers Hous was Burnt — About this Time Brother Pela^h Son Chester was Born — Chrismas Day Sister Lurene was Married

1751 In Feby Brother Elishas Lucy was Born — In March Lurene Movd Away — About this time old Serj^t Tracy Died — Carter Was Hangd at Tower Hill this Spring — This Sumer Carpenter was Here with His Dulcimer and Brickel was with Him with his Sights — Aunt Anna Andrus Died this Sumer — the Latter part of Sumer & Foll was a Vary Sickly time Ezekiel Story Died — Brother Asa was Sick A Great while this Foll — A Deep Snow Fell about Chrismas a Vary Hard winter Proceded

1752 In Febr^y I Built ye Stable — ye 18th of this Month old Mr Tracy was Drownded — This Spring was a Vary Sickly time of ye Throat Distemper Several Children Died in our Society — In May Jonathan Story was Ordaind — Some time in August Brother Asa was Married About this time He Built His Hous. ye 27th I went to Folontown with Him — Septr 2nd there was a Training at Brother Pelat^h — Now was ye Alteration from old Stile to New — About this time Father Had a Spel of ye Burning Ago — This Foll old Granny Story Died & Dan^{ll} Gates wife — About this time we Coverd ye Stable and fenst ye Yard — The Winter Following I Thrasht a Quantity of Flander Seed

— Chrismas Day I went to Church at ye Landing & Hered Mr Punderson

1753 This winter Thos Branch workt For Brother Asa — ye 4th of March Brother Asa went away on a Jurny & Never Returnd hom Again — About this Time there was A Remarkable Flash seen In ye air Which I Have Thought whether Mightnot be Cald ye Forruner of ye Calamitus Sickness ye Latter Part of Sumer and Foll Following — ye Latter End of March Mrs Haskill Died — June 27th Brother Asa Had a Son Born — about this Time old Joseph Avery was Drownded Zebulon Tylar & Zeb^n Button Died — John Fox Livd with Brother Pelatiah this Sumer — Augt ye 9th Brother Pelatiahs Sun Pelatiah was Born ye 23^d His Sun Elisha Died — ye Later Part of this Sumer & ye Foll was ye Most Remarkable for Sickness that Ever was Known in this Plais In About 2 Months 27 Persons Died of ye Camp Distemper In our Society — In November Sarah Bramble was Hangd at N London — This Winter I Workt with David Palmer

1754 In ye Spring we Got A Number of Shingles in Wales — In May Dec^n Roth Died About this Time I Had My First Acquaintance with ye Lyric Poems — June 4th Sister Rudds Lurene Died — Sam^{ll} Corning Livd with Brother Pelatiah this Sumer — August 23rd Aunt Maynor Died — In September our Uper Towns Was Alarmd By Som Mischief Soposd To Be Don By ye Stockbridg Indions Stephen Fitch was Married about this Time — Aunt Anna was Married To John Baley this Foll — In Decr I was at a Lanching at Pocatanec About this Time Mr Whitfield went Threw ye Cuntry — Doc^r Webster Came to Live with Brother Pelati^h I Begun to Studdi ye Accidenc about This time Lived Cheefly with Sister Anna this Winter

1755 Abijah Fitchs wife Jonathan Tracys wife & Thos Tracy Died Near one time — Joseph Williams Went His First Voig to Sea — I Spent Many Cheirfull Hours with My Companon Webster. one Night in Perticular ye 14th of February &c —

War Was Vary Much Discorst upon the Sceem of Taking Crown Point First Projected this winter — In ye Spring an

Army Raisd Under Command of Gen^{ll} Johnson &c — The Latter End of March Brother Asa Sent Home a Letter in Which He sent for His Cloths — About this time Sister Rudd Lost a Child — April ye 7th Old Mr Cook Died — Y^e 16th Brother Asa Died at SayBrook ye 17th ye News Came to Us in a Letter from Mr Worthington with ye Circumstances of His Sickness &c His Child Had then Ben Sick a Long time at Home May 1st It Died — Y^e 20th Rufus Mix Died At Norwich Town — About This time ye Solders were Marching of for ye Crownpoint Expadition — ye 31st I went to Groton to Se Sister Anna This Spring also Gen^{ll} Braddic Came over with an Army Intending an Expadition against Ohio — ye 9th of July After He Had Crost ye River Mononghale with Part of His Troops was Unhappily Beset By ye Enimy and Intirely Defeted with ye Loss of Near 800 Men a Valuable Artilery a Vast Sum of Cash with war Like Stors of all Sorts and in ye Contlusion His Own Life

ye Latter End of Augt our Army Sent Home for Reinforcements a Number of Men was Granted to Join Them — Roger Billings Had a Capt^{ns} Com^{sn} — Septr 1st I went to Stonington for Fear of a Press To Uncle Baldwains ye Next Day Set out Early In ye Morning Got in Company with Avery Denison & William Williams who were Going to Boston with a Drove of Sheep I Traveld with them to Judah Browns In Cituate Lodgd there That Night — ye Next Day Parted with Them & went to Uncle Knowltons — ye 5th I went to Sq^r Browns Had Considrable Conversation with him — Sunday ye 7th I Came Back to My Uncles — Y^e 8th went to Hunt Bairs with Cosen Thos ye 9th I Set out to Come Home Traveld all Day Alone at Night Came to Uncle Baldwains where I Staid Shut up all ye Next Day In ye Evening Came Home Hered A Variety of News — ye 11th Capt Billings Company Marchd

About This Time ye News of ye Late Ingagement of our Army at Lake George Reachd Us Which Fild ye Cuntry with So Much Discorce. The Battle was Fought Septr ye 8th 1755

Sunday ye 28th I Hered of ye Death of Jonathan Pride who Died Augt 14th — ye 29th This Evening I Se Doct^r

Webster and John Baley at Brother Pelatiahs This was ye Last Time that I Ever Se My Friend Webster — Octr 11th I went to Groton With Sister Anna — ye 29th I Drove a Pair of Oxen to Town for Brother Elisha — Novr 4th I went to Training at Serj^t Blunts. ye 5th I went to Se Dan^{ll} Whipple Ordained Got Some Acquaintance with Ichabod Packer. ye 6th I Went to Stonington to Nathan^{ll} Browns the Next Day went To Westerly & Then Home at Night Hered of ye Deaths of Sam^{ll} Fitch & Woodberry Starkweather who Died one on ye 29th & ye other on ye 30th of Octr Last — ye 13th was Thanksgiving Day Brother Rudd & His wife was At Fathers — ye 18th There was a Remarkable Earthquake at 4 oclok in ye Morning — ye 21st I Hered Mr Chapman Preach at our Meeting Hous from Those words : — Ye will not Com Unto Me that Ye Might Have Life &c ye 22nd I Se Dan^{ll} Cook Tried & Whipd for Stealing Sunday ye 23rd I Hered Mr Chapman at Newent from Colossans 3rd 4th and Geni^s 6th Chap^r 3rd Vers The Tuesday Following I Hered him again at New^t from Those words Blessed are They that Morn for they Shal be Comforted &c Decr ye 3rd I Went to Fishing with Mr Pride ye 6th I Se Seth Mix ye Next Day after He had Got Home from ye Camp — ye 17th Mr Katterlan was Reinstoild at Groton — Chrismas Day was Extream Cold I Thrasht Oats — ye 29th I was at Poccatanok Just as Mr Williams was Going to Sea Bid Him Fairwell — ye 31st I Rece^d A Letter from Mr Stoddard at Fort Edward

1756 January 13th I Hered ye Sorrowfull News of ye Death of My Harty Friend Doc^r Ebenezer Webster who Died at ye Camp at Lake George on or about ye 19th of Decr Last — ye 22nd Sister Anna Came Here — About this time I was Vary Industres in Lairning ye Accidence — ye 24th I Helpt Brother Elisha Move a Stable — ye 25th In ye Evening John Baley Came to Brother Pelatiahs I was there He Had a News Paper that Gave an account of ye Distruction of Lisbon in ye Late Earthquake &c — ye 26th Baley and Anna Went Home Sister Rudd Came Here ye 27th Elisha Rockwell & His wif was Here This Evening I Went to Mr Treets & Mr Rossaters for Som Books — ye 28th Sister Rudd went Home John Tracy was Married I entred on

Sententiae This Evening — February ye 2nd I Had Some Considrable Acquaintance with Shadrick Webster Brother to ye Doc^r — ye 3rd Sam^{ll} Brewster Came Here I Recei^d another Letter From Mr Stoddard this Day — ye 11th Brother Elisha Set out to Go to Cort — ye 12th Benjⁿ Brewster Came Here This Night we Lost a Stately Cow — ye 19th Harbud Prides old Hous was Burnt — ye 25th A Vary Cold Day I Spent Cheefly with John Baley ye Next Day He & Anna went Home — This Day Nathan Plais Came Here — ye 27th I Went to Pocatanock — Se Mr Katterlan — This Day Brother Elisha Came Home from Cort — March ye 1st There Fell a Deep Snow ye 16th Capt Gidings Daughter was Married — ye 24th James Burnam Was Married — ye 25th I Went to Town Se ye Tryal of Joseph Avery At Night I Went Up to Brother Rudds ye Next Day I Came Home — Avery & Spicer was Cropt and Branded this Day — Aprill 5th I Went over to Town there Lit of William Billings He & I Went Up to Bozrah To Se Col. Whiting I Had Some Discorce with ye Col. of Going with Him In the Intended Expadition — ye 8th Brother Pelatiah Movd away His Family & Benjamin Richards Movd Into His Hous — Uncle Haskel was Married This Day — ye 10th I Went to Town In Order to Meet Col. Whiting but was Disappointed I Got My wig at Lanmans & Came Home — ye 12th I Went to Town with Brother Elisha it was Fremans Meeting I Se Col. Whiting — ye 14th was our Training at David Andruss This Night I went To Fishing with Mr Pride. Staid There while Saturday Night — Tuesday Aprill 20th I went to Town and Inlisted into His Majesties Service ye 29th I went to Town again and Hered of Maj^r Diah & Lieu^t Watermans Being Taken By ye Indians I Came Home By Pocatanok — This Day Brother Pelatiahs Second Son Elisha was Born — May ye 1st I went To Groton to Uncle Baleys — Sunday ye 2nd I went to Mr Katerlans Meeting where I Lit of Brother Pelatiah At Night went Home from Meeting with Him & Toock a Prospect of Fort Hill — Monday Brother and I went Down to Noanc in ye Afternoon went to ye Ferry & Back to Fort Hill — Tuesday May 4th Brother & I Came Up to Norwich This Day our Company Mustred at Town

—Hered Mr Lord Preach a Sermon to us—May 10th Our Company Met at Bozrah Made our Serj^{ts} & Corp^{ls} Mr Troop Preachd to Us—At Night I went Up to Brother Rudds ye 11th Met in Town—ye 12th I went to Town Rec'd My First Months Wages Came Home That Night—ye Next Day I was at Layser* ye 14th we Met in Town again this Day we Rece^d our Arms at Night I went Up to Brother Rudds. ye Morning I Bid them Fairwell & Came Down to Town at Night as I Was Coming Home I Se Gen^{ll} Winslow—Sunday ye 16th I went To Preston Meeting Hered Mr Lord of Norwich—ye 17th We Met in Town Rec^d our Blankets Contluded to Go of ye Next wednesday— Tuesday I Went over to Brother Elishas He and I Shot at ye Mark I Went to Capt Gores and Stephen Fitchs Walter Came Home with Me Uncle Baldwain was Here— This Day I Fited My Pack ye 19th We Met Again in Town Expecting to Go of Those that Went By Land Did March this Day At Night I Put My things abord ye Vessel and Came Home—ye 20th I Set out to Go to ye Landing Before Day Got on Bord Just as they were Going off.

(*To be continued.*)

SCITUATE, MASS.
BIRTHS, MARRIAGES AND DEATHS.

Literally transcribed from the original records,

By GEORGE ERNEST BOWMAN.

The earliest entries of births, marriages and deaths at Scituate are found in Volume IV of the town records. This book is subdivided into four parts, paged independently. Part I contains many marriages between 1700 and 1800, with a few in the preceding century; Part II, the earliest marriages; Part III, births; Part IV, deaths, with a few pages of town accounts.

Some of the leaves of this volume are so badly worn that many of the entries are illegible. Fortunately the "Church

* Leisure.

Book" of the First Church, covering the years 1707–1791, contains many records of marriages and baptisms by Rev. Nathaniel Pitcher and his successors. A comparison of the two books has enabled the transcriber to perfect every record found on the first four pages of Vol. IV. The parts supplied from the Church Book are enclosed in parentheses.

The original paging of the town record is indicated by numerals enclosed in brackets placed before the first word of the page.

[Vol. IV, Pt. 1.]

[1] The Following persons were Married together by Shearj. Bourn Minis(*worn*)
Jedediah Dwelly was married to Eliz^a. House, Oct^o 7, 1725
Ensign Cole & Sarah Peaks, November 7, 1726
Abiezer Turner & Grace mott, February 1, 1726
Job Otis Junr & thankful Otis, February 16, 1726
John Merrit Junr & Hannah Peaks, July 10, 1727
John Stutson & Relief Ewel widdow, July 27, 1727
David Lapham & Rebecca King, December 4, 172(7)
Jonathan Merrit the third & Mehitabel Damon, Jany 8, 172(7)
Joseph Foster & Abigail Steel, January 11, 1727
Alexander Thorp & Eliz^a. Balch, February 25, 172(7)
David House & Silence French, February 29, 17(27)
(E)zekiel Vinal & Tabitha Stodder, April 4, 172(8)
James Hyland & Mary Tilden, July 3, 172(8)
Nicholas Powers & Bethiah Stutson, September 5, 172(8)
Edward Jenkins & Abigail Merrit widdo, September 12, 17(28)
John Nash & Hannah Buck, October 31, 17(28)
Thomas Tilden & Lettice Turner, December 12, (1728)
Eliab Studly & Mary Briggs, April 1(0, 1729)
Jacob Bailey & Ruth Palmer, June 1(0, 1729)
Joseph Young & Lydia Barrel, Septemb^r 5, (1729)
Joseph Dwelly & Mary Randall, October (9, 1729)
Stephen Vinal & Sarah Stodder, Novemb^r 12, (1729)
John Colman & Leah Nichols, N(ovember 12, 1729)
David Taylor & Eliz^a. Silvester, Nove(mber 20, 1729)
Joshua Rogers & Mehitable Chittenden, Novem(ber 26, 1729)
Nathanael Wade & Hannah Vinal, Decemb^r (3, 1729)

Jonathan Jackson Sarah Damon, February (16, 1729)
John Vinal y[e] third & Sarah Cudworth, February (16, 1729)
Solomon Bates & Deborah Whitten, (May 11, 1730)
Joseph Nash & Deborah Merrit, (May 21, 1730)
Elisha woodworth & Anna Clap, (May 21, 1730)
Peter & Cilia Negroes, (June 11, 1730)
(J)acob Lincoln & Mary Holbrook (July 16, 1730)
(J)onathan (P)ratt and Hannah Wh(itcomb, August 20, 1730)
Thomas (Jam)es & Hannah (Holbrook, October 8, 1730)
[2] Israel Bailey and Keziah Perry, November 12, 1730
Major Amos Turner & m[rs] Hannah Clap Widdow, November 19, 1730
Seth Turner and Mehitable Gould, December 10, 1730
Joseph Briggs & Sarah Morey widdow, January 14, 1730
David House & Eliz[a]. Dellys, February 11, 1730
Andrew Halliburton & Abigail Otis, February 22, 1730
Thomas Jenkins and Sarah Bailey, March 4, 1730
Hezekiah Hatch and Patience Elms, March 25, 1731
Samuel Brown and Hannah Nash, April 1, 1731
Timothy Bailey and Sarah Buck, May 27, 1731
Joseph Northey and Elanor Woodworth, September 16, 1731
(Jo)shua Staples and Mary Rogers, October 21, 1731
(J)ohn Cudworth Jun[r] and Mary Briggs, January 13, 1731
Benjamin Tilden and Grace Turner, February 24, 1731
David Hatch and Elizabeth Chittenden, March 7, 1731
(Ed)ward Curloo and Abigail Russel, April 21, 1732
(Josep)h Elms and Eliz[a]. Sutton, May 30, 1732
(James) Litchfield and Ruth Tilden, June 15, 1732
(Josiah Litch)field and Susannah Morey, July 4, 1732
(Ezra Pitc)her and Zeruiah Booth, August 13, 1732
(Joshua) Young and Eliz[a]. Cudworth, August 22, 1732
(Jeremiah) Pierce & Bathsheba Litchfield, August 24, 1732
(Timothy) White and Sarah Clap, October 26, 1732
(Jonathan) Jackson and Deborah Stutson, October 30, 1732
(David Cole and Sarah) Balch, December 7, 1732
(Solomon Bates and Deb)orah Studley, December 14, 1732
(Joseph Clap and) Hannah Briggs, December 21, 1732
(Jonathan Cole a)nd Sarah Vinal, January 8, 1732
(Martin Cahill) & Ann Hyland, January 18, 1732

Scituate, Mass. 45

(Robert Young and) Margaret Murfie, February 6, 1732
(Joseph Bailey Jr.) and Elizabeth White, March 1, 1732
(John Bates and Abigail) Bailey, May 21, 1733
(Job Cowing & Deborah Ga)nnett, May 24, 1733
(Jonathan Hatch & Mar)tha Allen, November 22, 1733
(Thomas Orcutt Jr. &) Thankfull Jenkens, Jany 17, 1733
(Benjamin Seabury & Reb)ecca Southworth, Jany 24, 1733
(Capt. Israel Cudworth & Martha) Baily, November 12, 1734
(David Little Jr. and Deborah Clap), February 19, 1734
(Ward Holloway & Mary Stud)ley, February 27, 1734
[3] Samuel Litchfield & Fear Turner, March 6, 1734
Caleb Torrey & Mary Clap, May 1, 1735
Benjamin Bailey & Ruth Litchfield, June 12, 1735
Joseph Carter & Sarah Perry, July 24, 1735
Nathanael Goodspeed & Deborah Briggs, August 18, 1735
John Field & Deborah Garrett, November 11, 1735
Thomas Hatch & Lydia Franklin, December 2, 1735
Israel Peaks & Lydia Cowing, January 1, 1735
Samuel Emms & Abigail White, March 15, 1735
Nathanael Studson & Mary Dellis, April 1, 1736
Israel Cudworth, Junr & Mary Merritt, June 24, 1736
Jacob Wade & Eliz^a. Vinal, July 12, 1736
Seth Bryant and Eliz^a. Barker, August 17, 1736
Joseph Hamon & Thankful Damon, Novemb^r 11, 1736
Ebenezer Bailey & Mary White, January 13, 1736
Morris Tubbs & Bethiah Holbrook, August 4, 1737
Winsor & Jenny Negroes, August 25, 1737
Josiah Edson & Ruth Baily, September 13, 1737
Samuel Stocbridge Junr & Sarah Tilden, Novemb^r 1, 1737
Nicholas Litchfield Junr & Sarah Studly, March 23, 1737
Thomas Young & Mary House, April 12, 173(7)
Jonathan Cudworth & Hannah Merrit, May 18, 173(8)
Joseph Tolman and Mary Turner, May 22, 173(8)
Joseph Otis & Eliz^a. Little, June 6, (1738)
Joseph Battles & Susanna Studly, August 22, 17(38)
John Fobes & Martha Pierce, October 19, 17(38)
John Garrett and Abigail Sutton, February 1, 17(38)
David Francis & Lydia Attiman Indians, April 19, 1(739)
John Caswell & Eliz^a. Franklin, April 29, (1739)

James Merrit Junr and Eliz^a. Cole, May 17, (1739)
Joseph Withrel & Lydia Turner, January 3, (173–)
Isaac Lincoln & Jail Garrett, February 7, (1739)
Bristol & Judith Negroes, June 19, (1740)
Lemuel Francis & Meriah Indians, June 2(9, 1740)
Peleg Bryant & Mary Jenkins, July (10, 1740)
Mordecai Ellis & Sarah Otis, September (30, 1740)
Benjamin Cudworth & Mary Little, N(ovember 13, 1740)
David Nash & Penelope Merrit, Nov(ember 20, 1740)
William Peaks & Priscilla Tur(ner, January 15, 1740)
[4] Joseph Otis & Mercy Little, February 2, 1740
Samuel Jenkins and Rebecca White, March 2, 1740
Jonathan Buck & Rachel Peaks, March 19, 1740
Cornelius Briggs & Lydia Stodder, April 9, 1741
Elisha Merrit & Priscilla Holbrook, Sep^tr 17, 1741
Israel Chittenden Junr & Deborah Vinal, Oct^o 29, 1741
Elisha Curtis & Sarah Chittenden, November 12, 1741
Daniel Damon & Judith Litchfield, Decemb^r 8, 1741
William Baily & Abigail Clap, December 24, 1741
David Jenkins & Eliz^a. Merrit, January 14, 1741
Jonathan Merrit Junr & Sarah Wade, January 21, 1741
Eleazer Litchfield & Desire White, Jany 21, 1741
Chess & Prudence Negroes, March 11, 1741
Issachar Vinal & Mary Chittenden, March 15, 1741
Ebenezer Keith & Mary Pierce, March 18, 1741
Samuel Litchfield Junr & Priscilla Vinal, April 1, 1742
George Stutson & Eunice Stutson, May 10, 1742
Job Clap & Susannah Litchfield, May 20, 1742
Noah Whitcomb & Mary Franklin, June 10, 1742
(Jo)seph Buck & Leah Peaks, August 22, 1742
Job Stetson & Mary Prouty, September 27, 1742
Joseph Damon & Joanna Damon, Novr 13, 1742
Thomas Man & Ruth Damon, December 30, 1742
(B)enjamin Woodworth and Hannah Cudworth, Jany 27, 1742
(Ja)cob Vinal ye third & Lydia Holbrook, June 21, 1743
(Ben)jamin Hyland & Sarah Hamon Widdow, July 14, 1743
(Isaac) Litchfield & Lydia Cowing, September 8, 1743
(John Soper) & Anna Woodworth, Oct^o 13, 1743
(Chess & Pri)scilla Negroes, February 5, 1743

(Josiah Dam)on & Leah Briggs, February 23, 1743
(Jonathan Fish) & Mary Merrit, March 18, 1743
(Seth Bailey) & Rachel Cudworth, April 24, 1744
(Thomas Orcutt) & Margaret Sutton Widdow, May 15, 1744
(John Briggs & Ju)dith Damon, August 19, 1744
(William Dwelly) & Deborah Jones, November 1, 1744
(John Mansel & Leah) Simons, November 29, 1744
(James Cudworth & Rac)hel Simons, Decemb^r 5, 1745
(Winsor & Content Negroes), December 5, 1745
(George Morton & Sarah) White, January 1, 1745
(Joseph Vinal & Martha Je)nkins, February 13, 1745

(*To be continued.*)

REPORTS FROM STATE SOCIETIES.

MASSACHUSETTS SOCIETY.

The Third Annual Meeting was held at the Hotel Vendome, Boston, on Monday evening, November 21, 1898, the Two Hundred and Seventy-Eighth Anniversary of the Signing of The Compact.

The Secretary reported that since the last annual meeting the Board of Assistants had elected 130 new members and accepted five resignations. There were also four deaths, leaving the total membership 399, a net gain of 121 for the year. The membership included a lady 105 years of age, a gentleman aged 101, two ladies, twins, aged 93, and a gentleman aged 91.

Nearly 800 different lines of descent have been filed by members, and the Library contains nearly 200 volumes, besides valuable original documents, photographs of old Bible records, and other historical material.

The Society has for two years rented Room 623, Tremont Building, where meetings of the Board of Assistants and the various committees are held, and the Library and records are kept. The Library may be freely consulted by members of any of the State societies.

The Treasurer's report showed a balance of $1,971.93 in addition to the value of the Library and the office furniture.

The following officers were elected : —

Governor,	Gamaliel Bradford.
Deputy Governor,	Nathan Appleton.
Captain,	Myles Standish, M.D.
Elder,	Rev. Charles Augustus Brewster, A.M.
Secretary,	George Ernest Bowman.
Treasurer,	Marcus Morton.
Historian,	Frederick Wesley Parker.
Surgeon,	Samuel Jason Mixter, M.D.
Assistants,	Winslow Warren, Mrs. Burr Porter, Morton Dexter, Mrs. John Anthony Remick, Francis Richmond Allen, Mrs. William Lawrie, Mrs. Henry Emmons Raymond.

After the business meeting dinner was served, Governor Gamaliel Bradford presiding. Addresses were made by Hon. Hosea M. Knowlton, Attorney General of Massachusetts, Prof. Victor Clifton Alderson, of the Illinois Society, Mr. Thomas Snell Hopkins, of the District of Columbia Society, and Hon. Winslow Warren, of the Massachusetts Society. Governor Bradford read a telegram from Walter Morton Howland, Governor of the Illinois Society, and letters from Herbert Jenney, Governor of the Ohio Society, and William Lowrey Marsh, Governor of the District of Columbia Society.

The following Standing Committees have been appointed by the Board of Assistants for the year 1898–1899 : —

Membership: Nathan Appleton, Mrs. Richard Arnold, Mrs. Charles Edward Grinnell, Mrs. Charles L. Pitkin, Francis Apthorp Foster.

Publication: Morton Dexter, Winslow Warren, Charles Augustus Hopkins, Frederick Wesley Parker, George Ernest Bowman.

Finance: George Adelbert Alden, Horace Homer Soule, Charles Allen Howland, William Minard Richardson, Silas Reed Anthony.

Library: Benjamin Franklin Stevens, Mrs. William Lawrie, Henry Francis Coe, Mrs. Daniel H. Lane, Mrs. George Francis Arnold.

Entertainment: Rev. Frederick Baylies Allen, Mrs. Edward Livingston Adams, James Myles Standish, Mrs. Sydney Harwood, Mrs. John Anthony Remick.

Historical Research: Francis Richmond Allen, Morton Dexter, James Atkins Noyes, George Ernest Bowman, Frederick Wesley Parker.

Marking Historic Sites: Gamaliel Bradford, Mrs. Burr Porter, Benjamin Delano Sweet, Mrs. Frederick Alden Barker, Miss Susan Barker Willard.

DONATIONS TO THE LIBRARY AND CABINET.

"The Allerton Family," from Mrs. James S. Peck.

"The John Robinson Memorial Tablet" and "The Story of the Pilgrims," both from the author, Morton Dexter.

"The Earliest Printed Sources of New England History, 1602–1629" and "The Surrender of the Bradford Manuscript," both from James Atkins Noyes.

"History of Hardwick, Mass.," from Mrs. William Mixter.

"New York Genealogical and Biographical Record, October, 1876," from Mrs. Dudley A. Sargent.

"Col. John Gorham's 'Wast Book,'" from the author, Frank William Sprague.

"Memorials of the Mauran Family," from William Mauran Stockbridge.

"The Bradford History," from Hon. William M. Olin.

"Truro, Cape Cod," from Mrs. Loriman S. Brigham.

Two photographs of the Paul Prince Bible, from Andrew Gray Weeks.

"Register of the Lynn Historical Society for 1897," from Nathan Mortimer Hawkes.

Six photographs of the Bibles of Oliver Soper and Oliver Soper, Jr., from Mrs. Nathan Anthony.

"John Rogers of Marshfield" and "The John Rogers Families in Plymouth and Vicinity," Second and Revised Edition, both from the author, Josiah H. Drummond.

Vol. I of *The Genealogical Advertiser*, from Mrs. Lucy Hall Greenlaw.

The Hingham Magazine, from Miss Susan Barker Willard.

Two photographs of "Family Record" of Abner Sowle (born 1747) and his son-in-law, William C. Manchester, from Mrs. Charles Ray Brayton.

Bradford's "History of Plimoth Plantation." Edition of 1856; purchased with fund subscribed by the following descendants of Governor Bradford: Miss Maud L. Atkinson, Miss Ann A. Bradford, George L. Bradford, Livingston W. Cleaveland, William C. Donnell, Mrs. John Holmes Morison, Mrs. Jonathan F. Pierce, Mrs. Samuel F. Smith, Benjamin D. Sweet, Frank R. Thomas, Mrs. Henry W. Wilkinson.

Bradford's "Memoir of Elder Brewster," from George Ernest Bowman.

Members Elected.

October 11, 1898.

398. Miss Mary Perkins Quincy, New Haven, Conn., seventh from John Howland.
399. Miss Mary Emma Wood, Brookline, eighth from John Howland.
400. Miss Abby Christina Howes, Quincy, ninth from William Brewster.
401. Miss Helen Elizabeth Keep, Detroit, Mich., ninth from William Bradford.
402. Freeman Foster, Abington, eighth from William Brewster.
403. Cordilla Walker Fitch, Morrisville, Vt., eighth from William Brewster.
404. Rev. Charles Augustus Brewster, Vineland, N. J., eighth from William Brewster, seventh from Love Brewster.
405. Daniel Clark Remich, Littleton, N. H., eighth from Isaac Allerton, seventh from Mary Allerton.
406. Mrs. James Erving Shepard, Lawrence, seventh from Myles Standish.

November 9, 1898.

407. Mrs. Fred Lawson Godding, Medford, eighth from John Alden.
408. Miss Mary Stimson Clarke, Duluth, Minn., ninth from Stephen Hopkins, eighth from Gyles Hopkins.
409. Asa Lansford Foster, South Orange, N. J., eighth from Myles Standish.

November 21, 1898.

410. Mrs. John Daugherty White, Manchester, Ky., ninth from William Bradford.

November 30, 1898.

411. Winfred Hervey Rogers, Woburn, eighth from John Howland.

December 14, 1898.

412. Silas Reed Anthony, Boston, eighth from Myles Standish.
413. Miss Sarah Haskell Crocker, Boston, eighth from John Howland.

December 31, 1898.

414. Edward Brinley Kellogg, M.D., Boston, eighth from Myles Standish.
415. John Standish Foster Bush, M.D., Boston, eighth from Myles Standish.

416. Edward Royall Tyler, Boston, eighth from Francis Cooke.
417. Mrs. Thomas E. Cannell, Maquoketa, Iowa, eighth from John Alden.
418. Mrs. Frank Moseley, Brookline, ninth from John Howland.
419. Cyrus Alger Hawes, Brookline, ninth from John Howland.
420. Mrs. Henry Vollmer, Davenport, Iowa, ninth from Stephen Hopkins, eighth from Gyles Hopkins.
421. Mrs. William Sawin Whiting, Brookline, seventh from John Howland.

SUPPLEMENTAL LINES FILED.

November, 1898.
368. Mrs. Elias A. Tuttle, ninth from William Brewster.

December, 1898.
51. Mrs. Solon W. Stevens, eighth from Richard Warren.
297. Archie L. Talbot, eighth from Francis Cooke, eighth from John Howland, ninth from Degory Priest.
369. Mrs. Charles R. Brayton, eighth from John Alden, eighth from Richard Warren.
389. Virgil C. Pond, tenth from William Brewster, eighth from Peter Brown, eighth from Francis Cooke, seventh from John Howland, eighth (two lines) from John Howland, ninth from Degory Priest, ninth from Richard Warren, tenth from Richard Warren.

NEW YORK SOCIETY.

Officers elected at the Annual Meeting, November 22, 1898:

Governor, Henry E. Howland.
Deputy Governor, John Taylor Terry.
Captain, Joseph Jermain Slocum.
Elder, Rev. Roderick Terry, D.D.
Secretary, Edward Wilkins Dewey.
Treasurer, William Milne Grinnell.
Historian, Richard Henry Greene.
Surgeon, Henry Brewster Minton, M.D.
Assistants, William Lanman Bull, J. Bayard Backus, Howland Davis, Waldo Hutchins, Walter Scott Allerton, Edward Loudon Norton, Frederic Horace Hatch.

Members Elected.

October 5, 1898.

483. Mrs. David Thomson, New York, seventh from Stephen Hopkins, sixth from Gyles Hopkins.
484. George Bradford Coggeshall, Brooklyn, eighth from John Alden.

November 2, 1898.

485. Warren C. Crane, New York, seventh from Thomas Rogers.
486. Charles Elliot Warren, New York, eighth from Richard Warren.
487. Mrs. Charles Borcherling, Newark, N. J., eighth from William Bradford.
488. Leon Brooks Bacon, Syracuse, eighth from Myles Standish.

December 7, 1898.

489. Edward Morrill Johnson, Minneapolis, Minn., ninth from James Chilton, eighth from Mary Chilton.
490. Mrs. James P. Woodruff, Litchfield, Conn., ninth from Richard Warren.
491. Frederick Sheldon Parker, Brooklyn, ninth from William Bradford.
492. Mrs. Charles G. Baldwin, Syracuse, eighth from William Bradford.
493. Miss Martha Murphey, Albany, eighth from John Alden.
494. Miss Virginia Hulburt Murphey, Albany, eighth from John Alden.

December 31, 1898.

495. Frank Warren Crane, New York, eighth from Thomas Rogers, seventh from Joseph Rogers.
496. Mrs. Richard S. Jefferies, Augusta, Ga., ninth from William Bradford.
497. Lucien Calvin Warner, Irving-on-Hudson, eighth from Francis Cooke.
498. Mrs. Seabury Cone Mastick, New York, ninth from Francis Cooke.
499. Frederic Rogers Kellogg, New York, ninth from John Howland.
500. Mrs. Cornelius T. Longstreet, Syracuse, seventh from John Alden.
501. Harry Ward Skerry, Brooklyn, ninth from Myles Standish.
502. Edward Franklin Weed, New York, ninth from John Howland.

503. Mrs. George Coit Butts, Norwich, Conn., tenth from James Chilton, ninth from Mary Chilton.
504. Theodore Bliss Cunningham, New York, eighth from John Alden.
505. George W. Taylor, Marinette, Wis., seventh from John Alden.
506. Mrs. Ogden H. Fethers, Janesville, Wis., ninth from William Brewster.
507. Mrs. Edward Morrill Johnson, Minneapolis, Minn., ninth from Richard Warren.
508. Mrs. Charles K. Billings, New Haven, Conn., seventh from John Alden.
509. Mrs. William H. Seward, Auburn, seventh from James Chilton, sixth from Mary Chilton.
510. Henry Kirke Bush-Brown, Newburgh, eighth from John Howland.
511. William Watts Jones Warren, New York, ninth from Richard Warren.
512. William E. Miller, Warsaw, eighth from John Alden.
513. Mrs. William E. McComb, Lockport, tenth from William Brewster.
514. Silas Brown Brownell, New York, seventh from John Howland.
515. Mrs. Frank V. Davis, Grand Rapids, Mich., ninth from Francis Cooke, eighth from John Cooke.
516. Mrs. Reice Marshall Newport, St. Paul, Minn., eighth from William Bradford.

SUPPLEMENTAL LINE FILED.

November, 1898.
318. Miss Marguerite T. Doane, tenth from William Brewster.

CONNECTICUT SOCIETY.

The Third Annual Meeting was held at the Crocker House, New London, on Wednesday evening, December 21, 1898, the Two Hundred and Seventy-Eighth Anniversary of the Landing of the Pilgrims at Plymouth.

The Secretary reported that twenty-seven members had been elected during the year, and two deaths had occurred. There were also eight transfers to new State Societies, leaving the net membership at this time 179.

Over thirty volumes have been presented to the Society's Library.

The following officers were elected to serve for the ensuing year: —

Governor,	William Waldo Hyde.
Deputy Governor,	Henry Augustus Morgan.
Captain,	Royal Bird Bradford, Captain U. S. N.
Elder,	Rev. James Gibson Johnson.
Secretary,	Henry Richardson Bond, Jr.
Treasurer,	Laurence Waterman Miner.
Historian,	Edwin Allston Hill.
Assistants,	William Molthrop Stark, Percy Coe Eggleston, Mrs. George D. Whittlesey, Mrs. Charles B. Jennings, Mrs. Frank H. Arms, Mrs. George J. Bramble, Miss Elizabeth Mussey Browne.

DONATIONS TO THE LIBRARY.

"Genealogy of the Howland Family," "The Standishes of America," "Cushman Genealogy," "White Genealogy," "The Doty-Doten Family," "History of Montville, Conn.," "Alden Genealogy," all from Henry A. Morgan.

Savage's "Genealogical Dictionary," Vols. III and IV, Bradford's "History of Plymouth," "The Story of the Pilgrim Fathers," "Signers of the Mayflower Compact," all from Mrs. N. Lansing Zabriskie.

"Year Book of Society of Colonial Wars, 1897–98," from John Crocker Foote.

"Allerton Genealogy," from the compiler, Walter S. Allerton.

"Stephen Lincoln, Ancestry and Descendants," from the compiler, John E. Morris.

"Claremont, N. H., Inscriptions," from Mrs. Mary S. David.

"The Allertons of New England and Virginia," from the compiler, Isaac J. Greenwood.

"Gov. Edward Winslow," from the author, Rev. Wm. Copley Winslow, D.D., LL.D.

"Reprints on the Gorham Family," from Frank W. Sprague.

"Seventeen Pedigrees, from Family Memorials," and "Twenty-Nine Pedigree Charts, from Family Histories and Genealogies," both from Prof. and Mrs. Edward E. Salisbury.

"Old Plymouth Days and Ways," Drew's "Burial Hill, Plymouth," "White Genealogy," "Diary of Hezekiah Prince," from *New England Magazine*, "The Pilgrim Fathers in Holland," "The Theology of the Puritans," "The Church Polity of the Pilgrims," all from Edwin A. Hill.

"The Alden-Fuller Record," from M. Percy Black.

Reports from State Societies. 55

"A Record of the Descendants of Samuel Denison of Floyd Co., N. Y.," from Mrs. George B. Denison.

"Relief Work of the Connecticut Chapters, D. A. R., May to October, 1898," from Mrs. Henry T. Bulkley.

"Lines of Descent from Honored New England Ancestors" (name of donor withheld).

MEMBERS ELECTED.

October 17, 1898.

178. William Converse Skinner, Hartford, eighth from John Alden.
179. Mrs. Frederick Abroy Bugbee, Willimantic, tenth from William Brewster.
180. George William Ellis, Hartford, tenth from William Brewster.
181. Mrs. William Edmond Reed, Norwich, New York, eighth from William Bradford.

December 19, 1898.

182. Charles Edward Gross, Hartford, ninth from William Brewster.
183. Mrs. Charles Edward Gross, Hartford, eighth from William White, seventh from Peregrine White.
184. Mrs. William C. Skinner, Hartford, eighth from William White, seventh from Peregrine White.
185. Mrs. James U. Taintor, Hartford, eighth from William White, seventh from Peregrine White.
186. Mrs. Oliver Joseph Geer, Brooklyn, N. Y., eighth from John Howland.
187. Mrs. John Quaintance, New York, N. Y., eighth from William Brewster.
188. Mrs. Christopher Colson Viall, Painesville, Ohio, eighth from John Howland.
189. Mrs. Henry Thorp Bulkley, Southport, seventh from John Howland.
190. Mrs. William Bradford Allen, Hartford, ninth from Isaac Allerton, eighth from Mary Allerton.
191. Nathan Holt Smith, New London, ninth from William Brewster.

December 21, 1898.

192. Lyman Dennison Brewster, Danbury, seventh from William Brewster.

SUPPLEMENTAL LINE FILED.

October, 1898.

34. Mrs. Nelson D. Robinson, seventh from John Alden.

PENNSYLVANIA SOCIETY.

The Annual Meeting was held at the Hotel Stanton, Philadelphia, on Tuesday evening, November 22, 1898. Hon. Thomas F. Bayard was the guest of the evening, and related his experience in obtaining from the Bishop of London Governor Bradford's manuscript "History of Plimoth Plantation," and returning it to the Commonwealth of Massachusetts.

The Secretary reported that sixteen members had been elected during the year and one had resigned, leaving the net membership eighty-five.

The following officers were elected: —

Governor,	Charlemagne Tower, Jr.
Deputy Governor,	Francis Olcott Allen.
Captain,	Charles A. Brinley.
Secretary,	William Henry Castle.
Treasurer,	James Mauran Rhodes.
Historian,	Josiah Granville Leach.
Surgeon,	Charles Harrod Vinton, M.D.
Assistants,	Edward Clinton Lee, Eben Francis Barker, E. Otis Kendall, Arthur Hale, Elihu Spencer Miller, Theophilus Parsons Chandler, Ashbel Welch.

Members Elected.

October 24, 1898.
88. Mrs. John Frederick Lewis, Philadelphia, eighth from William Bradford.

December 7, 1898.
89. Mrs. John Quincy Carpenter, Philadelphia, ninth from William Bradford.

December 30, 1898.
90. Mrs. Charles S. Hinchman, Philadelphia, eighth from Degory Priest.
91. Miss Mary Augusta Kent, Clifton Heights, seventh from Francis Cooke.
92. Amos Rogers Little, Philadelphia, seventh from Richard Warren.
93. Mrs. J. Bolton Winpenny, Philadelphia, ninth from William Bradford.
94. Ashbel Russell Welch, Philadelphia, eighth from William Bradford.

95. George Fales Baker, M.D., Philadelphia, eighth from John Alden.
96. George Edward Bartol, Philadelphia, seventh from George Soule.
97. Stephen Jarvis Adams, Pittsburg, eighth from John Howland.
98. Craige Lippincott, Philadelphia, ninth from William Bradford.
99. Mrs. Earl Bill Putnam, Philadelphia, ninth from John Alden.
100. Miss Elizabeth McKean Rhodes, Ardmore, ninth from John Howland.
101. James Crosby Brown, Philadelphia, eighth from William Bradford.
102. Wilfred Harvey Schoff, Philadelphia, eighth from Francis Cooke.
103. Mrs. Robert Knox McNeely, Philadelphia, eighth from Richard Warren.
104. Mrs. Josiah Granville Leach, Philadelphia, eighth from John Howland.
105. Miss Josephine Lippincott, [Philadelphia, tenth from William Bradford.

ILLINOIS SOCIETY.

The Second Annual Banquet was held at the Grand Pacific Hotel, Chicago, on Monday evening, November 21, 1898. The address of the evening was made by Dr. James Nevins Hyde, on "Some of the Remote Results of the Pilgrim Migration."

Before the members departed each was presented with a copy of "The Bradford History," the edition published by the Commonwealth of Massachusetts.

The Secretary's report showed that the net membership of the Society was fifty-six.

The following officers were elected at the Annual Meeting: —

Governor, Walter Morton Howland.
Deputy Governor, J. McGregor Adams.
Captain, John Smith Sargent.
Elder, Rt. Rev. Charles Edward Cheney, D.D.
Secretary, Mrs. Seymour Morris.
Treasurer, Frederick Morgan Steele.
Historian, Victor Clifton Alderson.

Surgeon, Harry Cushman Worthington, M.D.
Assistants, Josiah Lewis Lombard, George Whitefield Newcomb, Mrs. Edward Nevers, Lester Orestes Goddard, Mrs. John R. Wilson, Rollin Arthur Keyes, Mrs. Dwight W. Graves.

DONATIONS TO THE LIBRARY.

"Freeman Genealogy," from Volney W. Foster.
"Phineas Pratt and Some of his Descendants," from Franklin S. and Charles H. Pratt.
Vol. I of *The Genealogical Advertiser*, from Mrs. Lucy Hall Greenlaw.
"List of Genealogies now being Compiled," with Supplements, from Seymour Morris.

MEMBERS ELECTED.

October 12, 1898.
46. Hubert Cowles Downs, Chicago, ninth from William Bradford.
47. Arthur Orr, Evanston, eighth from William Bradford.
48. George Butters, Oak Park, eighth from Myles Standish.
49. Mrs. Carl Weber Preston, Chicago, tenth from William Brewster.
50. Mrs. Frederick Laforest Merrick, Chicago, ninth from Richard Warren.
51. Charles Frederick Quincy, Chicago, tenth from William Brewster.

November 9, 1898.
52. Fredrik Herman Gade, Chicago, eighth from William Bradford.
53. Mrs. Frank E. Fellows, Jefferson, Wis., ninth from William Brewster.
54. Albert Volney Foster, Evanston, tenth from William Brewster.

December 14, 1898.
55. Mrs. Eliphelet Wickes Blatchford, Chicago, seventh from William Bradford.

December 31, 1898.
56. Miss Eva Cornelia Foster, Evanston, tenth from William Brewster.
57. Isaac Burrows Snow, Chicago, ninth from Stephen Hopkins, eighth from Constance Hopkins.

58. Mrs. Thomas Foster Withrow, Chicago, seventh from Myles Standish.
59. Mrs. William Liston Brown, Evanston, eighth from John Alden.
60. Frank Bassett Tobey, Chicago, eighth from William Brewster.
61. Mrs. Ralph Emerson, Rockford, ninth from Edward Fuller, eighth from Samuel Fuller.
62. Miss Cornelia Gray Lunt, Evanston, tenth from Francis Cooke, ninth from John Cooke.

SUPPLEMENTAL LINES FILED.

October, 1898.
12. William E. Barbour, ninth (six lines) from William Brewster.

December, 1898.
32. Frederick M. Steele, eighth from William Bradford.
47. Arthur Orr, ninth from Stephen Hopkins, eighth from Constance Hopkins.

OHIO SOCIETY.

On the twenty-second of March, 1898, the General Board of Assistants granted a charter for the organization of the Ohio Society to Mrs. Frances Deering Jones, Mrs. Frances Delphine Rawson, Mrs. Carrie Rawson Davis, Herbert Jenney, Charles Davies Jones, Mrs. Evelyn Goss Curtis, Miss Clara Chipman Newton, Mrs. Mary Loring Williams, Mrs. Florence Carlisle Murdoch, Henry Christopher Yergason, Mrs. Susan Walker Longworth, Charles Bartlett, Mrs. Harriet Fisher Greve, James R. Webster, Mrs. Mary Rhodes Ellis, Mrs. Clara Anna Rich Devereux, Edward A. Handy, Miss Ellen Huldah Newton, Mrs. Elizabeth Watson Russell Lord, and Miss Emma C. B. Jones.

The organization was perfected at a meeting of the charter members held April 25, 1898, by the adoption of a constitution and the election of the following officers: —

Governor, Herbert Jenney.
Deputy Governor, Mrs. Frances Deering Jones.
Secretary, Miss Clara Chipman Newton.
Treasurer, Henry Christopher Yergason.
Historian, Charles Davies Jones.

Assistants, Mrs. Frances Delphine Rawson, Mrs. Evelyn Goss Curtis, Mrs. Nicholas Longworth, Mrs. Mary Rhodes Ellis, James Reed Webster, Edward A. Handy.

At the First Annual Meeting, held on Monday, November 21, 1898, the Officers and Assistants elected at the meeting for organization were reëlected to serve during the ensuing year.

MEMBER ELECTED.

December 6, 1898.

23. Mrs. James Dunn Lehmer, Cincinnati, ninth from Edward Fuller.

DISTRICT OF COLUMBIA SOCIETY.

The General Board of Assistants, at its meeting March 22, 1898, granted a charter for a Society of Mayflower Descendants in the District of Columbia, to the following twenty-two petitioners: William L. Marsh, William W. Case, Nathaniel E. Robinson, Hattie L. Alden, Sherburne G. Hopkins, Thomas S. Hopkins, William F. Alden, James Bowen Johnson, Henry P. R. Holt, Algernon A. Aspinwall, Isabel S. Chamberlin, Mary L. Robinson, Emily E. Robinson, Marcus Benjamin, John L. Ewell, George C. Gorham, Frank B. Smith, A. Howard Clark, Harry W. Van Dyke, William P. Metcalf, Edwin A. Hill, Ellen H. Smith.

The Society was duly organized at a meeting of the charter members, April 28, 1898, when a constitution was adopted, and these officers were elected:—

Governor, William Lowrey Marsh.
Deputy Governor, Marcus Benjamin.
Captain, William Park Metcalf.
Elder, Rev. John Lewis Ewell.
Secretary, Harry Weston Van Dyke.
Historian, Algernon Aikin Aspinwall.
Assistants, Miss Isabel Sargent Chamberlin, Miss Hattie Lucinda Alden, Frank Birge Smith, Thomas Snell Hopkins, James Bowen Johnson, Edwin Allston Hill.

June 2, 1898, Mrs. George Rochford Stetson was chosen to fill the vacancy in the Board of Assistants, and October 11, 1898, George Lyman Fox, M.D., was elected Surgeon.

The First Annual Meeting of the Society was held November 21, 1898, at the Congregational Church.

The Secretary's report showed the net membership to be thirty-one, ten members having been elected since organization, and one deceased.

The Officers and Assistants before mentioned were re-elected to serve during the ensuing year.

DONATION TO THE LIBRARY.

"The Keim and Allied Families," from Mrs. de B. Randolph Keim.

MEMBERS ELECTED.

October 11, 1898.
27. George Lyman Fox, Washington, ninth from William Bradford.
28. Joseph Edward Bradford, Woodside, Md., eighth from William Bradford.
29. Mrs. William Dennis Slaughter, Washington, ninth from John Alden.
30. William Humphrey Aspinwall, Sistersville, W. Va., eleventh from John Howland.

November 8, 1898.
31. Miss Mary Elizabeth Terry, Washington, ninth from William Bradford.
32. James Oscar Pierce, Minneapolis, Minn., ninth from John Alden.

December 13, 1898.
33. Miss Mary Louisa Peterson, Janesville, Wis., eighth from John Alden.
34. Caleb Rochford Stetson, Washington, tenth from William Bradford.

PILGRIM NOTES AND QUERIES.

NOTES.

THE ANCESTORS OF THE PILGRIMS. — The Massachusetts Society, through its Committee on Historical Research, is making arrangements for a systematic examination of English and Dutch records, with a view to obtaining information about the *Mayflower* passengers and their ancestors.

It is proposed to employ an expert genealogist, residing in England, and thoroughly familiar with the English records, to make exhaustive researches in such locations as are indicated by our present knowledge of the Pilgrims.

When this expert is engaged he will be furnished with every item of information which could possibly give a clue to the ancestry or former home of any one of the *Mayflower* passengers. He will also be given data concerning the passengers on the *Fortune*, the *Anne*, and the *Little James*, and will be instructed to preserve all material relating to them which may come to his attention. All persons interested in the Pilgrims are requested to assist in this work by sending to the Editor every item relating to the ancestry of the *Mayflower* passengers.

The examination of the Dutch records will be conducted on the same plan as that outlined for the English records.

The expense of this research will be great, and the Committee asks all *Mayflower* descendants for subscriptions to a fund for carrying on the work. If each member of the General Society should contribute five dollars only, the sum available would be over $6,000, an amount sufficient to secure a thorough examination of a very large amount of unpublished records.

The work will begin as soon as the subscriptions received will justify the engagement of an expert, and all information obtained will be published in THE MAYFLOWER DESCENDANT.

Subscriptions may be sent to the Editor, and will be acknowledged in this magazine.

The Massachusetts Society has appropriated two hundred and fifty dollars from its treasury to start the fund.

PHOTOGRAPHS OF FAMILY BIBLE RECORDS. — In a great many cases the only record of a marriage, a birth, or a death is that contained in an old family Bible or almanac or account book. There are numbers of such records scattered over the country, and a large proportion of them are in a very dilapidated condition and will not last much longer. These records should at once be put beyond the possibility of loss by further decay or by fire.

The best method of preserving the facts contained in these entries is by photography. A photograph not only shows the exact form of the record, but furnishes conclusive proof of its reliability, as the style of the handwriting will determine whether or not the entry was made by a person who was in a position to know the facts.

In any case where the line of descent of an applicant can be proved only by a record in a family Bible, or other old document in private hands, the Massachusetts Society requires the applicant to file with his pedigree papers a pho-

Pilgrim Notes and Queries. 63

tograph of such record. This not only furnishes the evidence in the best possible form, but preserves all other entries on the same document.

Every one owning or having access to private records of this character is urged to have them photographed without delay, and to deposit copies with this Society. All such donations will be acknowledged in this magazine, and records of especial interest will be published at the earliest opportunity.

The two illustrations in this issue are excellent examples of the necessity of preservation by photography.

A DESCENDANT OF TWENTY-TWO MAYFLOWER PASSENGERS. — Mr. Frederic Alonzo Turner, Jr., of Boston, has on file with the Massachusetts Society eight different pedigree papers, showing descent from 22 out of the 49 *Mayflower* passengers from whom descent can at present be proved. He also has second lines from seven of these passengers. Can his record be equaled or exceeded? It is as follows: —

Ninth from Dr. Samuel Fuller.
Tenth and eleventh from William and Alice Mullins.
Ninth and tenth from John and Priscilla (Mullins) Alden.
Tenth from Isaac and Mary (Norris) Allerton.
Ninth from Mary (Allerton) Cushman.
Tenth (2 lines) from John and Eleanor Billington.
Ninth (2 lines) from Francis Billington.
Tenth from William and Mary Brewster.
Tenth from James Chilton and his wife.
Ninth from Mary (Chilton) Winslow.
Ninth from Francis and Sarah Eaton.
Eighth from Samuel Eaton.
Tenth from John Tilley.
Ninth from John and Elizabeth (Tilley) Howland.

QUERIES.

1. SIRKMAN — FULLER. In the *Plymouth Colony Records* (Printed), Vol. II., p. 23, is the following entry: " Henry Sirkman & Bridgitt Fuller married the XXXth Septembr, 1641." Who were the parents of " Bridgitt," and is anything more known of this couple? Did they leave any descendants? A. L. F.

2. FULLER. What was the given name of Edward Fuller's wife? A careful examination of Bradford's " History," Mourt's " Relation," Morton's " New England's Memorial," Prince's " New England Chronology," and other original sources of information fail to reveal any foundation for the statement that her name was " Ann." H. W. L.

3. RAMSDELL. Was Thomas Ramsdell, who lived in Duxbury, Scituate, and Pembroke, a son of Daniel Ramsdell (Ramsden) and a grandson of Joseph Ramsden of Plymouth, who married, first, Rachel Eaton (Francis [1]), and second, Mary Savery? In 1674, about three months before his death, Joseph Ramsden of Lakenham (part of Plymouth) by deed of gift transferred all his property to "eldest son" Daniel. In 1702 Thomas Ramsdell of Duxbury sold land at Lakenham, and his marriage, 23 March, 1702-3, to Sarah (Alverson of Scituate, according to family records) is recorded on both Duxbury and Scituate records, showing that the wife must have been of Scituate. Thomas died in 1727, and Sarah 4 August, 1773, in her ninety-first year.

What was the maiden name of Daniel[2] Ramsden's wife Sarah? When and where were they married? W. K.

4. MOSES — BROWN. Was the Mary Brown who married John Moses at Windsor, Conn., 18 May, 1653, the daughter of Peter Brown of the *Mayflower*? E. M. B.

[Mary Brown, daughter of Peter of the *Mayflower*, married Ephraim Tinkham of Plymouth, before 27 October, 1647, six years earlier than Mary Brown of Windsor was married to John Moses. Bradford's "History" shows that Peter Brown's daughter Mary was the mother of two children before 1651. — *Editor.*]

5. SOULE. What was the maiden name of George Soule's wife Mary? It is frequently stated that she was Mary Bucket or Becket, but I can find no positive proof of this. When did she die? Was she the mother of all of the children?
F. W. P.

BOOK NOTES.

The John Rogers Families of Plymouth and Vicinity. Second and Revised Edition. By Josiah H. Drummond. Portland, Me., 1898. 8vo, paper, pp. 28. Price, fifty cents. For sale by H. W. Bryant, Portland, Me.

John Rogers of Marshfield, and Some of His Descendants. By Josiah H. Drummond. Portland, Me., 1898. 8vo, paper, pp. 194. Price, $1.00. For sale by H. W. Bryant, Portland, Me.

Mayflower Descendants, and especially those with Rogers blood flowing in their veins, are greatly indebted to Judge Drummond for identifying the various persons by the name of John Rogers who are found on the early records of Plymouth and vicinity. As the result of a critical examination of these records, he has conclusively proved that John Rogers of Duxbury was the son of Thomas Rogers of the *Mayflower*, and has thus settled a long-disputed question.

While engaged in this research the author accumulated a large amount of data concerning John Rogers of Marshfield and his descendants. This material seemed worthy of preservation, and has been published in a very attractive form. It will be of great value to the many persons who are connected with the Marshfield families.

In the name of God Amen

The Mayflower Descendant

Vol. I.   APRIL, 1899.   No. 2.

MARY (CHILTON) WINSLOW'S WILL AND INVENTORY.

LITERALLY TRANSCRIBED BY GEORGE ERNEST BOWMAN.

The original will of Mary (Chilton) Winslow is still preserved in the files of the Suffolk County Registry of Probate, at Boston, together with the bond of the administrators, signed by her son John Winslow and son-in-law Richard Middlecott. They were recorded in Vol. VI, pages 300 and 301, of the Probate Records.

The will was written on one side of a sheet of paper a little over eighteen by fourteen inches in size, and, as will be seen by the reproduction, is in excellent condition, except in some of the creases made by folding.

As William Tailer, the executor named in the will, came into court on the first of May and refused to serve, it is certain that Mary (Chilton) Winslow died before May, 1679, and probably only a short time before.

The original inventory is missing, and the copy has been made from Vol. XII, pp. 314, 315, of the Probate Records.

The copies of the will and bond were made from the original documents.

The will follows :

In the name of God Amen the thirty first day of July in the yeare of our Lord one thousand Six hundred seventy and Six I Mary Winslow of Boston in New England Widdow being weake of Body but of Sound and perfect memory praysed be almighty God for the same Knowing the uncertainety of this present life and being desirous to settle that outward Estate

the Lord hath Lent me. I doe make this my last Will and
Testam^t in manner and forme following (that is to say)
First and principally I comend my Soule into the hands of
Almighty God my Creato^r hopeing to receive full pardon and
remission of all my sins; and Salvation through the alone
merrits of Jesus Christ my redeemer: And my body to the
Earth to be buried in Such Decent manner as to my Execu-
to^r hereafter named shall be thought meet and convenient and
as touching such worldly Estate as the Lord hath Lent me my
Will and meaneing is the same shall be imployed and
bestowed as hereafter in and by this my Will is Exprest.

Imp^s I doe hereby revoake renounce and make voide all
Wills by me formerly made and declaire and apoint this
my Last Will and Testam^t Item I will that all the
Debts that I Justly owe to any manner of person or persons
whatsoever shall be well and truely paid or ordained to be
paid in convenient time after my decease by my Executo^r
hereafter named — Item I give and bequeath unto my Sone
John Winslow my great Square table Item I give and bequeath unto my Daughter Sarah Middlecott my Best gowne
and Pettecoat and my Silver beare bowle and to each of her
children a Silver Cup with an handle: Also I give unto my
grandchild William Paine my Great silver tankard: Item I
give unto my Daughter Susanna Latham my long Table: Six
Joyned Stooles and my great Cupboard: a bedstead Bedd and
furniture there unto belonging that is in the Chamber over
the roome where I now Lye; my small silver Tankard: Six
Silver Spoones, a case of Bottles with all my wearing apparell:
(except onely what I have hereby bequeathed unto my
Daughter Meddlecott & my Grandchild Susanna Latham :)
Item I give and bequeath unto my Grandchild Ann Gray that
trunke of Linning that I have alreddy delivered to her and is
in her possession and also one Bedstead, Bedd Boulster and
Pillows that are in the Chamber over the Hall: Also the sume
of ten pounds in mony to be paid unto her within Six months
next after my decease: Also my will is that my Executo^r
shall pay foure pounds in mony pr ann for three yeares unto
Mrs Tappin out of the Intrest of my mony now in Goodman
Cleares hands for and towards the maintenance of the said

Ann Gray according to my agreem^t with Mrs Tappin : Item I give and bequeath unto Mary Winslow Daughter of my sone Edward Winslow my largest Silver Cupp with two handles : and unto Sarah Daughter of the said Edward my lesser Silver cupp with two handles : Also I give unto my Said Sone Edwards Children Six Silver Spoones to be divided between them : Item I give and bequeath unto my grandchild Parnell Winslow the Sume of five pounds in mony to be improved by my Executo^r untill he come of age : and then paid unto him with the improvem^t Item I give & bequeath unto My grandchild Chilton Latham the sum of five pounds in mony to be improved for him untill he come of Age and then paid to him with the improvem^t Item my will is that the rest of my spoones be divided among my grandchildren according to the discression of My Daughter Middlecott : Item I give unto my Grandchild Mercy Harris my White Rugg : Item I give unto my Grandchild Mary Pollard forty shillings in mony. Item I give unto my grandchild Susanna Latham my Petty Coate with the silke Lace : Item I give unto Mary Winslow Daughter of my Sone Joseph Winslow the Sume of twenty pounds in mony to be paid out of the sume my said Sone Joseph now owes to be improved by my Executo^r for the said Mary and paid unto her when She Shall attaine the Age of eighteene yeares or day of Marriage which of them shall first happen Item I give and bequeath the full remainder of my Estate whatsoever it is or wheresoever it may be found unto my children Namely John Winslow Edward Winslow Joseph Winslow Samuell Winslow : Susanna Latham and Sarah Middlecott to be equally divided betweene them Item I doe hereby nominate constitute authorize and appoint my trusty friend Mr William Tailer of Boston afores^d merchant the Sole Executo^r of this my last Will and testam^t : In Witness whereof I the said Mary Winslow have hereunto set my hand and Seale the daye and yeare first above written

    Memorandum I do hereby also Give and bequeath unto Mr Thomas Thacher paster of the third Church in Boston the Sume of five pounds in mony to be pd convenient time after my decease by my Execut^r   Mary M Winslow
                                                                  her   marke   (Seal)

Signed Sealed and Published by the above named Mary Winslow as her Last Will & testam^t in the presence of us after the adding of foure lines as part of her will

        John Ilands
        Ffrancis H Hacker
         her marke
        John Hayward scr

Mr Wm Tailer nominat^d. Exec^r appeared in Court pr^o May : 1679 and renounced his Executorship. to this will.
      attests. J^sa : Addington Cler.

J^no Hayward and John Ilands made oath before the Honor^ble. Simon Bradstreet Esqr Govr and Edwd. Tyng Esqr Assist. 11th July 1679 that they did see m^rs. Mary Winslow Signe and Seale and heard her publish this Instrum^t to bee her last will and that then Shee was of disposeing minde to their best understanding.
      attests. J^sa : Addington Cler.

 24° July Ann^o : 1679.
  present.
Simon Bradstreet Esqr. Govr.
Edw. Tyng Esqr.
Joseph Dudley Esqr.
Humphry Davie Esqr.
      Assists

By the Honor^ble. Governo^r. and magistrates then met in Boston. power of Adm^con of all and singular the goods Estate and Credits of m^rs Mary Winslow late of Boston Widdow dece^d intestate is granted unto John Winslow and Richard Middlecott Merch^ts two of her sons in behalfe of themslves and others concerned they giving Security to Administer the s^d Estate according to law and the declared minde of the dece^d annext and bringing in an Invent^o thereof upon Oath   as attests. J^sa : Addington Cler.

(BOND OF ADMINISTRATORS.)

Know all men by these presents that wee John Winslow Richard Middlecott & Elisha Hutchinson all of Boston in New-England merchts are holden and stand firmly bound and obliged unto Edward Tyng Esqr Treasuror for the County of Suffolke in the Sume of ffour hundred pounds To

Mary Winslow's Will and Inventory.

bee paid unto the s^d Treasuror his Successo^{rs} in s^d Office or Assignes in currant money of New-England To the true payment whereof wee do binde our Selves our heires Exec^{rs} Adm^{rs} and every of them jointly and severally firmly by these presents. Sealed with our Seales Dated in Boston this 26º July. 1679.

The Condition of this present Obligation is such that if the above bound John Winslow and Richard Middlecott do well and truly Administer all and singular the Estate of their late mother m^{rs} Mary Winslow Widdow dece^d intestate according to Law and the declared minde of the dece^d and shalbee accountable and responsable for the same unto the County Court for Suffolke when called thereunto then this Obligation to bee void and of no Effect or else to remain in full force and Virtue.

Signed Sealed & Deliv^d.   John Winslow
in presence of   Richard Middlecott
Js^a: Addington Cler.   Elisha Hutchinson

(INVENTORY.)

Wee whose names are here underwritten, being desired by m^r John Winslow and m^r Richard Middlecott, do apprize the Estate of m^{rs} Mary Winslow of Boston. dece^d as followeth. July. 29th. 1679

	£	s	d
To .1. Silver beer Boule. 3£. Two Silver Cups .4£ .10	7	10	—
To .1. small Silver Tankard at 4£ .10. twelve Silver Spoons .6£	10	10	—
To .1. silver caudle Cup with two eares	2	18	—
To .1. small silver Cup at .10^s. one case wth 9 bottles 12^s.	1	2	—
To .1. silke gowne and petticoate at	6	10	—
To .1. gowne .6. petticoates .1 : pair. body's .1. mantle .1. pair Stockins	3	15	—
To .1. Bed and boulster with fflocks and ffeathers	1	10	—

Mary Winslow's Will and Inventory.

To .1. close bedsteed .2. coverlits & .2. old blankets .1. old Rugg .1. boulster .3. pillows & .1. p^r. curtains & vallents	4	—	—
To .2. Leather Chaires at 10^s. one ffeather Bed at 4£ .5	4	15	—
To : 11. old Sheets. at .35^s. one diaper Table Cloth .10^s	2	5	—
To .3. old ffustian .wastcoats at	—	7	6
To .22. old Napkins .7^s. Six Towels .2^s.	—	9	—
To .11. pillowbeers	—	11	—
To .6. Shifts at	1	18	6
To .6. white Aprons .18^s. Seven . neck handkercheifs 10/6	1	8	6
To .17. Linnen .Caps 8^s.6. ffourteen . headbands. 6^s.	—	14	6
To .3. Pocket handkercheifs .18^d. one Trunke .8^s.	—	9	6
To .1. old Chest 4^s. one round Table .10^s.	—	14	—
To .1. small cupboard 4^s. one small . Trunke .18^d	—	5	6
To .1 : p^r. of small Andirons .4/6. one old warmingpan 3/6	—	8	—
To .2. small brass kettles .15^s. one small Iron pot & hookes .6/6	1	1	6
To .1. gridiron .12^d. one great wicker chair .7/6	—	8	6
To .1. Close Stoole and a pan	—	6	6
To .1. great elbow chaire . 2/6. one brass candlestick .15^d.	—	3	9
To .1. voyder .18^d. one Iron. fender. 12^d	—	3	6
To .1. old bedsteed	—	3	—
To .3. great pewter dishes and .20. small peices of pewt^r	2	16	—
In debts by bills standing out	69	—	—
To one halfe of the house which was formerly m^r Joseph Winslows	67	—	—
To .1. Spit. 2/6. one p^r brass Scales .4/6	—	7	—
	£ 200	: 09	: 09.

At m^r John Winslows House

To .1. Long table and .6. joint Stooles. at	1	6	—
To .1 : p^r. small brass Andirons	—	16	—

To .1. old cupboard .7ˢ. one pothanger Iron Skillet and one .pᵃ. of Andirons .9ˢ.	— 16	—
To .9. Leather Chairs .36ˢ. one Bedsteed . 6ˢ	2 2	—
To .1. standing cupboard .20ˢ. one great Chest .10ˢ.	1 10	—
To .1. small table .8ˢ. two small bedsteeds .2ˢ.	— 10	—
To .3. chaires without Leathers .6ˢ. one pʳ. ffire Irons. 3/6.	— 9	6
To .1. Scotch. blanket .5ˢ. one pʳ. old striped stuffe curtains	— 6	—
To .1. woosted Rugg .18ˢ. one small ffeather pillow .3ˢ.	1 1	—
To .12. pˢ. of pewter and .6. plates	2 15	—
To .1. old Trunke	— 5	6
	£212 : 11	: 9

Witness oʳ hands
John Conney.   Jarvis Ballard.

mʳ Jnᵒ Winslow and mʳ Richᵈ Middlecott admitted Admʳˢ. made oath in Court .2ᵒ. Augᵗ. 1679. to the truth of this Inventory and wⁿ. more doth. appeare to discover it.

Jsᵃ. Addington Cler.

THE BREWSTER BOOK.

(Continued from page 8.)

(p. 209, *upside down.*)
Daniell Wetherell Maried
To Grace Brewster Agustt
the 4ᵗʰ : 1.6.5.9

Elisabeth Brewster Maried
To Peeter Brawly the
7ᵗʰ of Septemʳ 1653

Elisabeth Brawly Borne March
the 16ᵗʰ.— 1654

Hanah Brawly borne yᵉ 17ᵗʰ of
Septemʳ in New london 1656

Peeter Brawly was Borne at
New london ye 7th of Septem^r
1658

    The five preceding entries are in the handwriting of Daniel Wetherell. The next two are in that of Benjamin [3] Brewster (Jonathan [2] William [1]).

Lucretia the Daftre
of peter Bradle Borne at
New London August the 16 . 1661

peter Bradle the husbund of
Elisabeth deyed Aprell : 3 . 1662

(p. 208, *upside down.*)
Johnnathan Brewster Deyed
in the yere of our Lord : 1659
In August the 7th daye

Beniamen Brewster Mareed t(*worn*)
Ann Darte the last Daye of
Febeare : (Benjamin first wrote 1659, then drew his pen through it and wrote 1660. Later both dates were crossed out and 1669 added in another hand, with a different ink. The birth of the first child, Mary, shows that the date of this marriage was 28 February, 1659–60.)

Marre the dofter of Beniam(*worn*)
Brewster borne the : 10th : day
Desember 1660

Ann the Dafter of Beniamen
Brewster Borne at mohegin the
29th of September 1662

Johnnathan the sonn of
Benjamen Brewster borne
at mohegin November
the Last 1664

Dannell the Son of Benjamem
Brewster borne at mohegin th(*worn*)
first of march 1667

Lock in another plase

    The preceding entries on page 208 were written by Benjamin [3] Brewster. On the inside margin of this page is the following entry in a different

hand, but most of the words have been scratched through with the pen :
Ann Brewster : departed this life may the : 9 : 1708 the wife of Benjamin
Brewster.

(p. 206)

Ann Brewster the wif of Beniamen Brewster
Departed this Lif may thet 9 : 1708

The preceding entry is on the inside margin of the page, and is in the handwriting of Benjamin[3] Brewster.

(p. 201, *upside down*.)

Ruth Pickett widow ye daughter of Jonathan Brester
married to Charles Hill of Barley in Darbyshire
the second day of July 1668 :

Jane the Daughter of Charles & Ruth Hill
borne in New London the 9th day of December 1669.

Charles the sonne of Charles & Ruth
Hill was borne in New London the
16 day of October 1671 about fower
of ye Clock in ye morninge.

The handwriting of the three preceding entries is not identified. The following is probably that of Benjamin[3] Brewster, brother of Ruth (Brewster) (Pickett) Hill.

Ruth the wife of Charles
Hill deyed the first of may
1677.

(p. 200, *upside down*.)

Elisabeth Bradly Maried unto
Thos : Dymond The : Twenteth Second Day
of September : 1670

(p. 197, *upside down*.)

Jonathan Brewster son of
Benjamine Brewster & Anne his
Departed this Life November
the 20th : 1704 : Aged : 40 : yeares
and : 20 Days.

The two preceding entries are not identified.

The following entry was made by Nathan Freeman.

Preston June ye 14th Day 1756
then Daniel Brewste Departed

this Life and In the 69 year
of his Age

(p. 196, *upside down.*)

Willam Brewster thee sonn of
Benjamen Brewster borne at
mohegin the : 22th : of march 1669

Ruth the Dafter of Benjamen Bre(*worn*)
and Ann his weyfe Borne at
mohegin September : 16 : : 1671

Benjamen the sonn of Benjamen Bre(*worn*)
and Ann his weyfe borne at mohegin
November the : 25th : 1673 :

Elisabeth the Dafter of B(*worn*)
Brewster and Ann his wif(*worn*)
at mohegin June the 23 : 167(*worn*)

The four preceding entries were made, at different times, by Benjamin [3] Brewster.

(p. 193, *upside down.*)

Daniell Weherell Borne at
Maidstone in Kentt November
the 29th : 1630

Daniell Wetherell son of William
Wetherell Maried with Grace
Brewster Daughter to Johnathan
Brewster Agustt ye 4th 1659

Hannah the Daughter of
Daniel Wetherell & Grace his
wife was borne March ye 21
$16\frac{59}{60}$

Mary the Daughter of Daniell
Wetherell and Grace his wife
was borne the 7 of octobr 1668

Daniell the son of Daniell
Wetherell and Grace his

wife was borne January
the 26 : 1670

About one and a half inches has been torn off from the bottom of page 193. There is nothing to indicate that there had been an entry on the missing part.

(p. 192, *upside down.*)
Marye Wetherell the Daughter (*worn*)
Daniell Wetherell and Grace his
wife borne 1662 Lived but
2 month and Dyed

4 sons sucsesiv(*worn*)
borne and Dyed nameles
Imediatly after their Birth

All entries on page 193 and the first two on page 192 are in the handwriting of Daniel[2] Wetherell.

Grase wetherell Deyed
Aprell the : 22 : 1684

This entry was made by Benjamin[3] Brewster, brother of Grace.

(p. 189, *upside down.*)
Samwell fitch sonn to Jemes fitch
Se^r. marreed to mare Brewster Dafter
to Benjamen Brewster : 28th : day November
In the yere of our Lord 1678

mare the defter of Samwell fitch
and of mare his wife Borne at
mohegin march the 10th : 16$\frac{79}{80}$

Samwell fitch son of Samwell
fitch and mare his wife Borne
at mohegin the fift of October
In the yere of our Lord 1681 :

Hezeciah the son of Samwell
fitch and of mare his
wife Borne at mohegin
Jeneuare the : 7 : 1682

Eelesebeth the dafter of
Samwell fitch and mare

his wife borne feberare
the : 15 : 1684

The five preceding entries were made by Benjamin[3] Brewster. The following entry, and the first one on page 188, are in a different hand, not identified.

Abigell the dafter of Samuel
ffitch and Meary his wif
born feberae the 1
   1686

(p. 188, *upside down.*)

Samuell ffitch the son of
Samuell ffitch and mare his
wife borne november 28
   1688

Benjamen the son of Samwell fitch and
mare his wife borne at mohegin
march the 29 : 1691

The preceding entry is in the handwriting of Benjamin[3] Brewster. The next entry is in a different hand, not identified.

John ffitch the Son of Samuell ffitch &
Mary his wife was Borne the 17th day of
May 1693 att mohegan

Jabus fitch the son of Sam(*worn*)
fitch and mare his wife wa(*worn*)
born in the yere 1695 Ju(*worn*)
the 3 day

peltiel fitch the son of
Samwell fitch and of (*worn*)
his wife was borne in (*worn*)
yere 1698 feberare th(*worn*)
18 day

The two preceding entries were made by Benjamin[3] Brewster; the two following by Jabez Fitch, Jr., son of Jabez and Anna.

The above Jabez Fitch Died March 28th
1779 in ye 84th year of his Age.

His wife Anna Died Aug^t: 25th 1778 in ye 81st year of her Age

(p. 187, *upside down*.)

John Christopher the Sonn
of Christopher Christophers &
Elizabeth his wife was
Borne at New London Septem^r
3^d : 1668

The preceding entry is in an unknown hand; the following is probably by Benjamin[3] Brewster.

Christopher Christopher deyed
the : 23th : of July : 1687

(p. 186, *upside down*.)

Peter : Bradly ye Sonn of
peter Bradly marrid to Mary
Christophers dafter to Christo(*worn*)
Christophers y^e : 9 : day of
May in ye year of our Lord
 1678

The preceding entry is in an unknown hand; the following was made by Benjamin[3] Brewster.

peter Bradly Deyed the : 25 of
August 1687

THE MAYFLOWER COMPACT.

The Compact was drawn up and signed on board the Mayflower, 21 November, 1620 (11 November, old style).

The following copy, with the introduction, is taken literally from Bradford's "History," which does not give the names of those who signed the original document.

The earliest known list of the signers is that contained in Nathaniel Morton's "New England's Memorial," published in 1669. In the first edition of that book the names are arranged in the order here given, three columns of seven names each at the bottom of the page, and the others in three columns at the top of the next page. The line dividing the columns in the list appended indicates the bottom of the page in the "Memorial."

The remainder of An⁰ : 1620

I shall a litle returne backe, and begine with a combination made by them before they came ashore ; being ye first foundation of their govermente in this place. Occasioned partly by ye discontented, and mutinous speeches that some of the strangers amongst them, had let fall from them in ye ship ; That when they came ashore they would use their owne libertie ; for none had power to comand them, the patente they had being for Virginia, and not for Newengland, which belonged to another goverment with which ye Virginia Company had nothing to doe. And partly that shuch an Acte by them done (this their condition considered) might be as firme as any patent ; and in some respects more sure.

The forme was as followeth : —

In ye name of God Amen. We whose names are underwriten, the loyall subjects of our dread soveraigne lord King James, by ye grace of God, of great Britaine, Franc, & Ireland king, defender of ye faith, &c.

Haveing undertaken, for ye glorie of God, and advancemente of ye christian faith and honour of our king & countrie, a voyage to plant ye first colonie in ye Northerne parts of Virginia. Doe by these presents solemnly & mutualy in ye presence of God, and one of another ; covenant, & combine our selves togeather into a civill body politick ; for our better ordering, & preservation & furtherance of ye ends aforesaid ; and by vertue hearof to enacte, constitute, and frame shuch just & equall lawes, ordinances, Acts, constitutions, & offices, from time to time, as shall be thought most meete & convenient for ye generall good of ye Colonie : unto which we promise all due submission and obedience. In witnes wherof we have hereunder subscribed our names at Cap-Codd y^e .11. of November, in ye year of ye raigne of our soveraigne lord king James of England, France, & Ireland ye eighteenth, and of Scotland ye fiftie fourth. An^o: Dom. 1620.

John Carver*	Samuel Fuller	Edward Tilley*
William Bradford	Christopher Martin*	John Tilley*
Edward Winslow	William Mullins*	Francis Cooke
William Brewster	William White*	Thomas Rogers*
Isaac Allerton	Richard Warren	Thomas Tinker*
Myles Standish	John Howland	John Ridgdale*
John Alden	Stephen Hopkins	Edward Fuller*
John Turner*	Degory Priest*	Richard Clarke*
Francis Eaton	Thomas Williams*	Richard Gardiner
James Chilton*	Gilbert Winslow	John Allerton*
John Crackston*	Edmund Margeson*	Thomas English*
John Billington	Peter Brown	Edward Doty
Moses Fletcher*	Richard Britteridge*	Edward Leister
John Goodman*	George Soule	

PLYMOUTH COLONY WILLS AND INVENTORIES.

(Continued from page 34.)

[7] 1633   WYNSLOW GOV^R.

An Inventory taken the 10th of Octobr 1633 of the goods & Chattels of Peter Browne of new Plymouth deceased as they were prised by Capt Myles Standish & m^r Will Brewster of the same & presented upon oath in Court held the 28th of Oct. in the ninth yeare of the Raigne of our Soveraigne Lord Charles &c.

Inpr Corne 130 bushels	32	16 00
it Six melch goats prised at	18	00 00
it ffive young lambs	07	10 00
it 2 wether lambs & a Ram	02	00 00
it 4 Barrow hoggs at	9	15 00
it 3 sowes at	2	10 00
it 4 barrow Shotes	4	00 00
it 2 young sowes & a Bore	3	00 00

* Died the first year.

it 1 heyfer at	16 00 00
it 1 fowling peece	1 10 00
it 1 morter & pestle	00 15 00
3 wedges at	00 10 00
it 1 felling axe	00 1 6
it 1 other felling axe	00 2 00
it 1 handsaw	00 1 6
it 2 awgers & 1 chisell	00 1 6
it 1 how at	00 1 00
it 1 sute of Cloathes & 1 Cloake	00 3 00
it 1 flock bed in a fetherbed tick	00 16 00
it 1 bolster ticke	00 04 00
it 1 Coverlet & a blew blancket	01 11 00
it 1 old blancket & one old pillow	00 08 00
it 2 pr of sheets at 18	00 18 00
it 1 Iron pott	00 03 00
it 1 pr of pott hangers	00 02 00
it 1 Iron kettle at	00 12 00
it 1 pr of Cob Irons at	00 02 0(*)
it 2 Reape hookes at	00 01 0(*)
it 1 Twart Saw	00 03 00
it 5 peecs of pewter at	00 09 00
it 2 brasse Candlesticks at	00 03 00
it 1 quart pott of latten	00 08 00
it 1 latten pan & a dripping pan	00 04 00
it 1 brasse skellet	00 01 00
it 2 old brasse kettles at	00 04 00
it 1 chamber pott	00 01 00
it 1 pewter cupp	00 00 06
it 3 old chestes at	00 07 00
it 1 boxe at	00 06 00
it 1 Cradle	00 03 00
it an hogshead. a barrell & an harness bar	00 10 00
it 1 brush	00 00 02
it 1 Butt	00 05 00
it 1 bedsteed	00 10 00
it 1 pillowbeer of blew stuffe	00 01 04
it* 2 pr of Irish Stockins	00 03 00

* Worn.

it 2 pr of shoes	00 08 00
it 1 Coate	00 08 00
it 12 oz of shott	00 02 00
it 1 Iron pot & pot hangers & pot hookes	00 10 00
it 2 brasse kettles at	00 04 00
it 1 ffrying panne at	00 02 05
it 1 Gredyron & a trevet	00 02 00
it 1 Brush	00 14 00
it 1 ffetherbed & bolster & 3 pillowes	02 00 00
it 1 Chest	00 04 00
it 1 box	00 00 08
it 1 Smoothing yron	00 01 00
it 1 Spade	00 02 00
it 1 Axe	00 01 06
it 1 howe	00 01 00
[8] it 1 Bible	00 03 00
it 4 pr of pillowbeers	00 16 00
it 1 pillow	00 02 00
it 6 table napkins	00 02 00
it owing him by Joh. Jenny	01 00 00
it pr Jonath. Brewster 1 bushel of Corne	00 05 00
it pr goodman Rowly 1 bush. Corne	00 05 00
it pr goodm Rowly more	00 03 00
it pr Edw: Bangs	00 03 00
it pr H. Howland 9 oz of shott	
it pr Expr Michaell 1 oz of powder	

Peter Brown debtor to John Browne
eleaven bushels of Corne & a peck.

it more to Joh. Browne	00 01 00
it more to Joh Browne	00 08 00
it to Will Palmer	00 14 04
it more to Joh. Browne	00 02 08
it to mr Gilson 2/8 in beaver at 6/8	00 26 00
it to one at Massachusets 24 bushels of Corne	06 00 00
it to mr Heeks 5 bushels of Corne	01 05 00
it to mr Weston a bush. & 1/2 of Corn	00 07 06
it to Tho. Clark 1 bush of Corn & 6d	00 05 06
it to Josiah Wynslow 1/2 bush Corn	00 02 06

it to m^r ffog		00 00 06
it Joh Dunham		00 04 00
it to ffr. Sprague 5 pecks of Corne		00 06 03
it to Joh Cooke 2 pecks of Corne		00 02 06
it to m^r Collier for 1/2 bushell of pease		
it to m^rs ffuller for 1 peck malt & purgac		
it to the Surgion for letting her man bloud		
it to Kanelm Wynslow for a Coffin		00 12 00

Peter Brown aforesaid dying w^thout will : See how his estate was disposed on by a Court off assistants held the 11th of November An. 1633.

P — 37 — Court ord^rs (*this line is in a different hand.*)

Plym.   WYNSLOW GOV^R.
1633.

A true Inventory of the goods & Chattels of Martha Harding deceased as they were prised by James Hurst ffr Cooke & John Done & presented upon Oath at a Court held the 28th of Octobr. An. 9 Reg Dom nri Carol &c. wherein Joh. Done allowed to enter upon thestate & make it good to her Creditors so far as it would extend.

Inpr 2 Gownes	02 10 00
It 1 Coate & Apron	01 08 00
It A pcell of smale linnen	02 08 00
It A glasse	00 01 00
It 2 pr of sheets	00 16 00
It 3 aprons	00 04 00
It 2 pillowbeers	00 03 00
It 9 napkins & a tablecloath	00 05 00
It 5 towels	00 02 00
It A chest	00 06 00
It A kettle & a skellet	01 01 00
It A fire shovell & tongues	00 01 06
It A Cloake	00 05 00
It Pewter	00 09 00
It 3 Quaiffes	00 05 00
It. 1 pann	00 01 06

Plymouth Colony Wills and Inventories. 83

It A peece	00 12 00	
It Joyners tooles wth other things	00 13 00	
It A little kettle & an old pan & a pot	00 06 06	
It Corne	01 05 00	
It A serv^{ts} time sold	06 00 00	
It A sow	02 10 00	

(*This line is in a different hand*) summe 20 18 06

[9] 1633   Martha Harding

Martha Harding debitor
To m^r Done wherein he hath cleered & disbursed for her the sum of   09 09 01
It owing to divers prsons in driblets or smale pcels   04 00 00
It more to her husbands brs in Engl. to one eight pownds to another 9£ to another 3£
— Suma   20 00 00

    This Martha Harding dyed wthout will leeving one son in the custody of m^r Joh Done the Administrator of the said Martha in whose behalfe the said Joh. Done allowed to administer as pr order in Court Oct 28 before expressed

Vide — another old Book — P. 33 (*this line is in another hand*)

1633 Plym.   WYNSLOW GOV^R

    An Inventory of the goods of Rich Lanckford deaceased who dyed the 14th of Septembr as it was taken by Josuah Pratt & Edw : ffoster & presented upon Oath in Court the 28th of Octobr An° Reg Dom. nri Carol 9 &c.

Inpr. one sute of stuffe being dublet Cloake & Briches	00 07 00	
It 1 smale box of trifles being 42 in number	00 06 00	
It Two black dublets 1 black Cloake & 1 black pr of brieches	00 09 00	
It one Satten sute being dublet & hose	01 10 00	
It one dublet of mixed stuffe	00 10 00	
It 1 pr of old cloath brieches	00 00 04	

It 1 lining of a dublet of red wollen	00 00 06
It 1 white say waste & a rent pr of drawers of the same	00 01 00
It 1 Canvase sute	00 03 00
It 1 pr of lether linings	00 00 06
It 1 old wollen wastcoat	00 00 08
It 1 Cloath Coate	00 05 00
It 1 old white hat 1 munmoth Cap	00 01 10
It 1 pr boot legs & 1 pr of old boots	00 00 10
It 1 pr of mittens & 1 pr of spurs	00 01 00
It 1 mattrise bed	00 02 06
It 2 bolsters & 2 blanckets	00 03 10
It 1 Rug being in 4 peecs	00 06 00
It 3 sheets & 1 halfe sheet	00 13 00
It 3 sheets 1 towell & 2 napkins	00 03 06
It 7 pr of stockins	00 03 08
It 6 ells of new canvase	00 10 00
It 3 quarters of a pownd of beaver	00 07 06
It 1 Rapier	00 05 00
It 1 Axe	00 01 10
[10] It 1 Bill	00 00 06
It 1 Billhooke	00 00 03
It 2 howes & 1 sickle	00 01 00
It 1 melting ladle 3 powder hornes	00 01 10
It 1 ffowling peece	01 00 00
It A little birding peece	00 10 00
It A Carbine	01 06 00
It 2 girdles 1 pr of hangers	00 01 00
It 1 bag of smale nayles cont between 7 & 800	00 02 00
It one bunch of thongs for shoes	00 00 03
It 1 lether bag full of patches	00 00 06
It 1 hand shave 1 hand saw	01 04 00
It 1 Awger	00 00 06
It 1 pr of Taylers sheeres	00 00 06
It 1 prcer stock & a pod in it	00 01 00
It 1 brasen lamp & a frying pan	00 03 06
It 1 pr of pothooks	00 01 00
It 1 fire slice 1 baking plate of Iron	00 02 06
It 1 pewter platter 1 pewter bottle	00 03 04

It 1 old brasen skellet of som six pints	00 00 06
It 1 harnice barrell wth a rownd lock to it	00 01 04
It 1 firkin & 1 halfe firkin	00 01 04
It 1 oyle Jarre of a quart	00 00 04
It 1 old sack & 2 baggs	00 01 00
2 ffishing lines	00 04 00
It an old wastcoate	00 00 02
It 1 black hatt	00 01 00
It 1 pr of skie coloured garters	00 00 06
It 20 smale books & 2 singing ps. books	00 07 06
It 4 single bands	00 02 06
It 2 Ruffe bands	00 02 00
It A box wth thried & points in it	00 01 00
It Another box wth ginger cloves & buttens	00 00 07
It An Embroydered girdle	00 00 00
It 1 silke garter	00 01 00
A case wth smale Cisers & bodkin & penknife	00 00 06
A case to put bullets in	00 00 06
A cap wth silver lace on it	00 00 10
It 2 pr of lether gloves	00 00 06
It A little bag wth peppr & ginger	00 00 06
It A smale box wth yellow nayles	00 00 06
It 14 boot hose tops 3 old boot hose	00 01 00
It 9 old handcherchers	00 01 06
It 1 little here brush	00 00 04
It 3 nightcaps	00 01 04
It 1 pcell of points & thried	00 00 06
It 1 old trunck	00 02 00
It Aynsworth on Exodus	00 01 06
It Bifields works	00 01 06
It 1 pr of shoes	00 01 06
It 3 Iron wedges	00 03 00
It 3 shillings in one of the boxes	00 03 00
It halfe a boate & halfe a canoe	
It The Corn in the field	02 06 03

Rich. Lanckford dying w^thout will Edw Wynslow allowed his Administrator & to pay w^tsoever debts are owing by the sd Rich in new Engl.

[11] 1633 The debts of Rich Lanckford wch are knowne at prnt.

To Job Cole	00 03 09
To m^rs ffuller for phisick	00 06 08
To the widow Adams	02 06 00
To Edw ffoster	02 18 03
To Rich Sparrow	00 11 06
To m^r Gilson	00 1 06
To ffr Weston for divers charges & paines in sicknes & about his death	03 15 06
To the Church at Plymouth	00 14 00
To Josias	00 02 03
To m^r Isaack Allerton	
To Rich Church for a Coffen	00 12 00

PILGRIM ANNIVERSARIES.

As the Pilgrims used "old style" in writing their dates, it is necessary to change them to "new style" in order to determine the anniversary of any event.

The following table gives the proper dates on which to celebrate the principal events which occurred before the end of the year 1621: —

August 15.	Sailed from Southampton, England.	1620
September 16.	Sailed from Plymouth, England.	1620
November 16.	William Butten died at sea.	1620
November 19.	First sighted Cape Cod.	1620
November 21.	Signed "The Compact." Anchored in Cape Cod Harbor and went ashore.	1620
November 23.	Took the shallop ashore for repairs.	1620
November 25.	First exploring party set out by land.	1620
November 26.	Discovered Truro Springs, Pamet River, Cornhill.	1620
December 7.	Second exploring party set out with the shallop.	1620
December 10.	Found the wigwams, graves, etc.	1620
December 14.	Edward Thomson died. *The first death after reaching Cape Cod.*	1620

Pilgrim Anniversaries. 87

December 16.	Third exploring party set out with the shallop.	
	Jasper More died.	1620
December 17.	Dorothy (May) Bradford died.	1620
December 18.	James Chilton died.	
	First encounter with the Indians.	
	Reached Clark's Island at night.	1620
December 20.	Third exploring party spent the Sabbath on Clark's Island.	1620
December 21.	FOREFATHERS' DAY. Third exploring party landed on Plymouth Rock, and explored the coast.	1620
December 25.	The Mayflower set sail from Cape Cod for Plymouth, but was driven back by a change in the wind.	1620
December 26.	The Mayflower arrived at Plymouth Harbor.	1620
December 27.	First Sabbath passed by the whole company in Plymouth Harbor.	1620
December 28.	A party landed and explored by land.	1620
December 29.	One party explored by land, and another in the shallop. Discovered Jones River.	1620
December 30.	Decided to settle near what is now Burial Hill.	1620
December 31.	Richard Britteridge died. *The first death after reaching Plymouth.*	1620
January 2.	Began to gather materials for building.	1621
January 3.	Solomon Prower died.	1621
January 7.	Divided the company into nineteen families and laid out lots.	1621
January 11.	Degory Priest died.	1621
January 14.	Myles Standish with a party discovered wigwams, but saw no Indians.	1621
January 18.	Christopher Martin died.	1621
January 22.	Peter Brown and John Goodman lost themselves in the woods.	1621
January 24.	The thatch on the commonhouse burned.	1621

January 29.	Began to build their storehouse.	1621
January 31.	Kept their meeting on land.	1621
February 8.	Rose Standish died.	1621
February 19.	The house for the sick people caught fire.	1621
February 26.	Indians carried off tools left in the woods by Myles Standish and Francis Cooke.	1621
February 27.	Had a meeting to establish military orders, and chose Myles Standish Captain.	1621
March 3.	Got the great guns mounted on the hill. William White, William Mullins, and two others died.	1621
March 7.	Mary (Norris) Allerton died.	1621
March 17.	Sowed some garden seeds.	1621
March 26.	Had another meeting about military orders, but were interrupted by the coming of Samoset.	1621
March 28.	Samoset came again, with five others.	1621
March 31.	Another meeting about laws and orders, interrupted by coming of Indians. The carpenter fitted the shallop "to fetch all from aboord."	1621
April 1.	Another meeting for public business, interrupted by the coming of Samoset and Squanto to announce Massasoit, with whom a treaty was made.	1621
April 2.	The laws and orders concluded. John Carver chosen Governor for the ensuing year.	1621
April 3.	Elizabeth (Barker) Winslow, wife of Edward Winslow, died.	1621
April 12.	Governor Carver certified a copy of the will of William Mullins, which was carried back to England on the Mayflower.	1621
May 22.	Edward Winslow and Susanna (Fuller) White married. *The first marriage in the colony.*	1621

son to John & Rebecca Taylor
John Taylor was Borne the 21: Day of
November on Saturday between the hour
and Seven of the Clock in the morning
in the yeare one thousand Six Hundred
Seventy foure: 1674

william Taylor son to John & Rebeckah
Taylor was borne the twenty first of
May in the yeare one thousand Six Hundred
Seventy & Six: 1676

Ann ~~~~~~~~~~~~~~~~~~~~~~~~~~~~

Ann Winslow was Borne the seventh
day of August in the yeare 1618

Jn.o Taylor was Marryed to Ann
Winslow the fifth day of November
in the yeare 1662

John Taylor ye sonne of Jn.o & Ann Taylor was
borne ye 31 day of August 1664 and on ye 15 day of

July 12.	Stephen Hopkins and Edward Winslow set out to visit Massasoit.	1621
July 13.	They reached Sowams, and were welcomed by Massasoit.	1621
August 24.	Captain Standish set out for Namasket, with a party of armed men, to revenge the supposed death of Squanto.	1621
September 28.	Captain Standish set out with nine men, and Squanto and three other Indians, to visit the Massachusetts.	1621
September 30.	Landed at Squantum, in Quincy.	1621
November 20.	The Fortune arrived.	1621
December 23.	The Fortune set sail on her return to England.	1621

THE JOHN TAYLOR BIBLE.

Communicated by WILLARD ATHERTON NICHOLS, of Redlands, Cal.

This Bible is owned by John Taylor Gilman Nichols, M.D., of Cambridge, Mass. (seventh in descent from the John Taylor who owned the book in 1679), and is in the care of his brother, Willard Atherton Nichols. It was found in Cambridge in 1889, stored in the garret of the house formerly occupied by the owner's grandfather, Rev. Dr. Ichabod Nichols.

The owner's grandmother, Rev. Dr. Nichols' first wife, was Dorothea Folsom Gilman, whose father, Gov. John Taylor Gilman, of Exeter, N. H., was a grandson of the third John Taylor, "Borne 30th day of August 1704."

Ann Winslow, wife of the second John Taylor, was a daughter of Capt. Edward Winslow, and granddaughter of Mary (Chilton) Winslow.

The writer was elected a member of the Massachusetts Society of Mayflower Descendants, in right of his descent from James Chilton, and this Bible was an important link in the chain of evidence required to prove the line.

All of the pages as far as the first book of Kings have

been lost, but careful comparison with descriptions of early editions of the Bible lead to the conclusion that this is a "Geneva Bible." It is a small quarto. The binding is full calf, in fair condition, and as indicated by the clipping of the pages, noticeable in the entry at the top of the family record, it has been rebound at some date subsequent to the first entry. It contains the Prayer Book and Metrical Psalms, but not the Apocrypha.

The entries shown in the halftone are found on a blank leaf between the Old and New Testaments, and are as follows : —

John Taylor son to John & Rebeckah Taylor was Borne the :21: Day of November one Satturday betwene Nine and Tenn of the Clock in the morning in the yeare one thousand Six Hundred Seventy foure. 1674

William Taylor son to or of John & Rebeckah Taylor was borne the twenty first of May in the yeare one thousand Six Hundred Seventy & Six: 1676

Ann Winslow was Borne the seventh day of August in the year 1678

Jn⁰ Taylor, was Married to Ann Winslow the 5 fifth day of November in the yeare 1702

John Taylor ye son of Jn⁰, & Ann Taylor was Borne 30th day of August 1704 and on ye 4th day of ye weeke

At the bottom of a fragment of the last page, and in the *same handwriting as the first two entries*, appears the following entry : —

John Taylor His Book 1679

On the back of the last page of Revelation is inscribed the following record : —

my Grandfathear Tayntar Desesed this Life In thee 20 day of Feberuary In the yer of our lord — 1689

The preceding entry was probably written by John Taylor, born 1674 (son of John and Rebecca Taylor). It refers to Joseph Taintor, of Watertown, who had a daughter Rebecca, born 18 August, 1647, and whose will, made just before his death, mentions his son-in-law John Taylor.

PLYMOUTH COLONY DEEDS.

Literally transcribed from the Original Records at Plymouth, Mass.,
BY GEORGE ERNEST BOWMAN.

The first volume of the records of deeds was published in 1861, by the Commonwealth of Massachusetts, as Volume XII of the "Records of the Colony of New Plymouth," but the remaining volumes have never been printed.

On the flyleaf of Volume II of the original records appears the following inscription : —

"This volume of Deeds was originally bound up with wills and inventories in two different volumes. It was separated from the wills &c. and indexed, interleaved and bound anew at the expense of the Government of Massachusetts and under the direction of the Revd James Freeman, D.D., Samuel Davis and Benjamin R. Nichols, Esq^s, their Committee, A.D. 1818.

It consists of two parts, and has separate indexes at the beginning of each."

The original numbering of the pages is indicated by numerals enclosed in brackets, and inserted before the first word of each page.

(Volume II.)
[1] 1651 BRADFORD GOV^R

To all Christian people to whom this p^{r}sent writing shall com Samuell ffuller of Scittuate in the goverment of New Plymouth in New England in america sendeth greeting;

Know yea that I the said Samuell ffuller for and in consideracon of a sufficient sum of money in full satisfaction by mee in hand Receved by Peeter Collymore of Scittuate aforsaid planter wherwith I doe acknowlidge myselfe fully satisfyed contented and payed; and therof and every pt and pcell therof exonarate acquite and discharg the said Peeter Collymore his heires executors administerators and assignes for ever by these p^{r}sents have freely and absolutly barganed and sold enfeffed and confeirmed and by these psents doe bargan sell enfeffe and confeirm unto the said Peeter Collymore his heires and assignes forever one dwelling house and a barne and Cowhouse with sixteene acars of upland more or lesse being bounded on the west with the land of m^r Willam Varssall on the south with the land of Resolved White on the north with the hieway by the herring brook; and on the east with the mersh; as allsoe two pcells of mersh land conteining twelve acars more lesse being bounded (one pcell of it) on the west with the upland aforsaid on the south with the mersh land of Mr Willam Varss(*worn*) from a marked stake on the upland to a marked tree on the south end of beare Iland east with beare Iland and on the North to the herring brooke; a smale pcell lyinge betweene the herring brook and the upland; The other pcell of mersh conteining five acars being pt of a pcell of mersh land conteining ten acars being in the use of the aforsaid Samuell ffuller and Willam Wills of Scittuate aforsaid being yet undevided; an(*worn*) is bounded on the west with the mersh land of Walter Woodward tha(*worn*) was once in the tenure and occupacon of Willam hatch senior; on the North and East with the herring brook on the south with a little creek toward beare Iland; with all and severall the appurtenances therunto belonging or any way apperteining; and all my said title and enterest into the said p^rmeses and every pt and pcell therof To have and to hold the said houses upland and meddow unto the said Peeter Collymore his heires and assignes for ever To bee holden after the mannor of east Greenwidge in the Countey of Kent in free and common soccage and not in capite or by Knights service by the Rents or services therof and therby due or of Right acostomed and with Warrantice against all people whatsoever from by or under mee the said Samuell ffuller or by my Right or title claiming any Right title or enterest into the said pmises or any pt or pcell therof; And I the said Samuell ffuller doe allso covenant and promise and graunt by these psents that it shall and may bee lawfull to and for the said Peeter Collymore either by himselfe or his atorney to Record or enrowle these psents or Cause them to bee Recorded and enrowled in the Court at Plym : afor(*worn*) before the Governer for the time being according to the [2] The usuall mannor and order of Recording and enrowling evidences in such cases provided : In Wittnesse whereof I the said Samuell ffuller haue heerunto sett my hand and seale the five and twentieth day of March in the yeare of our lord one Thousand six hundred and fifty

Memorand the words (hieway by the) between the lynes of twelve and thirteene, in the originall evidence were enterlyned before the sealing and delivering heerof

Samuell ffuller

Signed Sealed and delivered   his seale
in the psence of
The Mark I of Isack Stedman
The Mark O of henery Adverd
    James Torrey

The 16th of May 1650 Jane ffuller the wife of Samuell ffuller did com before mee Timothy hatherley asistant to the Governer of New Plym : in New England and did freely acknowlidg her willingnes of the within Mencioned sale and did freely Resigne up her Right to Peeter Collymore

Timothy Hatherley

[3] 1651 To all people to whom these p^rsents shall come Thomas Robinson of Scittuate in the Goverment of New Plymouth in New England in America yeoman sendeth greeting &c.

Know ye that I the aforsaid Thomas Robinson for and in consideration of thirty and three pounds of corrant New England pay to mee in hand paied pr Josepth Shaw Planter and Willam Richards planter both of Waymouth in the Goverment of the Massachusets Bay in New England in America wherwith I the aforsaid Thomas Robinson doe acknowlidg my selfe fully satisfyed contented and paide and therof and of every part and pcell therof doe exonerate acquite and discharge the aforsaid Josepth Shaw and Willam Richards they and every of them theire and every of theire heires Exequitors aministrators and assignes for ever by these p^rsents have freely and absolutely barganed and solde infeoffed and confeirmed ; and by these p^rsents doe bargen sell enfeoffe and confeirme from mee the aforsaid Thomas Robinson and my heires to them the said Josepth Shaw and Williams Richar(*worn*) and theire & every of theire heires and assignes for ever ; All that pcell of upland called by the name of Springfeild lying and being in Scittuate aforsaid by that River commonly called and knowne by the name of the north-river and is by computation ninety acares more or lesse being bounded towards the east to the land of John Hewes seni^r of Scittuate aforsaid ; Towards the west to the common and butting towards the North to the common and butting towards the south to the mersh, likewise all the mersh meddow as shall belonge to the aforsaid ninety acars of upland on an equale devision which said mersh lyeth neare to the said upland ; With all and singular the appurtenances therunto belonging or any way appertaining to all or any part or pcell of the aforsaid ninety acars more or lesse of upland and the mersh meddow therunto belonging To have and to hold the aforsaid Ninty acars of upland and the mersh meddow therunto belonging unto the aforsaid Josepth Shaw and Willam Richards they and every of them theire and every of their heires and assignes for ever to the propruse and behoofe of them the aforsaid Joseph Shaw and Willam Richards theire and every of their heires and assignes for ever : To bee holden according to the Manor of East Greenwidge in the County of Kent in free and common Sockage and not in capite nor by Knights service pr the Rents and services therof and therby due and of Right accustomed and warranting the sale against all people whatsoever from by or under mee the said Thomas Robinso(*worn*) [4] or by my Right or title claiminge any Right title or enterest of or in the p^rmises or any p^t or pcell therof ; And the said Thomas Robinson doth allsoe Covenant promise and graunt to and with the aforsaid Josepth Shaw and Willam Richards that Silence Robinson wife of the aforsaid Thomas Robinson shall yeild up her Right in the thirds of the aforsaid Ninety acars of upland & the mersh therunto belonging within one month next ensueing the date heerof and that before a

maiestrate according to the usuall mannor and Costome of the Resigneing of Rightes in such case provided; And The said Thomas Robinson doth allsoe further covenant promise and graunt to and with the aforsaid Josepth Shaw and Willam Richards that it shall and may bee lawfull to and for the aforsaid Josepth Shaw and Willam Richards they or either of them or either of theire Attorne or Attorneys to Record or enrowle these p^rsents or to cause them to bee Recorded or enrowled in the court of New Plym : or any other place of Records before the Govn^r for that time being or any other maiestrate or offecer in that case provided according to the usuall mannor of Recording or enrowling evidences in such case provided In Witnese wherof I the aforsaid Thomas Robinson have hereunto set my hand and Seale the thirtieth Day of Aprell one Thousand six hundred fifty and one 1651
Signed Sealed   Tho : Robinson   his seal
and delivered in the
p^rsence of us videlecett
John Ramsden
Richard Garrett

The last of aprell 1651 Silence Robinson the wife of Thomas Robinson did freely acknowlidge the Resigning of her Right or enterest that shee had in the within named or mencioned deed before mee   Timothy Hatherley

[5] These p^rsents Witnesseth that I Josepth Shaw have allianated solde and made over unto Thomas Chambers fforty and five acars more or lesse of upland and eight acars of mersh more or lesse and is all my share of the within mencioned Land ; Aprell the 30th 1651   Witnesse my hand
                                                Josepth Shaw

These p^rsents Witnesseth that I Willam Richard(*worn*) have allianated sold and made over unto Gowin White fforty five acars of upland more or lesse and six acars of Mersh more or lesse and is all my share of the within mencioned land October the 22^{cond} 1651   Witnesse my hand
                                                Willam Richards

These breife Conveyances of land above mencioned doe stand in Reference to the Deed Recorded in the two pages ymediately goeing before and it with them were shewed in the open court holden at New Plym: the 2^{cond} of March 1651 and by order of the said court accordingly enrowled

Memorandum the 3^d of June 1652

That Willam Bassett senior of Duxburrow in the Jurisdiction of New Plym: doth acknowlidge that hee hath freely and absolutely given and made over unto his soninlaw Leiftenant Perigrine White forty acares of upland ground on which the said leiftenant White now liveth as alsoe all the meddow ground lying directly against betwixt the end (*worn*) the said upland and the south River the said upland to Range on the same mannor that It was layed out to him the said Willam Bassett the said upland and mersh soe lying and Ranging as aforsaid with all the emunities privilidges and appurtenances belonging therunto to appertaine unto the onely proper use and behoof of him the said Peregrine White hi(*worn*) heires and assignes forever

    Acknowlidged before mee Myles Standish
    June Court 1652.

[p. 6, blank]

[7] 1652   BRADFORD GOV^R

Memorand the 2^{cond} day of the 4th month called June.

These p^{r}sents doe Witnesse that John Reyner of Plymouth of New England for and in consideracon of the summe of five and twenty pounds to bee paid by Mr Ralph Partrich of Duxburrow in New England in mannor and forme following that is to say twelve pound and ten shillings in cattle or corn to bee payed the nine and twentieth of September commonly known by the name of michaelmas day 1652 the other twelve pounds and ten shillings to bee paied in corn or cattle the 29th of September 1653 hath freely and absolutly bargained and sould and by these p^{r}sents doth bargaine and sell unto the said Mr Ralph Partrich fifty nine acars of upland more or less lying in Duxburrow between the lands of John Browne and John Washburne senior alsoe six acars of meddow more or lesse adiacent and alsoe all and singulare the appurtenances therunto belonging and all his Right title and enterest of and into the same and every pte and pcell therof with all the ffencing

To have and to hold the said fifty nine acares of upland with the six acars of meddow and all the ffencing with all and every the appurtenances unto the said M[r] Ralph Partrich his heires and assignes for ever; and to the onely pper use and behoofe of him the said M[r] Ralph Partrich his heires and assignes for ever and with warrantice from him his heires & assignes In Witnesse Wherof I the said John Reyner hath heerunto sett his hand the Day and yeare above Written;

In the p[r]sence of us   John Reyner
Samuell Newman
Phillip Delano

[p. 8, blank]

[9] 1652   BRADFORD GOV[R]

The following writing bearing date March the 23[d] 1652 was Recorded July the 29[th] in the yeare abovesaid

Witnesseth these p[r]sents that wheras Henery Howland of Duxburrow and Experience Michell of the same Towne haveing theire Lands Joyning together and theire habitations neare eich other and the said henery howland haveing conveniency of a spring and smale brooke before his Land for watering of cattle and otherwise and the said Experience Michell being wholy defective of the aforsaid conveniency; And alsoe that there hath been Divers Differencies between the aforsaid pties conserning the Intrenchments upon the Lands of the said henery howland by the said Experien (*worn*) Michell; Now Know all men pr these p[r]sents that the aforsaid henery to end all Diferences heerafter hath for naighbourhood and continuance of frindshipp hath given and graunted unto the aforsaid Experience Michell to him his heires and assignes for ever free accesse to the aforsaid conveniency of water for the aforsaid uses; allwaies provided that the said Experience Michell Run his fence in his owne

Range between the aforsaid henery and Experience; and shall have his outlet for his cattle out of his owne land ; And when It shall seeme good to the aforsaid henery howland to ffence in his land severall ; then the said henery Doth give and graunt unto the aforsaid Experience to him and his heires forever his way to the aforsaid water; an outlett from an oake tree marked standing about six foote within henery howland northward and soe to another marked tree of oake southward ; and from this Range as aforsaid for the breadth all the upland to the mersh for a way for the said Experience to pase toe and fro without molestation for the ends afforsaid ; furthermore wheras there was exchange of a smale portion of upland by the said pties ; and diference likly to arise between them : It is confeirmed by this deed to stand as It was exchanged to the said henery and Experience to them and theire heires for ever ; It is further agreed and concluded by and between both the aforsaid pties that this agreement shall bee put upon Record to stand to all posteritie to end all future differences conserning the p^{r}mises aforsaid

June the sixt 1652   Acknowlidged by both pties
                               before Miles Standish
                               John Alden Asistants

[p. 10, blank]

[11] 1652   BRADFORD GOVN^R

Memorand ; The 2^{cond} of august 1652 That Thomas Little somtimes Inhabitant of the Towne of Plym : Doth acknowlidg that for and in consideration of the summe of fifteen pound; ten pound wherof is alreddy paied and the Remayning five pound to bee paied by the 2^{cond} of august 1653 in cattle or beefe by Richard ffoster of the Towne aforsaid Planter hee hath freely and absolutely barganed allianated and sould enfeafed and confeirmed and by these p^{r}sents Doth bargan sell enfeaffe and confeirm unto the said Richard ffoster all that his house and Land lying and being at the Eelriver in the Townshipp of Plymouth aforsaid wheron the said Thomas Little formerly lived videlecet all that his lott or share of land which hee had with his wife being twenty acres bee it more or lesse being bounded on the one side with the Land of Robert Bartlet and on the other side with the lands of Joseph Warren the netherend abutting upon the Eelriver aforsaid and soe extendinge Itselfe in ye length therof up into the woods together with an addition of land graunted sence unto the said Thomas Little att the upper end of the aforsaid Lott with a pcell of Land belonging to him att a place neare the said Eelriver commonly called the hoop place with a pcell of land hee bought of John Richards being twentyfive acres together with all the meddow Land of any kind belonging unto the said Thomas Little att the Eelriver aforsaid; with all the outhouses and houseing upon the said Land; with all the fenceing theron or in and about any pte or pcell therof; the said p^{r}mises with all and singulare the appurtenances belonging unto the said p^{r}mises or any pte or pcell therof; To have and to hold the said Lands houses out houses meddows fences; with all the enlargements belonging therunto and all graunts of Lands adioyning or belonging therunto with all and singulare the appurtenances and privilidges in any wise appertaining thereunto or unto any pte or pcell therof; unto the said Richard ffoster his heires and assignes for ever unto the only ppr use and behoofe of him the said Richard ffoster his heires and assignes for ever; provided that incase Nathaniel Warren or any of his heires shall molest or by law procure the abovesaid lott which the said Thomas Little had by marriage with his wife; from the said Richard ffoster or his heires; that then the said Thomas Little is to have Returned unto him or his heires what soever Lands now the said Richard ffoster hath bought of him; and the said Thomas Little or his heires is to Returne unto the said Richard ffoster or his heires the abovesaid fifteen pounds to bee paied att such severall paiments as it was paid to him

The day and yeare abovesaid Ann the wife of the said Thomas Little came before the Gove^r and together with her said husband; did give her free and full Consent unto the abovesaid bargan and sale

[p. 12, blank]

(*To be continued.*)

THE DIARY OF JABEZ FITCH, JR.

(Continued from page 42.)

November 19th 1756* We travel'd through the Clay banks & at 1 oClock came to Saratoge, where we waded through ye River & marched 8 miles furder where we Lodg'd by ye River a little below ye fly —

ye 20th In ye Morning we march'd Down to Still waters where we got some Refreshment — & then Set off for ye Half moon where we arrved before Sunset where we cros'd ye River & Lodg'd on a Mountain — In crossing the River Maj^r Saltonstall got ye Divel into him

Sunday ye 21st In ye morning we burnt each of us a Shurt and after Some time Set off & Traveled round in ye Woods to Shun ye Small Pox & about Sunset cam to Green Bush where we found Col. Wooster & got Some Refreshment & went into ye woods for a Lodging. This was the fifth night we had lain out & ye most Tedious of them all as ye weather was Extreem cold & ye bushes Small So we could make but little fire's but however we Spent ye Night in Eating raw Unyans Broyling Pork & Beef & Drinking Rhum Some of our Company Drunk &c —

ye 22nd We Spent chiefly In geting Provision to last us into Connecticut Toard night we March'd about Four miles & Lodg'd in a Large Dutch Barn Some of our men milk'd ye Cows — This Night there fell a Snow &c

ye 23rd We Travel'd By ye River about Ten miles & then Turn'd up Eastward & got within Seven miles of Canderhook where we Lodg'd again in a Dutch Barn

ye 24th We Traveled Down into Canderhook got some Brakefast & Traveled Down as far as ye Stone house where Somebody Stole my Musq^t, but it Happened So that I got another that answer'd as well as my own here we Lodg'd in a Barn this Night —

ye 25th We turn'd out very Early in the morning, Traveled Six miles & got Some breakfast then Turn'd out

---

* The part of the diary covering the period from 20 May to 19 November, 1756, has been lost.

in ye Snow & Travel'd Down to Nobles's where we Drink'd Something & Travel'd half a mile & found John Roben Drunk carried him back to the Barn & got about half a mile further & found Henry Shuntup as Drunk as tother — The Storm being very tedious & we just Assending ye Mountain we thought it Imprudent to Cary him back — So we cover'd him up in ye Snow with his blanket as well as posable & left him Then we Traveld four miles over ye mountain and got to Spurs tho' very wet & cold — This Night we Lodg'd in Spurs barn —

ye 26th The Snow had got to be Eighteen Inches Deep & no path ye weather Extreem cold and windy which made it uncomfortable Traveling, but however this Day we got into Canaan & Lodg'd at Night in Lawrence's Barn —

ye 27th We Travel'd threw Canaan Cornwell & Lodg'd at Woddams's in Gotion — This was ye First night that we Lodgd in any Dwelling house —

Sunday ye 28th We Traveled through Litchfield & Herrington & Lodg'd in ye Edg of Farmington at Strong's there we Se Abraham Hill he Infoms us of ye Death of old Jno. Richards of Preston

ye 29th We arrived at Hartford where we Lodg'd our Arms and Tock Receipts, Drink'd two Pottles of Wine & cross'd ye feny, and Lodg'd at Woodbridges in East Hartford —

ye 30th We traveled Down to Bolton before we could get breakfast, & Named ye plais ye Hungry March — Then we came to Howses in Andover Where we Lodgd that Night — here we met Several Norwich men

Decr ye 1st In ye morning we parted with most of our company before Sunrise about 10 oClock came to Lebanon Soon after we met Bro^r Rudd with a Horse for me to ride but I rather chose to go afoot, & we came to Land Lord Huntingtons where we Eat Dinner & at 2 oClock got into Town where we met Jno Andrus who carried our packs home for us — In ye Evening I got home to Fathers —

Decr ye 1st 1756 — I got Home to My Fathers from ye Camp — I Had Bin from Home More than Six Months this Time

ye 2nd Mr Powers was Ordain'd at Newent — This Day

I was at Brother Elisha's there I See Capt. Mix & Some other of our old Neighbors who were Going to Ordination —

ye 3rd I Bought a Deer Skin of Jos^h Bingham of Windham for three Dollars —

ye 7th I went to ye Landing & Bought Som Broad Cloath (of Lt Breed) for a Great Coat, I Lit of Brother Elisha there & Came Home with Him —

ye 11th I Heard of ye Death of Mr Worthington of Sea-Brook I Also Heard of ye Death of Sam^{ll} Tracy this Day who Died at Fort-Edward —

ye 16th Jacob Burnit was at Father's — This Day I went Up to Mr Fishers at Preston & Got My Great Coat — The Night Following there Fell a Concidrable Snow —

ye 21st I went over to Town. See Col. Whiting & Capt. Charles & Lt Billings at Lefingwell's after I Staid Som Time with them I went Up to Brother Rudd's

ye 22nd Bro^r Rudd & I went Up to His Father's after Som Time There we Tock Cos^n Jonathan with Us & went Up To Lieu^t Peck's To Se Serj^t Peck But He was Not at Home So went Down To Mr Waterman & there Found Serj^t Peck & After we Had Spent Som Time there Tock Him & Ezekiel Waterman with Us & Came Down To Bro^r Rudd's where We Had a Vary Good Supper Prepaird & Flip Vary Plenty — Also Lt Ichabod Fitch was there y^t Evening with David Waterman & Som Other Gent^n Who Had Concidrable Comacal Discorce of Capt. Whiting & His Wife —

ye 23rd was a Stormy Day I Staid there with Bro^r & Sister all Day —

ye 24th I Came Home to Father's Bro^r Rudd Came with Me Down to ye Mill —

Saturday ye 25th Chrismas Day I went over To Town again To Carry Som Accounts (in Order To Make Up a Muster Roll) To Capt. Whiting's — When I Came there I Found ye Col. there & Soon After Adj^t Russel of the Rhod-Island Reg^t Com in — Then We Had a Vary Good Dinner & was Treated Vastly Hansom — In Coming Home I Cros'd ye Riv^r on The Ise &c. —

Monday ye 27th Bro^r Elisha Help'd Me Chop wood —
This Night we Had our Chrismas Choras at Stephen Fitch's
a Concidrable Company we Had there Both of Young Men
& Women — About This Time I Se Sam^ll Stoddard (My old
Friend & Companion) Several Times & Had Much Discorce
with Him He Had Lately Ben Cast away as He was Going
a Vaig to Sea with Capt. Chester

Jan^u 11th 1757 In ye Evening I Was In Company at James
Cook's Where We Drink'd a Quantity of Mothegalen &
Had a Concidrable Choris — It was Vary Bad Riding this
Night &c.

ye 18th Stephen Fitch Met with a Sad Accident By a
Fall from a Hors which Hurt Him Concidrablely &c. —

ye 19th I Went over To Town Somthing Expecting to
Receive My Wages But was Disappointed & at Night
Went Up To Bro^r Rudd's —

ye 20th I Went Down To Town again & Rec^d the Whol
of My Wages of Col^o Whiting which was £14. s13. d1.
Then After I Had Had Somthing of a Tote with Serj^t Peck
Serj^t Andrus & Som other of My old Acquaintanc I Came
Home with a Ruff Company of My Neighbor's &c.

ye 24th I Went over to Town again Carried Som
Leather To Mr Hide & Got a Saddle there. I Went Up to
Bro^r Rudd's again I also Paid Lieu^t Breed Som Money
this Day at Night I Came Home ye Storm was Vary Considrable —

ye 26th I went Down To Bro^r Pelatiah's in Groton —

ye 27th Bro^r & His Wife Mr Stoddard & I Went over
To Mistick a Visiting To Capt. Burrows's Mr Ellet's To
Sam^ll Burrows's & To Thos Eldredg's where We Had Concidrable Company & Staid Som Time, at all Which Plaises
we was Treated Extreamly Well — In ye Evening We Went
to Bro^rs again only Left Stoddard at Eldredg's This Evening We Also Went Down To Mr Foot's Where was L^t
Fish & His Wife. There we Drink'd Yokheage & Sider &
Had a Good Supper. But ye People I Thought Not So
Agreable for Discorce. But However We Got Home So as
to Have Som Sleap —

ye 28th We Made a Visit at Mr Katerlin's Capt. Bellou's and Mr Gallup's, after we Got to Bro^rs again Mr Stoddard & I went Down To Sam^ll Burrows's &c.

ye 29th In ye Morning I Set out & went over to Uncle Baley's Where I Staid Som Time — And Then Came Hom To Father's

ye 3^d of February I was in Company at Jos^h Brewster Jn^rs In ye Evening & also Most of ye Night — ye Weather was Somthing Cold & it was Extream Slipery ye Nex Morning I Got Hom in Season To Fodder the Cattle — Then I Went over To Town & Accidentally Lit of My Cos^n Ichabod Downing &c. I also Se Col. Whiting this Day & Capt. Jabez Fitch of Canbury &c.

ye 7th Bro^r Elisha & I Went To ye Landing & Carry'd Som Oats to Market —

ye 9th Elisha & Wm Stewert Help'd Me Chop Wood in the Great Swamp Bro^r John Baley was at Father's this Day &c.

ye 14th In ye Evening I was at Mr Deming's — Dan^ll Deming was Then Sick of ye Pluricy — This was after He was Publish'd His Wife was there — This Night I Wach'd with Him — His Garl & Sist^r Lucy Set Up with Him Most of ye Night — The Next Morning after I Had Tock a Nap I went Home & To Clearing Swomp ye Evening Following I was at Bro^r Elisha's He was Gon to a Cort at Preston His wife & I Contluded y^t He was Run away with ye Wid^o Branch —

ye 25th I went over to Town & Inlisted Into a Comp^y To Be Commanded By Capt. Fitch for an Unknown Expadition — This Day In Town I Heard ye Sorrowfull News of the Distruction of ye Norwich Privatear (Commanded By Capt. Gale) which I Understand was Blown Up in Som Part of ye West Indies on ye 8th of Jan^u Last — About this Time also we Hered of ye Death of Sam^ll Mayson who Died in Old England &c.

ye 26th My Burth Day I Bought a Cow of Mr Pride for £2. *s*18.0

ye 1st of March Sister Rudd Was at Father's — I Went Part way Hom with Her — This Day Capt. Hull Got Home & Gave a More Perticular Account of ye Loss of ye Late

Privateer — This Day Thos Andrus Listed, as I was Coming Home I was in at His Hous — I also Se Lt Palmer of Sonington Had Som Discorce with Him &c — ye 1st of March 1757.

March 4th 1757 I Went to Town Se Sister Rudd at Lt Durkys

ye 5th Brother Pelatiah & His wife Came to Fathers Sunday ye 6th I Went to Meeting with Brother at Night a Numbber of ye Nabours was Here

ye 7th I Toock a Ride With Him First we went to Samll Tracys then Nathan Tracys Mr Buttons Decn Tracys Jedh Tracys Josh Morgans Mr Rosaters Coraries* Insn Lambs there went to Diner then to Hezkh Meechs Peter Yearingtons Ephraim Smiths Decn Tracys & then Home

ye 8th We Went to Town at Night to Brother Rudds there Se an old Noissy Solder

ye 9th Brother & I Sot out to Com Home Came Into Town I Staid there & Musterd that Day at Night Came Home Brother Elisha & his wife were Here

ye 10 was a Vary Snowy Day

ye 11th Brother Pelatiah & His wife went to Capt Averys

ye 12 I Met them at Mr Giless Went With em to Nathan Galleps then Home with em

ye 14th I went to Noanck With Brother to Se Jno Fanens Child that was Scolt then to Lamll Burrowss to John Lathams Thos Wolworths then Home With Him Trimd Some Peech trees at Night a Company of ye Nabors Was there Thos Eldridge & His wife & Josh Burrows Staid all Night Singing Anough we Had

ye 15th I Staid there all Day — Nathan Gallup was there at Night we went Down to Amos Burrowss

ye 16th I Went to Unkle Baleys at Night Back to Brothers

* Crary's.

(*To be continued.*)

SCITUATE, MASS.,

BIRTHS, MARRIAGES AND DEATHS.

(Continued from page 47.)

Rev. Nathaniel Eells was pastor of the Second Church, at South Scituate, now Norwell. Mr. George C. Turner, of Norwell, has kindly compared my copy of the town records with the original records of that church, and the additions furnished by him are enclosed in parentheses.

[5] The following persons were married together by Nathanael Ells Minister

Richard Bourn of Sandwich & Margaret Foster of Scituate were married April 12, 1731

Dr. Benjamin Stocbridge & Ruth Otis both of Scituate were Married June 3^d, 1731

Thomas Rose of Hanover & Faith Silvester of Scituate were Married August 19, 1731

Joseph Lovel & Desire Hatch both of Scituate were married September 23^d, 1731

James Neal & Jane Blair both Residents in Scituate were Married Oct^o 28, 1731

Christopher Fling of Pembrook & Martha Linsey of Scituate were Married Novr 4th, 1731

James Woodworth & Sarah Soper Both of Scituate were Married December 16, 1731

Nehemiah Hatch & Martha Stutson Both of Scituate were Married December 21, 1731

Joshua Lincoln & Mercy Dwlly Both of Scituate were married Feb. 18, 1731

Nathan Pickles Junr & Margaret Stutson Junr both of Scituate were married March 13, 1731–2

Thomas Faunce of Plym^o & Hannah Damon of Scituate were Married April 13, 1732

John Collamer of Scituate & Margaret Whitten of Hingham were married April 27, 1732

Enoch Whitten of Hingham & Leah Stutson of Scituate were married November 16, 1732

Scituate, Mass. 107

James Turner and Mary Turner Both of Scituate were Married November 23, 1732

Thomas Joslin of Hanover & Anna Stocbridge of Scituate were married Jany 1, 1732-3

Thomas Turner Junr & Mary Bryant Both of Scituate were Married Feb. 14, 1732-3

Joseph Cushing Junr & Lydia King Both of Scituate were Married March 29, 1733

Joshua Russel & Silence Damon both of Scituate were married August 23, 1733

Joseph Palmer & Jane Toby both of Scituate were married Septem^r 20, 1733

Samuel Perry & Eliz^a. Bryant both of Scituate were married Septem^r 20, 1733

Thomas Wason & Ann Canady both of Scituate were married Oct^o 11, 173(3)

Nathanael Eells of Stonnington in Connecticut and Mercy Cushing of Scituate were married Oct^o 18, 173(3)

William Prouty & Jemima Tower both of Scituate were married Novemb^r 15, 173(3)

Samuel Palmer Junr & Barsheba Bryant both of Scituate were married Jany 16, (1733 4)

Benjamin Clap & Grace Tilden both of Scituate were married Oct^o (23, 1734)

John House of Hanover & Anne Neal of Scituate were Married Nov^r (19, 1734)

Edward Prouty & Eliz^a. Sprague both of Scituate were married Novemb^r (21, 1734)

Elisha Silvester & Eunice Prouty both of Scituate were married Decem(ber 12, 1734)

Jesse Turner & Grace Dwelly both of Scituate were married Decem^r 1(8, 1734)

Arthur Mullin & Mary Forgason both of Scituate were married Decem^r 2(6, 1734)

Thomas Pincin & Agatha Hammon both of Scituate were married Jany 15, (1734-5)

Jedediah Beal of Hingham & Grace Hatch of Scituate were married February 5, 17(34-5)

Joseph Wade & Rachel Turner both of Scituate were married Feby 13, 17(34-5)

Gideon Stutson & Lydia Pitcher Both of Scituate were married June 5, 173(5)

Joseph Copeland & Eliz^a. Tollman both of Scituate were married July 23, 173(5)

Robert Woodworth & Mary Soper both of Scituate were married Sepr 11, 173(5)*

Samuel Hollis of Weymouth & Deborah Tower of Scituate were married Jany 15, (1)7(35-6)

Richard Turner & Ruth Foster Both of Scituate were married Jany 23, (1)73(5-6)

Tony & Phillis Negroes Slaves to Mr Ephraim Otis of Scituate were married Jan. (29), 173(5-6)

Jabez Standly & Deborah Tremere both of Scituate were married Feb. (9), 17(35-6)

Scipio Lock of Woburn & Meriah Samson of Scituate were married (April 2), 17(36)

Barnabas Barker & Mary Neal of Scituate were married May (24, 1736)

Ezekiel Turner of Hanover & Ruth Randall† of Scituate were married June 17, (1736)

David Merrit & Hannah Barrell both of Scituate were married (Oct^o 21, 1736)

David Stocbridge of Hanover & Deborah Cushing of Scituate were married (January 10, 1736-7)

Caleb Church of Scituate & Sarah Williamson of Scituate ‡ were married (Jan. 20, 1736-7)

Ebenezer Wing of Hanover & Mary Stoddard of Scituate were (married Feb. 3, 1736-7)

Benjamin Bowker & Hannah Prouty both of Scituate (mar. Feb. 24, 1736-7)

[6] Edmund Gross of Hingham & Olive Silvester of Scituate were married March 3, 1736-7

Joshua Lapham & Mary Wood both of Scituate were married March 3, 1736-7

---

* Robert Woodwart, aged 85, and Mary Soper, aged 65. *Church Records.*
† Mrs. Ruth Randall. *Church Records.*
‡ Marshfield. *Church Records.*

Josiah Cushing & Ruth Thomas both of Scituate were married Oct⁰ 20, 1737

Benjamin Stoddard Junr & Ruth Curtice both of Scituate were married Novr 24, 1737

William Brooks & Mary Brayman both of Scituate were married Decr 15, 1737

James Nash & Sarah Litchfield both of Scituate were married Feby 23, 1737-8

Samuel Garnet Junr of Hingham & Abigal Simmons of Scituate were married April 18, 1738

Ensign Man of Scituate & Tabitha Vinal Late of Scituate were married July 19, 1738

Seth Williams of Taunton & Mary Ells of Scituate were married Novr 7, 1738

Jonathan Turner & Abigal Stocbridge both of Scituate were married Novr 15, 1738

Michael Stocbridge & Mary Jones both of Scituate were married Novr 30, 1738

Isaac Lincoln & Abigail Mellus both of Scituate were married Decr 21st, 1738

Cuffe a Negro of Deacon Stoddard of Scituate & Meriah Negro of John Stevens of Hingham were married Dec^m 21st, 1738

The Following Persons were Married p^r Joseph Cushing Ju^r Jestice peac

Hezekiah Hatch & Mary Cudworth both of Scituate Ware married June ye 23^d, 1755

Joseph Nash Junr & Thankfull Hammon both of Scituate ware married Decem^r 16, 1755

(worn)mion Turner & Sarah Buck both of Scituate were Married January ye 20th, 1756

John Studly & Mary Benson Jones both of Scituate were Married February ye 10th, 1756

(worn)obart Peirce & Mercy Hatch both of Scituate were Married March ye 15th, 1756

Peleg Simmons & Ruth Bowker both of Scituate were Married July ye 6th, 1758 (*worn*)dworth of Freetown & Anne Bryant of Scituate were Married Decem^r ye 7th, 1758

(*worn*)urch & Hannah Franklin both of Scituate were Marrid May 24, 1759

(*worn*)tis & Sarah Jenkins both of Scituate were married June 3, 1762

(*worn*)etson & Deborah Stetson both of Scituate were married Oct^o 7, 1762

(*worn*)rry & Mary Stetson both of Scituate were married June 16, 1763

(*worn*) Laphum of Marshfield & Content Berker were married Septem^r ye 26, 1763

(*To be continued.*)

THE WILL OF GYLES HOPKINS.

Communicated by MISS MARY G. HINCKLEY, of Barnstable, Mass.

This will was recorded in the Probate Records of Barnstable County, at Barnstable, Mass., and is found in Volume I, page 32.

As the Codicil was signed 15 March, 1689 (new style), and the will was admitted to probate 26 April, 1690 (new style), the death of Gyles Hopkins must have occurred between these two dates.

The will follows:

To all Christian people to whome these presents shall com know ye that I Giles Hopkins of Eastham being sick and weak of Body and yet of perfit memory do declare this as my Last will and Testament on this ninteenth day of January in ye year of our Lord 1682

I bequeath my Body to ye grave in decent burial when this Temporal Life of mine shall have an end and my soul to god that gave it in hopes of a blessed Resurection at ye Last day

2ly my will is that my son Stephen Hopkins shall possess and Injoy all my upland and meadow Lying and being at Satuckit that is to say all my upland and meadow on y^e

southerly side of ye bounds of ye Towne of eastham that is to say all my Right and title Intrest and claime to all those Lands from ye head of Namescakit to ye southermost part of ye long pond where mannomoyet cart way goes over to Satuckit and from thence to ye head of manomoyet river and so as our Line shall run over to ye south sea all ye Lands between thos bounds and ye westermost bounds of ye purchesers at satuckit river all these Lands I give unto my son Stephen Hopkins and to his heirs forever: and half my stock of cattill for and in consideration of ye above sd Land and half stock of cattel my will is that after my decease my son Stephen Hopkins shall take ye care and oversight and maintaine my son William Hopkins during his natural Life in a comfortable decent manner.

3ly my will is that all my Lands at Palmet both purchesed and unpurchesed both meadows and upland and all my Lands at Pochet and my third part of Samsons neck and what other Lands shall fall unto me as a purcheser from ye fore mentioned Bounds of my son Stephen Hopkinses Lands and potanomacot all these fore specified Lands I give unto my sons Caleb and Joshua Hopkins to be equaly devided between them: further my will is that if either of my sons Joshua or Caleb Hopkins dye having no Issew that then these Lands which I have given them to be equally devided between them fall to him that surviveth.

4ly. I give unto my wife Catorne Hopkins and to my son William Hopkins the improvment of too acres of meadow Lying at ye head of Rock Harbor during my wifes Life and ye one half of that too acres I give unto my son william during his Life and after ye decease of and after ye decease of my wife and son william I do give this above sd too acres of meadow to my son Joshua Hopkins and his heirs forever: as also after my decease I give unto my son Joshua Hopkins a parcel of meadow Lying at ye mouth of Rock Harbor according to ye bounds thereof specified in ye Towne Records of Lands: it I give unto my son Caleb Hopkins a parcel of meadow Lying at Little Nameskeket according to ye bounds thereof specified in ye Towne Book of Records of Lands.

It I give unto my wife my now dwelling House and halfe my Land and halfe my orchard that is by my house: by Land I mean half my Land that is about my house both fenced and unfenced during my wifes natural Life, and then ye abovesd housing and Lands to fall unto my son Joshua Hopkins; the other half of my Land and orchard I give to my son Joshua Hopkins after my death that is to say ye other half of my Lands Liying about my house.

It. I give unto my son Caleb Hopkins one pair of plow Irons.

It. I give unto my son Joshua Hopkins one payer of plow Irons.

It. I give unto my son Joshua Hopkins my carte and wheels.

It. I give unto my wife ye other half of my stock and moveables I say to my wife and my son William or what parte of ye moveables my wife shall see cause to bestow on my son William Hopkins.

It. I do appoint my son Stephen Hopkins to be my true and Lawful executor of this my Last will and testament to pay what is payable and Receive what is due.

And to ye truth and verity hereof I have hereunto sett my hand and seal ye day and year above written.

Signed and sealed in
presence of us,   ye mark of
Jonathan Sparrow.   Giles H Hopkins (seal)
Samuel Knowles.

Jonathan Sparrow and Samuel Knowles witnesses to this will made oath in Court y^e: 16th: of April 1690 that they saw ye above sd Giles Hopkins signe seal and declare this to be his Last will and Testament.

                Attest   Joseph Lothrop. Clerk.

I ye abovesd Giles Hopkins do declare where as by ye providence of God my Life has been prolonged unto me and by Reason of age and disabillity of Body I am Incapatiated to provide for my owne support and my wifes, my will further is that my son Stephen Hopkins from this time and forward shall possess and Injoy all my stock and moveable estate provided he take effectual care for mine and my wifes Comfortable Support during our natural Lives witness my hand and seal this fifth day of march $168\frac{8}{9}$.

Witness Mark Snow   Giles H Hopkins (seal)
Jonath Sparrow.   (mark / his)

The within mentioned Mark Snow and Jonathan Sparrow made oath in Court April y^e : 16 : 1690 that they saw Giles Hopkins within mentioned signe seal and declare y^e latter part of this will within mentioned to be his Last will and Testament.   Attest. Joseph Lothrop, Clerk.

Duly Compared with the original and entered April y^e : 22 : 1690.   Attest. Joseph Lothrop, Recorder.

REPORTS FROM STATE SOCIETIES.

MASSACHUSETTS SOCIETY.

A meeting of the Society was held at the Hotel Vendome, Boston, on Saturday afternoon, January 7, 1899, the Two Hundred and Seventy-Eighth Anniversary of the laying out of the lots on Leyden Street.

Governor Gamaliel Bradford read from Mourt's "Relation" the account of this allotment, and Mr. Morton Dexter described the unveiling of the John Robinson Memorial Tablet, on St. Peter's Church, Leyden, July 24, 1891. The Secretary announced the death, on January 1, 1899, of Matthew Allen Mayhew, of Boston. Mr. Mayhew was eighth and ninth in descent from Richard Warren, and was elected a member of the Society June 23, 1897. His State Number was 231, and General Number, 737. Afternoon tea was served. Nearly two hundred members and guests were present.

On Tuesday evening, February 21, 1899, a meeting of the Society was held at the Hotel Vendome. Governor Gamaliel Bradford read extracts from Bradford's "History." Mr. Edwin Sanford Crandon delivered an address on "The Pilgrim and the Puritan." Secretary George Ernest Bowman read from the *Massachusetts Mercury* for December

27, 1799, an account of the *Feast of the "Sons of the Pilgrims,"* on Forefathers' Day, 1799. The Secretary announced the death, on January 12, 1899, of Joseph Davis Jones, of Boston, aged one hundred and one years, thirteen days. Mr. Jones was seventh in descent from John Howland. He was elected a member of the Society August 29, 1898, his State Number being 387, and General Number, 1121. The Secretary reported the purchase of a large fireproof safe for the preservation of the rapidly increasing collection of valuable documents; also that the Committee on Marking Historic Sites had collected, from descendants of Governor Bradford, over $200 towards the memorial on the Bradford Lot belonging to the Society, at Kingston, Mass. Refreshments were served after the exercises.

DONATIONS TO THE LIBRARY AND CABINET.

Photograph of the Tombstones of Joshua and Hannah (Bradford) Ripley, at Windham, Conn., from Mrs. Ashbel Welch.

"Genealogy of the Allen and Witter Families," from Francis Richmond Allen.

"History of the Ottowa and Chippewa Indians," from Mrs. Frank K. Owen.

Rhode Island Historical Society Quarterly, Vols. V and VI, from Mrs. Charles R. Brayton.

Records of the Town of Plymouth, Mass., two volumes, from Mrs. Edward L. Adams.

Records of the Town of Duxbury, Mass., from Mrs. Frank Moseley.

Hunter's "Founders of New Plymouth," from Mrs. Henry E. Raymond.

"First Church in Middleborough, Mass.," from Mrs. Dexter R. Puffer.

"The Richmond Family," from the compiler, Joshua Bailey Richmond.

"The Pilgrim and the Puritan," from the author, Edwin Sanford Crandon.

"The Pilgrim Fathers of New England," "Stafford's Almanack," for 1786; Probate papers (1717) signed by Judge Samuel Sewall; Summons (1758) signed by Benjamin Lincoln, afterwards General; Framed engraving (London, 1854) of the "Landing of the Pilgrims," from painting by Charles Lucy, all from Benjamin F. Stevens.

Miss Flora L. Brewster has presented to the Society a collection of seventy documents, including fifteen original deeds. The dates of the deeds with the names of the grantors follow: 1693, John Doty; 1714, James Thomas, Sr.; 1718, David Bradford; 1725, Israel Bradford; 1725, Caleb Stetson; 1727, Pelatiah West; 1735, Israel Thomas; 1741, Wrestling Brewster and Ephraim Holmes; 1751, Jonathan Holmes; 1756, Abiah Wadsworth; 1764, John Barce; 1785, Levi and Lydia Holmes; 1788, Levi and Polly Bradford; 1793, Amos and Priscilla Phillips; 1796, Ichabod and Silvia Washburn.

Mrs. Cyrus W. Bliss has presented to the Society a collection of seventy-nine documents, including sixteen deeds of land in Rehoboth and Bristol, bought by Benjamin Munro between 1770 and 1808; the inventory of Capt. Joseph Rosbotham's personal estate, taken 7 November, 1757; also indentures, bills of sale, receipts, etc.

MEMBERS ELECTED.

January 18, 1899.
422. Mrs. John Bradshaw Howarth, Detroit, Mich., eighth from John Alden.
423. Mrs. Eugene Hoyt, St. Paul, Minn., eighth from William Bradford.
424. Mrs. John Tyler, Boston, seventh from Francis Cooke.

February 8, 1899.
425. Andrew Gray Weeks, Boston, eighth from William Brewster.
426. Ray Greene Huling, Cambridge, ninth from Francis Cooke, eighth from John Cooke.
427. Francis Henry Raymond, Somerville, eighth from William Brewster.
428. Miss Susanna Reed Blanchard, South Weymouth, eighth from John Alden.
429. Mrs. Edward Foote, Boston, eighth from Francis Cooke.
430. Mrs. Edward Everett Capehart, Portsmouth, N. H., ninth from Samuel Fuller.
431. Miss Sarah Crocker Brewster, Boston, eighth from William Brewster.
432. Mrs. George Washington Percy, Oakland, Cal., eighth from Myles Standish.
433. Miss Henrietta Rogers Anthony, Boston, eighth from Myles Standish.
434. John Goddard Stearns, Brookline, eighth from Richard Warren.
435. Miss Paulina Freeman, Everett, ninth from William Brewster.

436. Miss Louise Freeman, Everett, ninth from William Brewster.
437. Mrs. Washburn Eddy Page, South Boston, tenth from William Brewster.
438. George Holley Stevens, Boston, eighth from Richard Warren.
439. Arthur Cox Anthony, New York, N. Y., eighth from Myles Standish.
440. David Thomas, Waltham, seventh from Peter Brown.
441. Mrs. Edward Lewis Johnson, Central Falls, R. I., tenth from John Howland.

February 21, 1899.
442. Miss Grace Woods Slocum, Providence, R. I., ninth from Francis Cooke, eighth from John Cooke.
443. Mrs. Ten Eyck Wendell, Cazenovia, N. Y., ninth from Francis Cooke.
444. Alfred Winslow Cole, Newtonville, seventh from Richard Warren.
445. James Edward Seaver, Taunton, seventh from Stephen Hopkins.
446. Mrs. Daniel Kimball Snow, Brookline, eighth from Myles Standish.
447. James Huntington Ripley, Springfield, eighth from William Bradford.
448. Mrs. Henry Martyn Smith, Enfield, eighth from William Brewster.
449. Arthur Irving Nash, Springfield, ninth from William Brewster.
450. Miss Anna Morton Latham, Deering Centre, Me., ninth from James Chilton, eighth from Mary Chilton.
451. Mrs. George Arthur Ward, Newton Centre, ninth from James Chilton, eighth from Mary Chilton.
452. Mrs. George Agry, Jr., Newton, eighth from William Bradford.
453. Mrs. Silas Reed Anthony, Boston, ninth from William Brewster.
454. Miss Catherine Swanton Eaton, Boston, seventh from John Alden.
455. Miss Lucy Houghton Eaton, Boston, seventh from John Alden.
456. William Flint Rogers, Hingham, seventh from John Alden.

February 28, 1899.
457. Volney William Foster, Evanston, Ill., ninth from William Brewster.

Reports from State Societies.

458. Ralph Stone, Lansing, Mich., ninth from William Bradford.
459. Mrs. Charles William Underhill, Brookline, eighth from Isaac Allerton, seventh from Mary Allerton.
460. Mrs. William Theodore Curtis, Boston, tenth from James Chilton, ninth from Mary Chilton.
461. Prof. Asa Clinton Crowell, Ph.D., Providence, R. I., ninth from John Howland.
462. Caleb Mills Saville, Malden, eighth from John Alden.
463. Mrs. Caleb Mills Saville, Malden, eighth from Myles Standish.
464. George Washington Webb Saville, Malden, seventh from John Alden.
465. Henry Richardson Plimpton, 2d, Boston, ninth from William Brewster.
466. Mrs. Henry Richardson Plimpton, 2d, Boston, eleventh from William Brewster.
467. Miss Harriet Arline Shaw, Boston, eighth from John Howland.
468. Lemuel Foster Morse, Boston, ninth from William Brewster.
469. Mrs. Walter Merrick Farwell, Boston, tenth from William Brewster.
470. Miss Annie Conant Morse, Boston, tenth from William Brewster.
471. Mrs. James Ellsworth Allard, Buffalo, N. Y., ninth from William Bradford.

SUPPLEMENTAL LINES FILED.
January, 1899.
45. Miss Orilla P. Ames, eighth from Edward Doty.
46. Miss Harriet S. Ames, eighth from Edward Doty.
180. Mrs. Charles H. Fisher, ninth from William Brewster.
266. Edwin S. Crandon, eighth from William Brewster, seventh from Love Brewster.
272. Mrs. Bradford D. Davol, seventh from George Soule; eighth from Richard Warren.
296. Mrs. Charles T. Stran, eighth from William White.
307. Miss Carolyn S. Varney, ninth from John Alden; ninth from William Bradford; ninth from Richard Warren; tenth from Richard Warren.
325. William C. Donnell, ninth from John Alden.
331. Miss Lois D. McCobb, ninth from John Alden; ninth from George Soule.
356. Mrs. Ella G. S. Pease, ninth from John Alden; eighth from George Soule.

357. Mrs. George H. Quincy, ninth from John Alden; eighth from George Soule.
370. Mrs. Dexter R. Puffer, eighth (2 lines) from Peter Brown; eighth from Francis Cooke; seventh from John Howland; ninth (2 lines) from Richard Warren.
388. Benjamin D. Sweet, eighth from John Alden; ninth from John Alden; eighth from Isaac Allerton, seventh from Mary Allerton; eighth from William Brewster, seventh from Love Brewster; ninth from William Brewster, eighth from Love Brewster; tenth from William Brewster, ninth from Love Brewster; ninth from James Chilton, eighth from Mary Chilton; eighth from Francis Cooke; eighth from Stephen Hopkins, seventh from Damaris Hopkins; ninth from Richard Warren; tenth from Richard Warren.
393. Horace A. Keith, eighth from John Alden; ninth (2 lines) from Francis Cooke; tenth from Francis Cooke; ninth from Richard Warren; tenth from Richard Warren.
407. Mrs. Fred L. Godding, eighth from Thomas Rogers.
408. Miss Mary S. Clarke, tenth from William Brewster.
412. S. Reed Anthony, eighth from John Alden.
418. Mrs. Frank Moseley, ninth from Francis Cooke; ninth (3 lines) from John Howland.
419. Cyrus A. Hawes, ninth from Francis Cooke; ninth (3 lines) from John Howland.
422. Mrs. John B. Howarth, eighth from Francis Eaton; eighth from George Soule; eighth from Myles Standish.

February, 1899.
78. Henry S. Shaw, eighth from Richard Warren.
88. Miss E. Leora Pratt, ninth from Peter Brown; ninth from Francis Cooke; tenth from Francis Cooke; ninth from Francis Eaton; ninth from George Soule.
89. Miss Edith F. Pratt, ninth from Peter Brown; ninth from Francis Cooke; tenth from Francis Cooke; ninth from Francis Eaton; ninth from George Soule.
112. Charles L. Parsons, ninth from Richard Warren.
129. Miss Antoinette Clapp, eighth (3 lines) from John Howland.
142. Edward T. Barker, sixth from John Alden.
180. Mrs. Charles H. Fisher, ninth from William Brewster.

Reports from State Societies. 119

186. George H. Leonard, ninth from Thomas Rogers, eighth from Joseph Rogers.
203. Mrs. Ebenezer T. Atwood, eighth (2 lines) from Stephen Hopkins, seventh (2 lines) from Constance Hopkins.
212. Henry J. Bowen, ninth from William Brewster; tenth from William Brewster; eighth from William White; ninth from William White.
220. Arthur W. Clapp, eighth (3 lines) from John Howland.
255. Miss Ann A. Bradford, eighth from John Alden; ninth (2 lines) from John Alden; eighth (2 lines) from John Howland; ninth (2 lines) from Thomas Rogers.
256. Edric Eldridge, ninth from John Howland.
266. Edwin S. Crandon, eleventh from John Alden; tenth from Francis Cooke; ninth from Edward Doty; tenth from Stephen Hopkins, ninth from Damaris Hopkins; ninth from Richard Warren.
280. Walter E. Blanchard, ninth from William Bradford; ninth from James Chilton, eighth from Mary Chilton; eighth from Francis Cooke; ninth from Richard Warren.
283. Miss Betsey R. Freeman, eighth (2 lines) from Stephen Hopkins, seventh (2 lines) from Constance Hopkins.
284. Mrs. Elmer E. Hudson, tenth (2 lines) from William Brewster; eleventh from William Brewster; tenth from Stephen Hopkins, ninth from Gyles Hopkins.
322. Mrs. James E. Freeman, eighth from John Alden; eighth from George Soule; eighth from Myles Standish; eighth (2 lines) from Richard Warren; ninth (3 lines) from Richard Warren; tenth (2 lines) from Richard Warren.
323. Mrs. Matthew Cushing, ninth from Francis Cooke.
327. Harry C. Philbrick, eighth from John Alden; eighth from Edward Doty; ninth from Stephen Hopkins, eighth from Constance Hopkins; tenth from Richard Warren.
340. Mrs. Loriman S. Brigham, ninth from Edward Fuller.
370. Mrs. Dexter R. Puffer, eighth from John Howland.
371. Mrs. John M. Rice, eighth (2 lines) from Peter Brown; eighth from Francis Cooke; seventh from John Howland; eighth from John Howland; ninth (2 lines) from Richard Warren.
382. Josiah Thompson, seventh from John Alden.
389. Virgil C. Pond, D.M.D., eighth from John Howland; ninth from Degory Priest.
392. Wallace C. Keith, M.D., eighth from John Alden;

ninth from Francis Cooke; ninth from Richard Warren.
394. Nathaniel A. Shaw, ninth from William Brewster.
406. Mrs. James E. Shepard, seventh from John Alden; seventh from John Howland; eighth from Degory Priest.
410. Mrs. John D. White, eighth from John Alden; tenth from James Chilton, ninth from Mary Chilton; eighth from Francis Cooke; ninth from Richard Warren.
411. Winfred H. Rogers, ninth from William Brewster; eighth from Stephen Hopkins, seventh from Gyles Hopkins; ninth from Stephen Hopkins, eighth from Constance Hopkins.
418. Mrs. Frank Moseley, ninth from William Brewster; ninth (2 lines) from John Howland.
419. Cyrus A. Hawes, ninth from William Brewster; ninth (2 lines) from John Howland.
422. Mrs. John B. Howarth, ninth from Edward Fuller; ninth from John Howland.
426. Ray G. Huling, tenth from Francis Cooke, ninth from John Cooke; ninth from Richard Warren; tenth from Richard Warren.
430. Mrs. Edward E. Capehart, tenth from Francis Cooke; ninth from Francis Eaton, eighth from Samuel Eaton.
432. Mrs. George W. Percy, eighth from John Alden, eighth from Stephen Hopkins.
433. Miss Henrietta R. Anthony, eighth from John Alden.
435. Miss Paulina Freeman, ninth from William Brewster.
436. Miss Louise Freeman, ninth from William Brewster.
439. Arthur C. Anthony, eighth from John Alden.
440. David Thomas, seventh from John Howland; eighth (2 lines) from Richard Warren.
442. Miss Grace W. Slocum, ninth from Richard Warren.
446. Mrs. Daniel K. Snow, eighth from John Alden.
450. Miss Anna M. Latham, ninth from James Chilton, eighth from Mary Chilton; tenth from James Chilton, ninth from Mary Chilton; ninth from Francis Cooke; ninth from Stephen Hopkins, eighth from Damaris Hopkins.
451. Mrs. George A. Ward, ninth from James Chilton, eighth from Mary Chilton; tenth from James Chilton, ninth from Mary Chilton; ninth from Francis Cooke; ninth from Stephen Hopkins, eighth from Damaris Hopkins.

452. Mrs. George Agry, Jr., eighth from John Alden; ninth (2 lines) from John Alden; ninth from William Brewster, eighth from Love Brewster; ninth from Thomas Rogers; ninth from Richard Warren.
466. Mrs. Henry R. Plimpton, 2d, ninth from John Alden; ninth from William Brewster; tenth (2 lines) from William Brewster; tenth from Stephen Hopkins, ninth from Constance Hopkins; tenth from John Howland.
467. Miss Harriet A. Shaw, eighth from Peter Brown; eighth from Francis Cooke; seventh from John Howland; ninth from Degory Priest.

NEW YORK SOCIETY.

The following Standing Committees have been appointed by the Board of Assistants for the year 1898–1899:—

Membership: Howland Davis, Pelham Winslow Warren, Roderick Terry, William Milne Grinnell, Thomas Lincoln Manson, Jr.

Finance: William L. Bull, Augustus L. Hutchins, William Ripley Strong, Frederick C. Seabury, George H. Warren.

Publication: Frederick H. Hatch, Henry Clark Coe, Henry Herbert Warren, James Dougal Bissell, M.D., Wyllys Terry.

Exercises: Waldo Hutchins, George Herbert Warren, Jared Weed Bell, William H. Doty, William W. Ellsworth.

Entertainment: Walter S. Allerton, Mrs. Daniel M. Stimson, Mrs. Hobart H. Porter, Jr., Mrs. Richard H. Greene, James Le Baron Willard.

Room and Property: J. Bayard Backus, Mrs. Russell Sage, Mrs. Edward L. Norton, Robert Sage Sloan, Henry Colvin Brewster.

Genealogical: Edward L. Norton, Henry R. Howland, Henry Farnam Dimock, Hamilton B. Tompkins, Alonzo Howard Clark.

MEMBERS ELECTED.

February 1, 1899.
517. Alden Freeman, Orange, N. J., ninth from John Alden.
518. Mrs. Almeric Paget, New York City, ninth from William Bradford.

February 28, 1899.
519. Mrs. William D. Bishop, Jr., Bridgeport, Conn., ninth from Francis Cooke.
520. Mrs. Benton McConnell, Hornellsville, N. Y., eighth from William Brewster.
521. Mrs. James L. Morgan, Jr., Brooklyn, ninth from John Howland.
522. William M. Adams, Brooklyn, eighth from William Bradford.

CONNECTICUT SOCIETY.

Members Elected.

February 20, 1899.
193. Mrs. Charles William Barnum, Lime Rock, eighth from William Bradford.
194. Mrs. Edward Joseph Pearson, Hartford, ninth from William Brewster.

PENNSYLVANIA SOCIETY.

On Tuesday evening, January 31, 1899, the Society gave a dinner at the Stratford Hotel, Philadelphia, in honor of the Governor General, Hon. Henry E. Howland. Hon. Winslow Warren, Deputy Governor General from Massachusetts, and Rev. Edward Everett Hale, D.D., were also present and made addresses.

Members Elected.

February 1, 1899.
106. Miss Alice Nicholson Coates, Philadelphia, tenth from John Howland.
107. George Champlin Mason, Ardmore, ninth from John Howland.

March 1, 1899.
108. Mrs. Henry Carney Register, Ardmore, seventh from George Soule.
109. Mrs. Joseph Harrison Brazier, Philadelphia, seventh from George Soule.
110. Jay Bucknell Lippincott, Philadelphia, ninth from William Bradford.
111. Henry Thomas Kent, Clifton Heights, seventh from Francis Cooke.
112. Miss Louise Leonard Kent, Clifton Heights, eighth from John Alden.

Reports from State Societies. 123

SUPPLEMENTAL LINES FILED.

January, 1899.
44. Mrs. Henry La B. Jayne, eighth from John Howland.
105. Miss Josephine Lippincott, tenth from Richard Warren.

February, 1899.
110. Jay B. Lippincott, tenth from Richard Warren.

ILLINOIS SOCIETY.

DONATIONS TO THE LIBRARY.

"Walworths of America," and Hayward's "History of Gilsum, N. H.," both from Mrs. Henry C. Purmort.
"Clarke–Clark Genealogy," from Walter M. Howland.

SUPPLEMENTAL LINES FILED.

February, 1899.
37. James N. Hyde, M.D., eighth from William Bradford; ninth from Thomas Rogers.
49. Mrs. Carl W. Preston, tenth from James Chilton, ninth from Mary Chilton.
58. Mrs. Thomas F. Withrow, seventh from John Alden; seventh from Stephen Hopkins; eighth from Richard Warren.

OHIO SOCIETY.

At a meeting of the Board of Assistants, held February 17, 1899, Rev. John Hugh Ely was elected Elder of the Society.

MEMBERS ELECTED.

February 17, 1899.
24. Mrs. Albert Hayden Chatfield, Cincinnati, eighth from Edward Fuller, seventh from Samuel Fuller.
25. Rev. John Hugh Ely, Cincinnati, eighth from Richard Warren.

SUPPLEMENTAL LINES FILED.

February, 1899.
4. Herbert Jenney, seventh from John Alden; eighth from Francis Cooke; sixth from Edward Doty; eighth from Stephen Hopkins, seventh from Damaris Hopkins; eighth from Thomas Rogers, seventh from Joseph Rogers.

10. Henry C. Yergason, ninth from Stephen Hopkins, eighth from Constance Hopkins.

DISTRICT OF COLUMBIA SOCIETY.

At the regular meeting held Tuesday, February 21, 1899, addresses were made by Historian General Richard Henry Greene and Mr. William Wallace Case.

A committee was appointed to co-operate with other patriotic societies, with a view to securing a room in the proposed Carnegie Library as headquarters for all such societies.

MEMBERS ELECTED.

January 10, 1899.
35. Mrs. Frank Friday Fletcher, Washington, ninth from William Bradford.
36. Mrs. William Henry Claflin, Boston, Mass., ninth from William Bradford.

February 21, 1899.
37. Mrs. Oscar Lawrence Hascy, Albany, N. Y., ninth from John Alden.
38. Miss Marion Oscar Barnes, Colorado Springs, Col., ninth from John Alden.
39. Mrs. Frank Sherman Smith, Washington, eighth from John Alden.
40. George Rochford Stetson, Washington, seventh from John Alden.
41. Jerome Fletcher Johnson, Washington, seventh from John Alden.
42. Solomon Elmer Faunce, Washington, seventh from William Bradford.
43. Mrs. Medad Chattman Martin, Washington, ninth from Edward Fuller, eighth from Samuel Fuller.

PILGRIM NOTES AND QUERIES.

[*This department is limited to subjects connected with Pilgrim genealogy and history. Queries can be inserted for subscribers only.*]

MAYFLOWER GENEALOGIES. — The Massachusetts Society is to begin the compilation of the genealogies of the Mayflower passengers and all of their descendants, *in all male and female branches*. This work will be under the direction

Pilgrim Notes and Queries. 125

of the Committee on Historical Research, and especial attention will first be given to perfecting the early generations, in order that a reliable foundation for future work may be established.

Meantime the later generations will not be neglected, all available material being collected and filed, for use as opportunity offers.

The Society already has in its possession a large amount of unpublished data. In order to render this material available for all persons wishing to perfect lines of descent from Mayflower passengers, the Committee will, on receipt of a fee of two dollars, cause a preliminary examination of the Society's records to be made, and if the desired information is not thus found, suggestions as to additional research will be given. All communications in regard to this work should be addressed to the Editor.

FOREIGN RESEARCH FUND (see pp. 61, 62). — The following subscriptions have been received: Mrs. Burr Porter, $5; Mrs. Oliver Ditson, $5 ; Frederick W. Parker, $25 ; Sumner B. Pearmain, $5 ; George H. Earle, Jr., $10; Jeremiah Richards, $5 ; Mrs. James Moses, $5.

THE PREPARATION OF PEDIGREE PAPERS. — In order to secure uniformity in pedigree papers, and to make sure that all applicants avail themselves of the opportunity for getting correct information, the Massachusetts Society will hereafter require that all dates given in an applicant's papers shall correspond with those published in THE MAYFLOWER DESCENDANT prior to the time of filing the pedigree papers with the Society. The proper references to the volume and page of the magazine must also be given.

Another important rule in the interest of uniformity and simplicity is, that *no pedigree paper will be accepted* unless the line of descent begins with one of the following twenty-two names : John Alden, Isaac Allerton, John Billington, William Bradford, William Brewster, Peter Brown, James Chilton, Francis Cooke, Edward Doty, Francis Eaton, Edward Fuller, Dr. Samuel Fuller, Stephen Hopkins, John Howland, Degory Priest, Thomas Rogers, Henry Samson, George Soule, Myles Standish, Richard Warren, William White, Edward Winslow.

A single example will suffice to show the necessity for this rule. Every descendant of John Alden is also a descendant of William and Alice Mullins and their daughter Priscilla. Hence the filing of a pedigree paper proving descent from John Alden must necessarily prove descent also from his wife Priscilla and from her parents, and it would be a waste of time and a useless multiplication of papers to file a separate set of papers for each of these four ancestors. After an Alden paper is accepted, the applicant's record is made according to the following form : —

Ninth in descent from William and Alice Mullins.
Eighth in descent from John and Priscilla (Mullins) Alden.

Papers showing descent from any one of the persons named in the foregoing list will cover all known Mayflower ancestors, and make the applicant's record complete without farther action on his part.

THE HARTFORD BIBLE. — In view of the many inquiries received as to the trustworthiness of the annotations referring to the Pilgrims in this Bible, it seems advisable to say, in advance of a critical study which will appear in a future issue of this magazine, that the book adds nothing to the knowledge of Pilgrim genealogy or history. Its alleged additions cannot be substantiated. It deserves no approval by critical scholars.

GOVERNOR BRADFORD'S HISTORY "OF PLIMOTH PLANTATION." — Every Mayflower descendant will be interested to know that the Commonwealth of Massachusetts has published an edition of Bradford's History, containing, in addition to the text, a full account of the proceedings incident to the return of the original manuscript to Massachusetts. The book also contains portraits of U. S. Senator George F. Hoar, Ambassador Thomas F. Bayard, the Archbishop of Canterbury, the Bishop of London, Gov. Roger Wolcott, and Gov. Edward Winslow, with five illustrations from the manuscript itself. This beautiful book of five hundred and fifty-five pages can be obtained for the sum of one dollar, by addressing the Secretary of the Commonwealth, State House, Boston, Mass. If the book is to be sent by mail, thirty-two cents must be added for postage.

THE MAYFLOWER ASCENDANTS. — In the following list will be found the name of every Mayflower passenger from whom descent has been proved : —

John Alden (see also under William Mullins).
Isaac Allerton and
Mary (Norris) Allerton, his wife.
Remember (Allerton) Maverick and
Mary (Allerton) Cushman, daughters of Isaac and Mary.
John Billington and
Eleanor (———) Billington, his wife.

Francis Billington, son of John and Eleanor.
William Bradford.
William Brewster and
Mary (———) Brewster, his wife.
Love Brewster, son of William and Mary.
Peter Brown.
James Chilton and
——— Chilton, his wife.
Mary (Chilton) Winslow, daughter of James and his wife.
Francis Cooke.
John Cooke, son of Francis.
Edward Doty.
Francis Eaton and
Sarah (———) Eaton, his wife.
Samuel Eaton, son of Francis and Sarah.
Edward Fuller and
——— Fuller, his wife.
Samuel Fuller, son of Edward and his wife.
Dr. Samuel Fuller.
Stephen Hopkins and
Elizabeth (———) Hopkins, his wife.
Gyles Hopkins and } children of Stephen by his
Constance (Hopkins) Snow, } first wife.
Damaris (Hopkins) Cooke, daughter of Stephen and Elizabeth.
John Howland (see also under John Tilley).
William Mullins and
Alice (———) Mullins, his wife.
Priscilla (Mullins) Alden, daughter of William and Alice.
Degory Priest.
Thomas Rogers.
Joseph Rogers, son of Thomas.
Henry Samson.
George Soule.
Myles Standish.
John Tilley.
Elizabeth (Tilley) Howland, daughter of John.
Richard Warren.
William White and
Susanna (Fuller) White, his wife.
Resolved White and
Peregrine White, sons of William and Susanna.
Edward Winslow.

MAYFLOWER RELICS. — The Editor is compiling a list of articles supposed to have been brought over in the Mayflower, and requests that any one who knows of such relics will send him a description of each article, with its history, and the name and address of the present owner.

QUERIES.

6. EATON. What was the maiden name of Elizabeth, the first wife of Samuel[2] Eaton (Francis[1])? They were married prior to 20 March, 1647, and had one child living in 1651.* Elizabeth died before 1661.   B. S. E.

7. STANDISH — COBB. Who were the parents of Rachel Cobb, born 8 December, 1702, died 24 June, 1769 (both dates from family Bible), married Moses[4] Standish (Ebenezer[3], Alexander[2], Myles[1]), of Plympton?   P. F. R.

8. CHANDLER. Who were the parents of Lieut. Zebedee Chandler, of Plympton (born October, 1712, died 2 December, 1777), who married first, Lydia Loring, 8 August, 1737; second, Repentance (Lucas) Bennett, 16 August, 1761?   F. W. P.

9. WARREN. When were Richard[3] and Jabez[3] Warren (Nathaniel[2], Richard[1]) born? How old were they when they died? Is there any deposition or other record giving the age of either at any period?   A. L. B.

BOOK NOTES.

The Richmond Family, 1594-1896. By Joshua Bailey Richmond. Boston, 1897. Imperial 8vo, pp. xviii + 614. Price, $7.50. For sale by the compiler, at 114 State Street, Boston, Mass.

In this beautiful work Mr. Richmond has preserved in permanent form the data collected in fifteen years of careful research. Nearly eighteen thousand names, including over eleven hundred descendants, of female Richmonds, are mentioned in the book, and its value and interest are greatly enhanced by the numerous insertions, fac-similes of deeds, commissions, and other old documents. It is handsomely bound in russet leather and canvas, and the paper is deckle-edged, with broad margins, head-bands, and initials.

This genealogy is of especial interest to Mayflower descendants, as John[2], Richmond (John[1]) married Abigail[3] Rogers (John[2], Thomas[1]), and thus a very large proportion of the eighteen thousand persons mentioned in the book are descended from Thomas Rogers, of the Mayflower.

---

*MAYFLOWER DESCENDANT, Vol. I, p. 15.

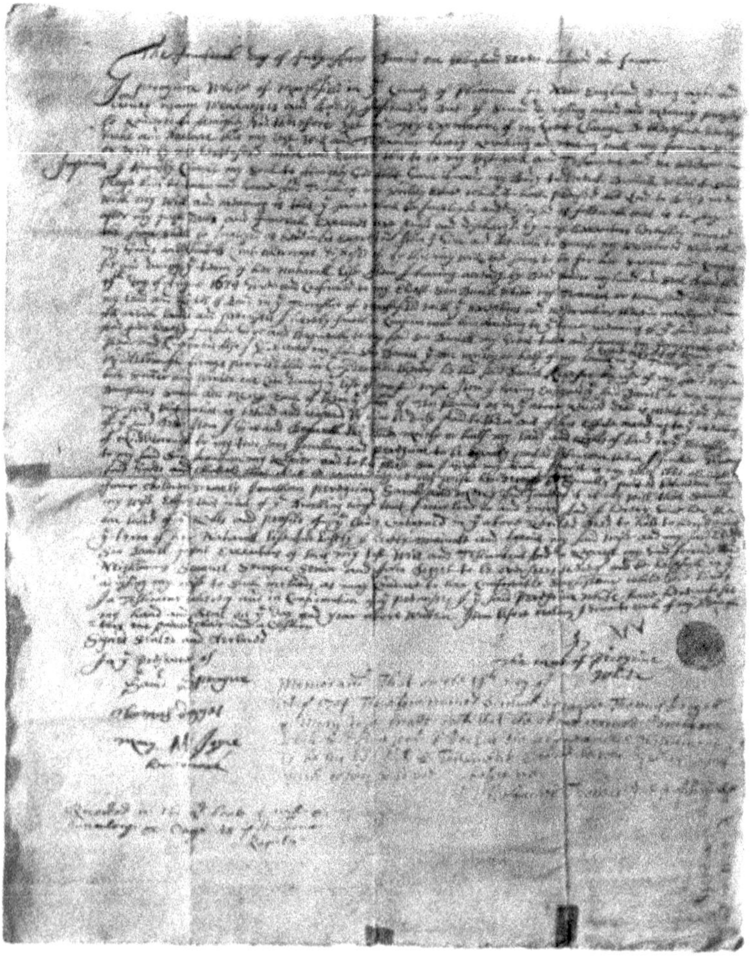

The Mayflower Descendant

THE WILL OF PEREGRINE WHITE.

Communicated by HERVEY N. P. HUBBARD, Curator and Librarian of the Pilgrim Society, Plymouth, Mass.

The original will of Peregrine White is in the collection at Pilgrim Hall, Plymouth, Mass. It is loaned to the Pilgrim Society by the courtesy of Mr. William T. Davis, to whom it belongs, and who has allowed it to be photographed for this magazine. The will is written on paper twelve by fifteen inches in size, and is well preserved. It was probated August 14, 1707, and recorded in Book 2, page 48, Nathaniel Thomas being Judge of probate at that time. The copy is made from the original will.

The fourteenth day of July Anno Domini one thousand seven hundred and four.
I Peregrine White of Marshfield in ye County of Plimouth in New England Being aged and under many Weaknesses and Bodily Infirmities But of Sound disposing mind and memory praises be Rendered to Almighty God therefore yet in dayly Expectation of my Great Change Do therefore hereby make and Declare this my last Will and Testament hereby Revoking and making null any former Will or Wils by me heretofore made and declare this to be my last Will and Testament and no other —

Imprimis I Humbly Commit my Soul to Almighty God that Gave it and my Body to decent Buriall when it Shall Please him to take me hence And Touching my Worldly Estate which it hath pleased the Lord to Bless me with my Will and meaning is that ye same Shall be Imployed and disposed as followeth that is to say after my just debts and funerall expenses are payd and discharged by my Executors hearafter named the same shall be Imployed as herein is expressed   Item I Give and Bequeath to Sarah my welbeloved Wife all my Goods and Chattels not otherways disposed of by this my Will the same to be for her Support and Comfort for and during ye term of her naturall Life.   Item I having already by Deed under my hand and Seal Dated the 19th day of August 1674 Given and Confirmed to my Eldest Son Daniel White my Tenement or Homestead with other my land and Rights of Land in ye Township of Marshfield with ye Exceptions and Reservations therein mentioned — All which lands and premisses I hereby further Confirm unto him according to ye true meaning of ye said Deed   And I do hereby further Give and Bequeath to my said Son Daniell my Great table and fourms my Joynworke Bedstead and Cupboard   Also I Give unto my said Son Daniel ye one moiety or half of my lands and Rights of land in ye Township of Middleborough Always provided that in Consideration thereof he the said Daniel Keep for the use of my said wife both Sumer and Winter one Cow during ye life of my said wife   Item I having enjoyned ye said Daniel to pay unto my Daughters Sarah and Mercy each of them ye sum of Ten pounds as in ye above Recited Deed is mentioned.   It is my will that what is behind and unpaid by him be duly paid to them out of his Estate according to ye meaning of ye said Deed.   Item I Give and Bequeath the other moiety or half my land and Rights of land in ye Township of Middleborough to my two sons Jonathan and Peregrine to be equally parted betweene them   I further Give to my said son Jonathan my Rapier and to his Eldest son I Give my Gun.   Item It is my will that all my said Goods and Chattels that shall be remaining at my wife her decease be Equally parted betweene my four children namely Jonathan Peregrine Sarah and Mercy   And further it is my will that Sarah my wife enjoy that part of ye Dwelling house that I now live in and enjoy   And I hereby Give her the one third of ye Rents and profits of ye lands contayned in ye above Recited Deed to hold to her during ye term of her Naturall life   And lastly I hereby nominate and Appoint my said Wife and my said Eldest Son Daniel joynt Executors of this my last Will and Testament And do Request my Good friends and Neighbours Samuel Sprague Senior and John Dogget to be overseers thereof and be helpfull in ye advising my wife to such methods as may conduce to her comfortable subsistance while she lives   In Testimony whereof and in confirmation of ye promisses I ye said Peregrine White have hereunto set my hand and seal on ye Day and year above Written.   Item before sealing I Give to Each of my sd Daughters one painted chair and a cushion.

Signed sealed and Declared   **P W**   (Seal)
In ye Presence of   The mark of Peregrine
    Saml Sprague   White
    Thomas Dogget
    Mary **M** Joyce
    her mark.

Memorand That on the 14th day of Augt 1704 The afore named Samuell Sprague Thomas Doggett & Mary Joyce made oath that the above named Perregreen White did signe seale & Declare the above written Instrument to be his last Will & Testament & that he was of Disposeing mind when he so did   before me

                      Nathaniel Thomas
                      Judge of Probate

Recorded in the 2^d booke of wills &
    Inventorys &c. Page 48   pr **N** Thomas
                              Register

PLYMOUTH COLONY DEEDS.

(Continued from page 99.)

[13] 1652   BRADFORD GOVN^R

Memorand: the twentysixt of august 1652 That Samuell Dunham in the behalfe of himselfe and his wife together with Gabriell ffallowell and Robert ffinney all of Plymouth Came before the Govr and did covenant and give consent unto That Jonathan ffallowell sonne of Willam ffallowell deceased; shalbee and dwell Remaine and continew with the said Robert ffinney untill hee bee twenty yeares of age; being at the day of the date heerof about eight yeares old; the said tearme of twenty yeares being fully accomplished hee is then to bee free; And incase the said Robert ffinney or his wife shall depart this life before the said Tearme of twenty yeares bee expired; that then notwithstanding the said Jonathan ffalloway shalbee and Remaine with him or her of them that shall survive untell the aforsaid tearme of twenty yeares bee fully accomplished and then to bee free; provided alsoe that it shall not bee in the power of either Robert ffinney or·his wife they or either of them to despose of the said Jonathan to any other pson or psons to bee with; any pte of the aforsaid tearme of twenty yeares either while they or either of them live or at theire decease; except it bee to work for and in the behalf of the said Robert or his wife for som smale time but alwaies to bee accounted as theires and under theire Goverment untell the said tearme of twenty yeares bee accomplished in mannor as abovesaid; and incase both the said Robert ffenney and his wife shall both decease before the said tearme of twenty yeares bee expired; That then the said Jonathan is free from the abovesaid engagement; And the said Robert ffinney and his wife they or either of them that shall Survive untell the said term of twenty yeare or there abouts bee accomplished and expired shall find and provide unto and for the said Jonathan ffallowell competent and sufficient meate drinke apparell washing and lodging fitt for one in his degree and calling

Know all men by these p^rsents that I Thomas Pope of New Plymouth Cooper doe Remise Release acquite and discharge George Bonum of the Towne aforsaid husbandman hee his heires executors and adminestrators of and from all bills bonds debts dues specialties summes of money and demaunds whatsoever due owing and payable unto mee the said Thomas Pope from him the said George Bonum at any time whatso-

ever from the begining of the world unto this p^rsent day being the 30th of October Anno 1652
In Witnesse wherof I have heerunto put my hand in the p^rsence of } Thomas Pope
        Nathaniell Morton   Clarke

[p. 14, blank]

[15] 1652   BRADFORD GOVN^R

    The following deed bearing date the one and twentieth of ffebrewary was shewed in the open court holden att Plymouth the 29th of June 1652 and by the said court appointed to be Recorded

This Indenture made the one and twentieth day of ffebrewary in the fourteenth yeare of the Raigne of our Soveraigne Lord Charles by the grace of God of England Scotland ffrance and Ireland King Defender of the faith &c Between Christopher Winter of the plantation of Scittuate in New England on the one pte; and Joseph Coleman of the same plantation on the other pte Witnesseth that the said Christopher Winter for and in consideracon of the summe of twenty pounds of currant money of England to be paied unto the said Christopher Winter by the said Josepth Coleman; hath barganed and sold and by these p^rsents doth absolutely bargaine and sell unto the said Josepth and to his heires for ever all my house and Lott which was my brother John Winters which Lott conteineth by estemacon foure acres bee It more or lesse and all the mersh therunto belonging; And alsoe a ten acars Lott allreddy layed out all which was given unto the said John Winter by the ffreemen of Scittuate; in consideracon of which money above specified and paied at the sealing and delivery heerof; I the said Christopher Winter doe by this p^rsent Indenture Surrender up unto the said Josepth Coleman all my Right title and enterest in the house and Lott above mencioned; in Witnesse wherof I have

heerunto sett my hand and seale the day and yeare above written
Sealed and delivered in the p^rsence of us
  James Torrey
  John Winter
  Thomas Chambers

Christopher
The mark of **W** | his seale
Winter

Att the court abovesaid the said Christopher Winter came into the said court and owned and acknowlidged the above written deed to bee his acte and deed and gave consent it should bee Recorded

[p. 16, blank]

[17] 1652   BRADFORD GOVN^R

 Memorandum the 20th of october 1652
 That Nathaniell Masterson of manchester in the Jurisdiction of the massachusets in new England in america planter doth acknowlidge that for an in consideracon of two young steers to him alreddy delivered by John Churchill of the Towne of Plymouth in the Jurisdiction of New Plym : in new England Planter; hee hath barganed allianated and sold unto the said John Churchill a pcell of upland ground lying at Wellingsley in the Townshipp of Plymouth aforsaid being ten acres or therabouts bee it more or lesse which hee bought of John Dunham Junier together with all the houses out houses in and upon the said Land with all the ffences and ffencing upon the said Land with all and singulare the appurtenances belonging unto the said Land or any pte or pcell therof onely all the apple trees excepted which the said Nathaniel Masterson hath sold unto Nathaniell Morton and the said John Churchill doth heerby give libertie unto the said Nathaniell Morton either by himselfe or any for him to take up and Remove the said apple trees at any time betwixt the day of the date heerof and the ordinary time of the takeing up and Removeing of trees in the spring of the yeare; the said ten acres of Land bee it more or lesse with all the said houses ffences and all other emunities privilidges and

appurtenances with all the said Nathaniell Masterson his Right title and enterest of and into the said p^rmises and every pte and pcell therof the apple trees above mencioned excepted, to belonge unto the said John Churchill his heires and assignes for ever unto the onely pper use and behoofe of him the said John Churchill his heires and assignes for ever, provided that the said John Churchill is to winter the said steers the following winter into the bargan and incase that one of them die before they are housed then the said John Churchill is to pay unto Nathaniell Masterson ten shillings if both die then twenty and according to the same Rate if either or both of them die before the first of May next ensuing the date heerof onely Nathaniell Masterson is to run the venter of the said steers; and the said steers are to Run with the cattle of the said John Churchill the next summer and hee is to look unto them as his owne; and incase any controversy shall fall out about the said land or appurtenances; that then the said John Churchill is to cleare the said Nathaniell Masterson of whatsoever trouble shall or may fall in that behalfe; onely whatsoever power the said Nathaniell hath to defend the Right and title that hee hath unto the said Land, hee doth by these p^rsents convay over unto the said John Churchill; in as full mannor as hee the said Nathaniell held it

[18] 1652   BRADFORD GOVERNER

Memorandum the 4th of october 1652
That Willam Merricke of Eastham in the Jurisdiccion of Plymouth in New England in america doth acknowlidge that he hath freely and absolutly sold and made over unto Gorge Partrich of Duxburrow in the Jurisdiction of Plym: aforsaid Tailer; all the Right title and enterest that hee either hath or for the future may have unto all or any Lands meddowes or any appurtenances belonging unto them; at the new plantation graunted unto Duxburrow; called and knowne by the name of Satuckquett or therabouts; to have and to hold The said lands meddows and all and singulare the appurtenances belonging therunto unto the said Gorg Partrich his heires and assignes forever to appertaine unto the onely pper

use and behoofe of him the said Gorge Partrich his heires and assignes for ever Morover the said Willam Merrick doth acknowlidge that the said Gorge Partrich hath fully paied and satisfyed him for his said Right and title in the abovesaid Lands Meddowes &c

      This bargane and sale of land was acknowlidged by both pties before Captaine Miles Standish the day and yeare above written ;

[19] 1652 BRADFORD GOVN^R

This writing underneath was Recorded
  by order from the governor the 27 of october 1652, Wee have graunted to Nathaniell Masterson our Lands in Wellingsley with our house there and the fences and the mersh and the upland in the woods ; Reserving our trees for John Wood to enioy for our good and his, to bee Removed the next autume ; And this wee doe upon consideracon ; agreed betweene us the 15th day of the fift month 1648 and heerunto have sett our hands

The trees are to bee	Ralph Smith
Johns whiles they beare	and Mary Smith her **M** marke
and halfe the fruite	
to bee sent to Boston	
for us while either of	
us live if God please	

Memorand the day and yeare first above written ; That Nathaniell Masterson above mencioned doth acknowlidge that for such consideracon as wherwith hee is satisfyed hee hath freely and absolutely made over unto John Wood of Plymouth senior ; all his Right hee hath in the one halfe of all the mersh meddow hee hath att goose point neare plym : aforsaid ; which said mersh the said Nathaniell bought of his fatherinlaw Mr Smith To have and to hold the said one halfe of the said marsh and all the appurtenances belonging therunto unto the onely pper use of the said John Wood his heires and assignes for ever to belonge unto the onely

Plymouth Colony Deeds.   137

pper use and behoofe of him the said John Wood his heires and assignes for ever;

The Range betweene the Lands of Samuell Eaton and Widdow Brewster by agreement of both pties Runeth North west and by west; and south east and by East the line being Run by   John Alden
            Phillip Delanoy
            and henery Sampson

[21] 1652   BRADFORD GOVN^R

A deed appointed to bee Recorded
To all Christian people to whom these p^rsents shall come Thomas Allyn of Barnstable within the Goverment of new Plymouth in New England in america yeoman sendeth greet : &c
Know yea that I the said Thomas Allyn for and in consideration of sixty five pound sterling to mee in hand paid by Lieutenant Mathew ffuller and Samuell ffuller both of Barnstable aforesd planters wherof and wherwith I doe acknowlidge my selfe fully satisfyed and payed and therof and of every pte and pcell therof doe for myselfe and my heires executors and administrators and every of them exownarate acquite and discharg the said Lieutenant Mathew ffuller and Samuell ffuller themselves and theires heires executors and administrators and every of them for ever by these p^rsents ; have freely and absolutely given graunted barganed sold enfeofed and confeirmed and by these p^rsents doe give graunt bargan sell and confeirme unto the said Lieutenant Matthew ffuller and Samuell ffuller them theire heires and assignes for ever all that my Lands lying and being in Barnstable aforsaid conteining nine score acres of upland and four score acres of mersh meddow bee it more or bee it lesse with all and singulare the appurtenances to all the said p^rmises belonging ; seaven score acres of the said upland lying upon the mayne adioyning to Sandwidge bounds on the norwest side therof; and on the southeast to a p^rcell of Land somtimes Samuell houses but now in the possession of the said Samuell ffuller

butting northeast upon the mersh and southwest into the woods and forty acres of the said upland lying upon Scauton neck adioyning to Sandwidge bounds, Norwest ptely to the mersh and ptly to an acre of Land somtimes Thomas Shaues now in the possession of the said Mathew and Samuell ffuller Southeast and buting upon the sea Northeast and on the Mersh Southwest; and forty six acres of the aforsaid mersh bounded Norwest by Sandwidge bounds; Southeast by ptly upon that mersh which was Isacke Robensons now Thomas Dexters and ptly upon what was Austine Beirces; and northeast by Scauton and Southwest by the aforsaid upland on the mayne and thirty and three acres of mersh bounded Norwest upon Scauton and ptly upon what was Willam Crockers mersh but now the said Mathew and Samuell ffullers Southeast upon John halls mersh northeast upon Sandy necke and Southwest upon the Creeke To have and to hold all the said nine-score acres of upland [23] upland and eighty acres of mersh bee it more or bee it lesse with all and singulare the appurtenances to all the said p^{r}mises belonging and alsoe all buildings and edifices upon the said p^{r}mises and all and every theire appurtenances whatsoever unto the said Lieutenant Mathew ffuller and Samuell ffuller theire heires and assignes for ever; and to the onely pper use of them the said Mathew ffuller and Samuell ffuller theire heires and assignes for ever To bee holden according to the privilidges of our pattent graunted to New Plymouth by his late Matie as of his Mannor of East Greenwidge in the Countey of Kent in the Realme of England in free and common Sockage and not in capite and by Knights service by the Rents and services therof due and of Right accustomed; and with warrantice against all people whatsoever from by or under mee the said Thomas Allyn mine heires executors and administrators or any of us claiming any use Right title or enterest of or in the said p^{r}mises or any pte or pcell therof And I the said Thomas Allyn doe by these p^{r}sents make good the sale therof and of every pte and pcell therof; And I the said Thomas Allyn doe alsoe covenant promise and graunt by these prsents that it shall and may bee lawfull to and for the said lieutenant Mathew ffuller and Samuell ffuller theire heires or assignes by themselves or theire attorney to enrowle these p^rsents or cause them to bee enrowled in the court att Plymouth aforsaid before the Govr for the time being according to the usuall mannor and order of Recording and enrowling evidences in such cases provided, In Wittnes wherof I the said Thomas Allyn have heerunto sett my hand and Seale This 2^cond of october Anno Dom : 1652

Sealed and delivered   Thomas Allyn
   in the p^rsence of   Winnefred Allyn (Seal)
Thomas Hinckley
Samuell Mayo
John Dickinson

Att the generall court holden att New Plymouth the 4th of october 1652 Mis Winnefred Allyn the wife of Mr Thomas Allyn came into the said court and gave her free consent unto the sale of the abovesaid Lands and Meddows and theire appurtenances and in wittnes therof sett her hand unto the deed above written accordingly as is above entered

(To be continued.)

PLYMOUTH BIRTHS, MARRIAGES AND DEATHS.

Literally transcribed from the Original Records at Plymouth, Mass.,
By GEORGE ERNEST BOWMAN.

On the title page of the oldest book is written, in a very bold hand :

PLIMOUTH TOWNE BOOK
FOR BIRTHS MARRIAGES
AND BURIALS
ANO DOMINIE
1699
THOMAS FAUNCE
TOWNE CLERK

On the back of this leaf is written :

on ye 3^d Day of June 1715, The Metinghouse at plimouth was mu(*worn*) The Thunder on The 4th day of ffebruary 1722-3 was a Dreadfull (*worn*) Raised the Tide 3 or 4 foot higher Then had ben kno(*worn*)

The next page seems, from its earlier date, to have been the original title page. It has the following inscription:

PLIMOUTH TOWNE
BOOKE
ANO DOMINE 1696-7
FOR BIRTHS BURIALS
AND MARRIAGES
PER THOMAS FFAUNCE
TOWNE CLERKE

These three pages contain also much scribbling in various hands.

The numbering of the pages begins with that on the back of the second title page. The third leaf, containing the second and third pages, is missing. The original paging is indicated by numerals enclosed in brackets, and inserted before the first word of each page.

[p. 1]

The Children of Mr. John Co(*)ton pastore of the of plimouth and of mistres Joanna Cotton his wife

1 John borne at guilford in Conecticut Colony August (*) 3th
2 Elzabeth Borne att guilford August the 6th 1663
3 Sarah borne att Marthins vinyard January the 17th 1665
 She dyed at guilford September the 8th 1669
4 Bowland borne at plimouth december the 27th 1667.
5 Sarah borne at plimouth Aprill ye 5th 1670
6 Maria borne at plimouth Jannuary the 14th 1671
7 A Son borne at plimouth September the 28th 1674
 he dyed the day following September the 29th
8 Josiah borne at bostorn September the 10th 1675
 he dyed at plimouth January 9th 1676.
9 Samuel borne February 10th 1677:
 he dyed at plimouth December the 23th 1682
10 Josiah borne at plimouth January the 8th 1679

* Worn.

11 Theophilos borne at plimouth May the 5ᵗʰ 1682
Abraham Peirce son of Abraham Peirce & Rebeckah his w(*) was born January 1638. Deceased January 1718 †

Mehitabel Nelson born Aprill the 5ᵗʰ 1670
(Pages 2 and 3 are missing)

[p. 4]

The Children off Eliazur Downham and Bathshaba his Wif(*)
1 Eliazur borne the 15ᵗʰ day of Janawary 1682
2 Nathannell borne the 20ᵗʰ day of March 1685 Decasd feb(*)
3 Mercy borne the 10th day of december 1686
4 Israil born october 1789 ‡
5 Elisha born in August 1692
6 Josiah born June 1794 ‡
7 Barshua born Aprill 26 1696
8 Susannah born in June 1698
9 Joshua born Aprill first 1701

The Children of John Cobb and martha Cobb his Wife
1 John Borne the 24ᵗʰ of august 1662
2 patience borne the 10ᵗʰ of august 1668
3 Ebenezor borne the 9ᵗʰ day august 1671
4 Elisha Borne the 3ᵗʰ of aprill 1679
5 James Borne the 20ᵗʰ of July 1682

The Children of Thomas Clerk and Rebeckah his Wife
1 Suzannah Borne the 21 day feburay 1684
2 Thomas Borne the 25ᵗʰ day of desember 1685

The Children of Thomas Clarke & Elizabeth Clarke his wife
Josiah Born on the 15ᵗʰ of december 1690
Eliazebeth born 12 day of July 1692
Rebeckah born June yᵉ 2ᵈ 1694

The Children of The above Named Thomas Clark & Susanah his Wife
1 Annah born January 24 1700
2 Abigall born on the 9ᵗʰ of december 1701
3 Sarah born february 10 170$\frac{4}{3}$

* Worn.
† The birth and death were both entered at the same time.
‡ These are plainly mistakes of the town Clerk for 1689 and 1694.

Plymouth Births, Marriages and Deaths.

John atwood Son to Nathanill atwood and Mary his wife
1 was born the first day of may 1684
2 Elizabeth born the 24th of Aprill 1687
3 Joannah born the 27th of february 1689 deceased March 30 169(*)
4 Mary borne on the 26 of aprill 1691
5 Nathaniell borne on the 3^d of october 1693
6 Isaac born on the 29 december 1695
7 Barnabus born on the 1 day of January 169$\frac{7}{8}$
8 Joannah born June 8th 1700

[p. 5]
The Chldren of Nathaniell Southworth & Desier his Wif
1 Constant borne the 12th day of august 1674
2 Mary Born the 3th day of aprill 1676 Decea^d being y^e wife of Jo : Rider Feb^{ry} 2nd 1757
3 Ichabod born Aboute the midle of march 1678
4 Nathaniell born the 18th day of may 1684

The Chldren of Elkanah Cushman and Elizabeth his wife
1 Elkanah born the 15th day of September 1678
2 Jams born the 20th of october 1679
3 Jabes born the 28th of december 1681
died the may following 1682

The Children of Elkanah Cushman and Martha his Wife
1 Allerton born the 21th day of November 1683
2 Elizabeth born the 17th day of Janawary 1685
3 Josiah born the 21th of March 168 $\frac{7}{8}$
Mehittable borne october the 8th 1693

The Children of Joseph ffaunce and Juduth his Wife
1 hannah born the 12th of Jun 1678
2 Mary born the 2 day of June 1681
3 John born the 3 day of december 1683
4 mercy born the 30th of June 1686
Shee dyed the 26 of Aprill 1687
5 Mehittale born May 27th 1689
6 Joseph borne May 21 1693
7 Eliazar born ffebruary 6 169$\frac{5}{6}$

* Worn.

8 Thomas born July 15 1698
9 Benjamin born february 17th 1703 : deseased June 28th 1704

[p. 6]

The Chil of Abraham Jacson Junor and Margareat his wif(*)
1 Abraham borne the 9th day december 1686
2 Samuel Borne August ye 15th 1689
3 Sarah Borne february ye 14th 1691 Deseased May 4th 16(*)
4 Israiel Borne December 11th 1693
5 Lidia Borne March ye 22d 1696
6 Seth Borne June ye 7th 1698

The Children of Edward Doty Senior and Sarah his Wife
1 Edward born the 20th of May 1664
2 Sarah born the 9th day of June 1666
3 John born the 4th day of august 1668
4 Mary & martha born the 9th day of July 1671
5
6 Elizabeth born the 22 of december 1673
7 patience born the 7th of July 1676
8 mercy born the 6th of febuawary 1678
   Shee dyed the last day of november 1682
9 Samuel born the 17th of may 1681
10 mercy born the 23 of September 1684
11 Benjamin Born the 30th of may 1689

The Children of Gorg bonan Junor and Elizabeth his w(*)
1 Elizabeth born the 18th day of June 1684
2 Samuell born the 15th day of october 1686
   he deceaced the 9th day of January 1686
4 Ruth borne the 29th december 1688
5 Ann born November 28 1690
6 Sarah born July 27 1693
7 Lidiah born october 20 1696
8 Ebonazar born march 3d 1699
9 Suzannah born Aprill 25 1702

The Child of Thomas Doty and Mary his wife
   Hannah Doty was born December 1675

* Worn.

The Child of Jerusha Finney, daught^r of Robert Finney
  Lydia Finney, Born Decemb^r 8. 1747.

The Child of Elizabeth Wood Widdow
  Mary Wood, Born Jan^{ry} 12. 174$\frac{5}{6}$

[p. 7]

The Children of Isaak Lobdell and Sarah lobdell his Wife
1 a daughter born the 13th of february 1680
  Shee dyed the 22th of the Same month
2 Sarah : born the 27th of September 1682
3 Martha : Born the 24th of february 1684
  She died the 13th of aprill 1686
4 Samuell born the 17th day of february 1686 : 87

The Children of John Doty & Elizabeth his Wife
1 John Born the 24th of August 1668
2 Edward Born the 28th of June 1671
3 Jacob Born the 27th of May 1673
4 Elizabeth Born the 10th of ffebruary 167$\frac{5}{6}$
5 Isaac Born the 25th of october 1678
6 Samuell Born the Last of Januawary 1682
7 Elisha Born the 13th of July 1686
8 Josiah borne in october 1689
9 Martha borne in october 1692

The Children of John Rickard Junor & mary Rickard his wife
1 John born the last of february 1679
2 Mercy born the 3th day of february 1682
3 John born the 3th day of february 1684
4 Ester borne the first of aprill 1691
  James Born september 25 (or 26 ?) 1696 *

[p. 8]

The Children of Josiah Morton and of Suzannah Morton his
    Wife
1 Suzannah born the first day of ffebruary 1686
  Shee dyed the first day of March 1687
2 Josiah born the 13th of Aprill 1688

---

* Between Ester and James space was left for two more names.

3 Suzannah born the first day of september 1690
4 Henerey born on the 7th day of January 1692 he deceased in Novem 1697

The Children John Briant Junor & Sarah Briant his Wife
1 John Born the first of September 1678
2 Jams born the 26th of July 1682
3 Ruth born the 26th of September 1685
4 Sarah born the 28th of february 1688
5 Joanah born on the 13th of november 1690
6 George born on the 3d of desember 1693

The Children of John Gray and Joanah his wife
Edward Borne the 21 day of September 1687.
he dyed the 20th of february 1687-88
Mary born the 7th of december 1688. desceased on the 17th of March 1703
Ann Born the 5th of Agust 1691
desire borne on the first day of desember 169(*)
Shee deceased on the 6th of december 1695
Joannah born the 29th of January 169$\frac{5}{6}$
Samuel born on the 23d of desember 170$\frac{1}{2}$
Marcey born on the 4th of february 170$\frac{3}{4}$

[p. 9]

The Children of John Churchill and Rebeckah Churchill his Wife
1 Elizabeth Borne the 7th day of october 1687
2 Rebeckah borne August 29th 1689
3 John borne december 20th 1691
4 Sarah borne ffebruary 10th 1695
5 Hannah borne 27th of Aprill 1697

The Child of John Sturtevant and hannah Stirtevant his Wife
1 hannah Borne the tenth day of Aprill 1687.
on A Sabbath day att 4 Clock afternone

The Child of John King and Hannah King his Wife
Amariah King was born March 4. 1752.
was Born in Plymouth —

* Worn.

William Green Sonẹ to William Gren
and Elizabeth his wife was born the 24th of Aprill 1684

[p. 10]

The Children of John Mordow and Lidiah Mordow his Wife
1 John Borne the 13th of december 1687
  he dyed the 8th of Januawary 1687
2 : Jonat borne the 3d of febraary 1689 deceased Aprill 24th 1697
3 : John Borne June the 8th 1691
4 : James Borne June 13th 1693 at 3 of the clock in the afterno(*) : he deceased March the 11th 169$\frac{3}{4}$
5 : Robert born on the 14 of March 16$\frac{6}{7}$ he deceased July 28 : 1699
6 : Robert born october 8th 1699 he deceased 7 weks after
7 James born January 14 169$\frac{4}{5}$ att 11 Clock at Night
8 Thomas borne on the 19 of november 1701 att 8 Clock at nigh(*)

The Children of John Drew and hannah Drew his Wife
1 Elizabeth borne the 5th day of february 1673
2 John borne the 29th of August 1676
3 Samuel borne the 21 of february 1678
4 Thomas borne the 1 day of may 1681
5 Nicolus borne about the middle of october 1684
6 Lemuell borne August the 4th 1687

The Children of James Easdell, & Rebeckah his wife
1.
2. *(No names were entered.)*
3

The Children of Samuel Garner and Suzannah his wife
1 Samuel borne September the 27th 1683
2 Nathaniel borne September the 10th 1685
3 Suzannah born the 10th of September 1687
  She dyed the first of september 1689

[p. 11]

* Worn.

Plymouth Births, Marriages and Deaths. 147

The Children of Thomas ffaunce and Jean his Wife
1 patience borne the 7th of november 1673 (She Marryd Ephm Kempton & Died at Dartmouth Aged 105 year 6 months & 5 Days.*)
2 John borne the 19th of September 1678
3 Martha borne the 16th of December 1680
4 pricilah borne the 20th of August 1684
5 Thomas borne the 18th of May 1687
6 Joannah borne the 24th of June 1689
7 Jean born the 18th of November 1692

The Children of Ephraim Morton and hannah his wife
1 hannah borne november the 7th 1677
2 Ephraim borne october the 31th 1678
3 John borne July 20th 1680
4 Joseph borne March the 4th 1683
5 Ebenezur borne Aprill the 11th 1685

The Children of Nathaniel Holmes and Mersey his Wife
1 Elisha borne the 19th of Aprill 1670
2 Mersy borne the 10th of September 1673
3 Nathaniel borne the 10th of november 1676
4 Sarah borne the 2 of october 1680
5 John borne the 17th of Aprill 1682
6 Elizabeth borne the 25th of Aprill 1686
7 Eliazur holmes borne the 16th october 1688
   Deceasd Augst 21st 1754*

[p. 12]
The Children of John Bradford and Mersey his Wife
1 John borne the 29th of december 1675
2 Alse borne the 28th of January 1677
3 Abigal borne the 10th of december 1679
4 Mersy borne the 20th of december 1681
5 Samuel borne the 23th of december 1683
6 pricilla borne the 10th of March 1686
7 Wiliam borne the 15th of Aprill 1688

The Children of William Churchill and lidiah his Wife
1 William borne on the 2 day of August 1685

* This entry is in a modern hand.

2 Samuel borne on the 15th day of Aprill 1688
3 James borne on the 21th of September 1690
4 lidiah born on ye 17 of Aprill 1699
5 Josiah born August 21 1702

(*To be continued.*)

THE DIVISION OF CATTLE IN 1627.

The oldest volume of the Plymouth Colony Records is entitled

"Plimouths great Book of Deeds of Lands Enrolled: from An° 1627 to An° 1651:"

On pages 50-57 of this book is entered the record of the Division of the Cattle which was made June 1, 1627, new style. This record is of great value to students of Pilgrim genealogy, as it contains the names of all members of the Pilgrim families in Plymouth on that date, including even Jonathan Brewster's little daughter Mary, born but five weeks before.*

It will be noted that forty-two of the ninety-nine persons who reached Plymouth on the Mayflower were still living there.

1627.}
At a publique court held the 22th of May it was concluded by the whole Companie, that the cattell wch were the Companies, to wit, the Cowes & the Goates should be equall devided to all the psonts of the same company & soe kept untill the expiration of ten yeares after the date above written. & that every one should well and sufficiently pvid for there owne pt under penalty of forfeiting the same.

That the old stock with halfe th increase should remaine for comon use to be devided at thend of the said terme or otherwise as ocation falleth out, & the other halfe to be their owne for ever.

* MAYFLOWER DESCENDANT, Vol. I, p. 7.

The Division of Cattle in 1627.   149

Uppon wch agreement they were equally devided by lotts soe as the burthen of keeping the males then beeing should be borne for common use by those to whose lot the best Cowes should fall & so the lotts fell as followeth. thirteene psonts being pportioned to one lot.

1 The first lot fell to ffrancis Cooke* & his Companie Joyned to him his wife Hester Cooke
   3 John Cooke*
   4 Jacob Cooke
   5 Jane Cooke
   6 Hester Cooke
   7 Mary Cooke
   8 Moses Simonson
   9 Phillip Delanoy
 10 Experience Michaell
 11 John ffance
 12 Joshua Pratt
 13 Phinihas Pratt

To this lot fell the least of the 4 black Heyfers Came in the Jacob, and two shee goats.

2 The second lot fel to Mr Isaac Allerton* & his Companie ioyned to him his wife ffeare Allerton.
   3 Bartholomew Allerton*
   4 Remember Allerton*
   5 Mary Allerton*
   6 Sarah Allerton
   7 Godber Godberson
   8 Sarah Godberson
   9 Samuell Godberson
 10 Marra Priest
 11 Sarah Priest
 12 Edward Bumpasse
 13 John Crakstone*

To this lot fell the Greate Black cow came in the Ann to which they must keepe the lesser of the two steers, and two shee goats.

3 The third lot fell to Capt Standish* & his companie Joyned to him his wife
   2 Barbara Standish

To this lot fell the

* Came in the Mayflower.

  3 Charles Standish
  4 Allexander Standish
  5 John Standish
  6 Edward Winslow*
  7 Susanna Winslow*
  8 Edward Winslow
  9 John Winslow
 10 Resolved White*
 11 Perigrine White*
 12 Abraham Peirce
 13 Thomas Clarke

Red Cow wch belongeth to the poore of the Colonye to wch they must keepe her Calfe of this yeare being a Bull for the Companie. Also to this lott Came too she goats.

4 The fourth lot fell to John Howland* & his company Joyned to him his wife
  2 Elizabeth Howland*
  3 John Howland Juno^r
  4 Desire Howland
  5 William Wright
  6 Thomas Morton Juno^r
  7 John Alden*
  8 Prissilla Alden*
  9 Elizabeth Alden
 10 Clemont Briggs
 11 Edward Dolton*
 12 Edward Holdman
 13 Joh. Alden

To this lot fell one of the 4 heyfers Came in the Jacob Called Raghorne.

5 The fift lot fell to Mr Willm Brewster* & his companie Joyned to him
  2 Love Brewster*
  3 Wrestling Brewster*
  4 Richard More*
  5 Henri Samson*
  6 Johnathan Brewster
  7 Lucrecia Brewster
  8 Willm Brewster
  9 Mary Brewster
 10 Thomas Prince

To this lot ffell one of the fower Heyfers Came in the Jacob Caled the Blind Heyfer & 2 shee goats.

* Came in the Mayflower.

The Division of Cattle in 1627.   151

 11 Pacience Prince
 12 Rebecka Prince
 13 Humillyty Cooper*

6 The sixt lott fell to John Shaw & his companie Joyned
 1 to him
 2 John Adams
 3 Eliner Adams
 4 James Adams
 5 John Winslow
 6 Mary Winslow*
 7 Willm Basset
 8 Elizabeth Bassett
 9 Willyam Basset Juno^r
 10 Elyzabeth Basset Juno^r
 11 ffrancis Sprage
 12 Anna Sprage
 13 Mercye Sprage

To this lot fell the lesser of the black Cowes Came at first in the Ann wth which they must keepe the bigest of the 2 steers. Also to this lott was two shee goats.

7 The seaventh lott fell to Stephen Hopkins* & his companie Joyned to him his wife
 2 Elizabeth Hopkins*
 3 Gyles Hopkins*
 4 Caleb Hopkins
 5 Debora Hopkins
 6 Nickolas Snow
 7 Constance Snow*
 8 Willam Pallmer
 9 ffrances Pallmer
 10 Willm Pallmer Jno^r
 11 John Billington Seno^r*
 12 Hellen Billington*
 13 ffrancis Billington*

To this lott fell A Black weining Calfe to wch was aded the Calfe of this yeare to come of the black Cow, wch fell to John Shaw & his Companie, wch pveing a bull they were to keepe it ungelt 5 yeares for common use & after to make there best of it. Nothing belongeth of thes too, for ye copanye of ye first stock: but only halfe ye Increase.

* Came in the Mayflower.

To this lott ther fell two shee goats: which goats they posses on the like terms which others doe their cattell.

8 The eaight lott fell to Samuell ffuller* & his company Joyned to him his wife
  2 Bridgett ffuller
  3 Samuell ffuller Junior
  4 Peeter Browne*
  5 Martha Browne
  6 Mary Browne
  7 John fford
  8 Martha fford
  9 Anthony Anable
  10 Jane Anable
  11 Sara Anable
  12 Hanah Anable
  13 Damaris Hopkins*

To this lott fell A Red Heyfer Came of the Cow wch belongeth to the poore of the Colony & so is of that Consideration. (vizt) thes psonts nominated, to have halfe the Increace, the other halfe, with the ould stock, to remain for the use of the poore.

To this lott also two shee goats.

9 The ninth lot fell to Richard Warren* & his companie Joyned wth him his wife
  2 Elizabeth Warren
  3 Nathaniell Warren
  4 Joseph Warren
  5 Mary Warren
  6 Anna Warren
  7 Sara Warren
  8 Elizabeth Warren
  9 Abigall Warren
  10 John Billington*
  11 George Sowle*
  12 Mary Sowle
  13 Zakariah Sowle

To this lott fell one of the 4 black Heyfers that came in the Jacob caled the smooth horned Heyfer and two shee goats.

* Came in the Mayflower.

The Division of Cattle in 1627.

10 The tenth lot fell to ffrancis Eaton* & those Joyned wth him his wife
  2 Christian Eaton
  3 Samuell Eaton*
  4 Rahell Eaton
  5 Stephen Tracie
  6 Triphosa Tracie
  7 Sarah Tracie
  8 Rebecka Tracie
  9 Ralph Wallen
10 Joyce Wallen
11 Sarah Morton
12 Robert Bartlet
13 Tho : Prence.

To this lott ffell an heyfer of the last yeare called the white belyd heyfer & two shee goats.

11 The eleventh lott ffell to the Governo^r Mr William Bradford* and those with him, to wit, his wife
  2 Alles Bradford and
  3 William Bradford, Junior
  4 Mercy Bradford
  5 Joseph Rogers*
  6 Thomas Cushman
  7 William Latham*
  8 Manases Kempton
  9 Julian Kempton
10 Nathaniel Morton
11 John Morton
12 Ephraim Morton
13 Patience Morton

To this lott fell An heyfer of the last yeare wch was of the Greate white back cow that was brought over in the Ann, & two shee goats.

12 The twelveth lott fell to John Jene & his companie joyned to him, his wife
  2 Sarah Jene
  3 Samuell Jene
  4 Abigall Jene
  5 Sara Jene
  6 Robert Hickes
  7 Margret Hickes

To this lott fell the greate white backt cow wch was brought over with the first in the Ann, to wch cow the

* Came in the Mayflower.

8 Samuell Hickes
9 Ephraim Hickes
10 Lidya Hickes
11 Phebe Hickes
12 Stephen Deane
13 Edward Banges

keepeing of the bull was joyned for thes psonts to pvide for.
heere also two shee goats.

1627, May the 22. It was farther agreed at the same Court: That if anie of the cattell should by acsident miscarie or be lost or Hurt: that the same should be taken knowledg of by Indifferent men: and Judged whether the losse came by the neglegence or default of those betrusted and if they were found faulty, that then such should be forced to make satisfaction for the companies, as also their partners dammage:

PLYMOUTH COLONY WILLS AND INVENTORIES.

(Continued from page 86.)

1633 PLYMOUTH   WYNSLOW GOVR.

An Inventory of the goods of Godbert Godbertson & Zarah his wife who dyed wthout will as it was tendered in Court upon Oath & as they were prised by m^r Joh. Done & m^r Steph. Hopkins the 24th of Octobr. & presented in Court the 11 of Novr Anno Reg Dom. nri Carol 9º.

Inpr one fowling peece	01 00 00
It 1 twart Saw	00 06 00
It 1 broade Axe	00 00 06
It An handsaw	00 00 06
It 2 wedges	00 01 06
It 2 pr of sheeres	00 00 08
It 1 pr of pinsers a drawing knife a file an hamer	00 01 06
It 1 hay hooke	00 00 06
It A melting ladle	00 00 06
It 3 howes	00 01 06

It A picaxe	00 01 06
It a chisell & Auger	00 00 06
It A table cloath	00 03 00
It A bed & bolster	00 14 00
It A pillow & pillow beere	00 01 00
It 2 deare skins & a net	00 01 06
It Barley wheate & oates	00 15 00
It A pottage pot pothookes & ladle	00 12 00
It A paire of pothangers & an Iron bar 2 hookes	00 05 00
It a slice	00 01 00
It 2 kettles	00 04 00
It A writing table of slate	00 00 04
It An earthen pan	00 00 06
It A Rugge	00 02 06
[12] It A felling Axe & a frow	00 01 04
It A Curtaine	00 00 06
It A warmingpan	00 02 06
It A paire of sheets	00 06 00
It A kettle	00 01 06
It A great bible	00 10 00
It Comunion of S^{ts} in ffrench	00 00 06
It Dod on the Comets*	00 01 00
It A looking glasse	00 00 04
It Salt 1 bushell 3 pecks	00 08 00
It pease wth the tub & oill	00 07 00
It A trunck	00 06 00
It A peece of Irish cloath	00 02 00
It A paire of sheets & pillow beere	00 05 00
It A Rug & blancket	01 10 00
It A box	00 00 08
It A Rownd box	00 02 06
It A Chest	00 01 06
It A Table	00 01 00
It A Chaire	00 02 00
It A Cupp	00 00 08
It A porrenger	00 00 06
It A salt	00 00 08
It 3 Trayes	00 01 06

*Commandments.

It A ffrying panne	00 02 06
It A drypping panne	00 04 00
It 4 pewter platters & a bason	00 07 00
It 5 trenchers & a platter	00 00 08
It A pistoll	00 01 00
It An other pistoll	00 05 00
It A lathing hamer	00 00 06
It An hatchet	00 00 04
It A felling Axe	00 00 08
It A spade & 2 Runlets	00 01 00
It A whipsaw & box & file	00 07 00
It A sickle	00 00 06
It old hogsheads bords & hemp	00 05 00
It 3 barrow hogs a sow & bore	08 10 00
It A Canoe & sayle	01 00 00
It 5 young hogs	03 00 00
It Six shares in a Cow	10 00 00
It Due debt owing by m^r Combs for a goate & other things	09 00 00
Due fro m^r Weston for a steere	03 00 00
It m^r Weston debtor for another steer	01 10 00
It A shovell	00 01 06
It A pcell of hemp	00 03 00
It 90 bushels of Corne at 6sh pr bush	27 00 00
It A box wth implem^{ts}	00 01 06
It A Cloake	01 10 00
It Another Cloake	01 00 00
It A hatt	00 06 00
It A paire of breeches	00 08 00
It A jerkin	00 04 00
It A hatt	00 02 00
It A Band	00 03 00
It A wastcoate & kirtle	00 12 00
It A yock	00 01 06
It A wastcoate & petticoate	00 06 00
It An Apron	00 04 00
It A paire of stockins	00 00 08
It 2 Aprons	00 02 00
It 1 old croscloath 2 old quoines &c	00 01 06

It a paire of shoes	00 00 06
[13] It A Gowne	02 00 00
It A Coate	00 03 00
It Another Coate	00 02 00
It A wastcoate	00 00 08
It A band	00 01 06
It A paire of stockins	00 00 06
It Coyfes & handcherchiefes	00 02 00
It An old Cloake	00 03 00
It A Coate	00 08 00
It The Dwelinge house & fence & garden	14 00 00

The debts of Godbert Godbertson.

Inpr debitor to Joh. Jenny in Corne at 5sh pr bushell	00 19 04
It To m^r Collier for comforts in sicknes	01 00 00
It To m^rs ffuller for phisick in sicknes	02 10 00
It To m^r Raph ffogg	04 14 03
It To Manasseh Kempton	00 10 00
It To Web Addy	00 03 00
It To Rich Sparrow	00 01 06
It To Will Richards for worke	00 16 06
It To Edm. Chandler	02 05 00
It To m^rs Warren for labor	00 06 00
It To Will Basset for labor	00 12 00
It To Nath. Morton	00 04 09
It to Rich Higgens	02 16 00
It To m^r W. Bradford & ptners	09 01 04
It To Company	
It To m^r Isaack Allerton	75 10 03

Vid. 1. Lib. C^rt orders, P. 37 & 41, 43. (*This line is in a later hand.*)

[14] PLYMOUTH   WYNSLOW GOV^R
1633

An Inventory of the goods & Chattels of John Adams late of Plymouth as they were prised by John Wynslow & John Jenny the 24 of Oct^o & presented in Court upon Oath the 11th of Novbr An^o 9° Regni Dom. nri Carol. &c.

Inpr. ¾ of a Cow one heyfer & a cow calfe	37	10	00
It 6 Swine	07	16	00
It 28 bushels of Corne	07	00	00
It 1 ffether bed & bolster	03	00	00
It 1 green Rug 2 blanckets	02	10	00
It 4 pr sheets	02	10	00
It 2 Table cloathes	00	04	00
It 6 Table napkins	00	04	00
It 6 pillowbeers	00	12	00
It 2 pillowes	00	04	00
It 2 Chests & a trunck	00	16	00
It 2 Cushens	00	03	00
It A chaire	00	03	00
It A smale wool bed	00	06	00
It 2 Iron pots	00	14	00
It 3 kettles	01	03	00
It 2 ffrying pannes	00	04	00
It pewter vessell	01	10	00
It 1 peece	01	10	00
It debts due for goods sold	03	10	00
It wooden vessell	00	05	00
	71	14	00

The above menconed Joh. Adams dyed w{th}out will. ffor the disposing of this estate see the order of Court Novbr 11. A⁰ Regni Dom. nri Caroli nono &c.

Book of C{rt} Ord{rs} from 1632 P. 39 — (*This line is in a later hand.*)

[15] PLYM.   WYNSLOW GOVR.
1633

An Inventory of the goods of Joh Thorp Carpenter late of Plym. deceased as they were taken by Capt. Myles Standish the & mr Will. Brewster the 15 of Novbr & presented in Court by Alice the late wife of the said Jn⁰. the 25 of the same. An⁰ 9⁰ Reg. Dom nri Carol. &c.

Inpr of Indian Corne 29 Bushels at 6 sh pr bushell 08 14 00

Plymouth Colony Wills and Inventories. 159

More Indian Corne that Stephen Tracy owes 9 bushell at 6 sh pr bushel	02 14 00
It 1 Canoe valued at 30 sh	01 10 00
It Indian Corne that Edw: Bumpas oweth 6 bushels at 6 sh pr bush	01 16 00
It Tho. Boreman oweth 2 lb of bever	01 00 00
It 1 ffowling peece at 35 sh	01 15 00
It Will Palmer thelder owes for a servt	02 00 00
It pt of a fframe of an howse that is neere Wellingsly	02 00 00
It 1 Latten lamp at	00 01 00
It 3 Trayes at	00 01 06
It 1 Great gouge	00 00 06
It 1 Green cloake at	01 10 00
It 1 pot, hangers, & 1 Iron ladle	00 07 00
It 1 pewter bason at	02 06 00
It pewter quart pot & 1 pewter pint pot	00 04 06
It other broken peecs of pewter	00 01 00
It 1 looking glasse	00 01 00
It one gr brush & 1 little brush at	00 00 10
It 1 square at	00 02 00
It 2 Gerdles at	00 01 06
It 1 Wastband of listes	00 00 06
It 1 sifting sive at	00 00 06
It one powder horne at	00 00 04
It 1 Chest at	00 14 00
It 1 stoole	00 00 02
It 1 ffishing line	00 00 06
It 3 howes at	00 00 04
It one hatchet	00 02 00
It 1 kettle	00 05 00
It Bend leather	00 01 00
It 1 Cradle	00 05 00
It 1 Cheire	00 02 00
It 1 ffyle	00 00 04

These following were prised pr Will Holmes & Josuah Prat being elsewhere.

One Square	00 02 06

It 1 short 2 handsaw	00 02 00
It A broade Axe	00 02 00
It An holdfast	00 01 06
It A handsaw	00 02 00
It 3 broade chisels	00 01 06
It 2 gowges & 2 narrow chisels	00 01 00
It 3 Augers Inch & ½	00 01 00
It 1 great auger	00 01 04
It inboring plaines	00 04 00
It 1 Joynter plaine	00 01 06
It 1 foreplaine	00 00 00
It A smoothing plaine	00 00 00
It 1 halferound plaine	00 01 00
It An Addes	00 02 06
It A felling Axe	00 03 00
It A doublet	00 18 00
It An hatt	00 01 00
It A paire of Breeches	00 01 00
[16] It A psalme booke	00 01 00
It A Bible	00 06 00

See the order in Court Nov. 25. 1633 concerning this estate, *in another Book**

Joh. Thorp debtor to

Joh. Holman of the Massachusets	02 00 00
To goodwife Pontus for keeping his wife in sicknes	00 13 00
To m^r Smith for boards	00 10 00
To m^{rs} ffuller	01 16 00
To m^r Hopkins for divers ptic^s	05 07 00
To Will. Richards	00 05 06
To widow Wright	01 09 09
To m^r Robt Heeks	02 17 06
To goodman Kempton	00 13 06
To Rich Higgens	00 07 00
To Sam. Chandler	02 08 06
To ffr Billington	03 12 06
To m^{rs} Warren	01 10 08

* The words in italics are in a later hand.

To m^r Gilson	00 15 00
To m^r Bradford	01 04 00
To m^r Done	00 01 00
To Edw Dowty	
To Jno Rogers	00 16 00
To m^r Hatherly as appeareth pr bill	02 04 00
To Edw. Bangs	00 15 00
To Edw Bumpasse for nursing his childe	00 11 00
To ffrancs Sprague	01 02 00
To Edm. Gyles	00 02 00
To m^r Isaack Allerton	09 04 04
To m^r Bradford & ptners	
To Lieuten^t Will Holmes 4 of br	02 00 00

(*To be continued.*)

THE DATE OF GOVERNOR BRADFORD'S PASSENGER LIST.

BY GEORGE ERNEST BOWMAN.

To the question, "When did Governor Bradford write his list of the Mayflower passengers?" the reply heretofore has been, "In 1650."

Such an answer seemed too indefinite, in regard to the record which is the foundation of all Mayflower genealogies, and I undertook to determine more closely, if possible, the time within which it must have been written. The success of the effort was greater than I expected, and the time has been reduced from one year to four weeks, as will be shown in the following notes.

In studying the records left by the Pilgrims it is necessary to keep constantly in mind the fact that they used "old style" dating, and that, according to their calendar, the year 1650 began on the twenty-fifth day of March, and ended on the twenty-fourth day of the following March.

Governor Bradford leaves no opportunity for doubt that he wrote his account of the Mayflower passengers during the year 1650, "old style," for, near the middle of the list, he writes "till this year .1650," and, in the last paragraph, "this present year .1650."* The list, therefore, must have been written before March 24, 1650, old style, that is, before April 3, 1651, new style.

Turning again to Bradford's History we find: "And seeing it hath pleased him to give me to see .30. years compleated, since these beginings. And that the great works of his providence are to be observed. I have thought it not unworthy my paines, to take a veiw of the decreasings, & Increasings of these persons, and such changs as hath pased over them, & theirs, in this thirty years." †

As Bradford distinctly says that thirty years have been "compleated, since these beginings," it is clear that he must have written this paragraph after the thirtieth anniversary of the Landing of the Pilgrims, that is, after December 21, 1650, new style. Thus Governor Bradford's own statements, in his account of the passengers, limit the time within which it was written to the three and one half months between December 21, 1650, and April 3, 1651, new style.

Continuing the investigation, a statement in the account of Elder Brewster's family attracted my attention. After mentioning the Elder and his wife, Bradford writes: "His sone Wrastle dyed a yonge man unmaried; his sone Love, lived till this year .1650. and dyed, & left .4. children, now living." ‡

As the exact date of Love Brewster's death is not known, I examined the probate records at Plymouth, and found that his will was dated October 11, 1650, new style, and his inventory was taken, by William Collier (his father-in-law) and Myles Standish, February 10, 1651, new style.§ The latter date is important, because the Pilgrims usually took an inventory of a man's property within a very few days after his death,¶ and as Love Brewster's inventory was not taken until the tenth of February, it is probable that he died very late in January, or even after the first of February. This

* MAYFLOWER DESCENDANT, Vol. I, pp. 12, 16.   † Ibid. p. 11.
‡ Ibid. Vol. I, p. 12.
§ Plym. Col. Prob. Records, Vol. I, p. 89.
¶ The inventory of Henry Samson's property was taken on the day of his death.

The Date of Governor Bradford's Passenger List. 163

would reduce to less than two and one half months the time within which the list could have been written.

After studying without results the other references to the deaths of the passengers, attention was turned to the children and grandchildren mentioned by Bradford, and in his account of the family of William Mullins was found the following statement: "Only his dougter priscila survied, and maried with John Alden, who are both living, and have .11. children. And their eldest daughter is maried & hath five children."*

John Alden's eldest daughter Elizabeth married on December 26, 1644, old style, William Pabodie, who was for many years the town clerk of Duxbury. While holding this office William Pabodie entered on the town records his own marriage, and the births of his children. The names of these children and the dates of their births I have copied directly from the original record made by their father: John, October 4, 1645; Elizabeth, April 24, 1647; Mary, August 7, 1648 †; Mercy, January 2, 1649 †; Martha, February 24, 1650; Priscilla, November 16, 1652 †; Priscilla, January 15, 1653 †; Sarah, August 7, 1656; Ruth, June 27, 1658; Rebecca, October 16, 1660; Hannah, October 15, 1662; William, November 24, 1664; Lydia, April 3, 1667.

It will be seen that the fifth child was Martha, who was born February 24, 1650, "old style," or March 6, 1651, "new style," and Bradford must have learned of her birth before he wrote: "And their eldest daughter is maried & hath five children."

It has therefore been demonstrated that Governor Bradford wrote his account of the Mayflower passengers and their "decreasings, & Increasings" during the four weeks between March 6, 1651, and April 3, 1651, both dates being in "new style."

---

* MAYFLOWER DESCENDANT, Vol. I, p. 13.
† Those not familiar with the difference between "old style" and "new style" dating will, doubtless, think it impossible that Mary should have been born August 7, 1648, and Mercy, January 2, 1649; but when we change these dates to "new style" they become respectively August 17, 1648, and January 12, 1650, and the apparent contradiction disappears. So in the case of the two children named Priscilla. The first one was born November 26, 1652, new style, and evidently died soon, for the next child, a girl, was born January 25, 1654, new style, and was also named Priscilla.

SCITUATE, MASS.,
BIRTHS, MARRIAGES AND DEATHS.

(Continued from page 110.)

Rev. Jonathan Dorby and Rev. David Barnes were pastors of the Second Church, at South Scituate, now Norwell, and Mr. George C. Turner of that place has again kindly compared my copy of the imperfect town records with those of the church, but the latter were so incomplete they were of no assistance.

Fortunately the town records of the "Intentions of Marriage" are preserved, and by comparison with them I have been able to perfect every name, and nearly every date. The parts supplied from the "Intentions" are enclosed in parentheses.

[7] The following Persons were married together by Jonathan Dorby minister

Ezra Randall & margaret Foster both of Scituate were married Novr 14th 1751

Elisha Silvester Junr & Grace Ruggles both of Scituate were merried Decr 17th 1751

Jonah Stetson Junr & Elizabeth Hatch both of Scituate were married Decr 19th 1751

Lemuel Ford of Marshfield & Priscilla Turner of Scituate were married Feby ye 20th 1752

Nehemiah Prouty & Lettice Taylor both of Scituate were married August ye 3^d 1752

Luke Bowker & Joanna Dunber both of Scituate were married Decr ye 14th 1752

Abijah Whiten of Hingham & mary Lambart of Scituate were married Jany ye 22^d 1753

Willm Gray & Abigail Perry both of Scituate were married Jany ye 30th 1753

Willm Davis of Freetown & Serviah Hatch of Scituate were merried march ye 1st 1753

Nehemiah Liscom of Stoughton & Rachel Clap of Scituate were merried march ye 26th 1753

Nath[ll] Brooks Ju[r] & Sarah Collamer both of Scituate were married april the 26th 1753

Cornelius Briggs & Jerusha Church both of Scituate were married may the 23[d] 1753

The Following Persons were married together by David Barns Minister

Isaiah Stodder & Mary Bowker both of Scituate were married Decem[r] y[e] 5th 1754

Nehemiah Hatch & Kezia Torrey both of Scituate were married June y[e] 17: 1755

Will[m] Carlile & Elizabeth Davis both of Scituate were married Novem[r] y[e] 17: 1755

Benjamin Curtis Jun[r] & Mary Cole both of Scituate were married Decem[r] y[e] 3. 1755

Benj[a] Stutson of Hingham & Zibiah* Elmes of Scituate were married February y[e] 5. 175(6)

Tho[s] Young & Jael Whitten both of Scituate were married Feb[y] y[e] 19th 175(6)

Elijah Curtis & Abigail Sole both of Scituate were married June y[e] 28. 17(56)

Edmond Bowker & Lydia Lambert both of Scituate were married Decem[r] y[e] 2[d] (1756)

Anthony Eames of Marshfield & Hannah Eells of Scituate were married Janu[y] y[e] 4: (1757)

Joseph Clap Jun[r] & Eliz[a]. Turner both of Scituate were married August y[e] 2† (1757)

Gidion Stutson Jun[r] & Eliz[a]. Perry both of Scituate were married Novem[r] y[e] 15 (1757)

Anthony Collamer & Marcy Barker both of Scituate were married Decem[r] y[e] 13: 175(7)

Galen Clap & Patience Brooks both of Scituate were married January y[e] 12: 175(8)

M[r] John Elmes & M[rs] Betty Perry both of Scituate were married January y[e] 19: 175(8)

Nicholas Vinal & Desier Cole both of Scituate were married July y[e] 13. 175(8)

* The " Intention " calls her Surviah.
† It is impossible to determine whether this date should be 2, or some number between 20 and 29.

Benj^a Bryant & Ruxby Perry both of Scituate were marrid July ye 16. 175(8)

Nath^{ll} Church and ye Widdo Mary Curtis both of Scituate were Married Novr 2. 175(8)

John Jacob & Hannah Tolman both of Scituate were Married Novr 2. 1(758)

Willm Baker of Marshfield & Hannah Linclon of Scituate were married Novr 2 (1758)

Mordacai Lincoln of Taunton & Abiah Eells of Scituate were Married Novr 30 (1758)

Simion Swift & Caturn Turner both of Scituate were married Decem^r 2 * (1758)

The Revd Mr Samuel Boldwin of Hanover & Miss Hannah Cushing of Scituate were married January ye 4th (1759)

Jonathan Brown Ju^r & Mary Cowing both of Scituate were married ye 1st (Nov. 1759)

Michael Clap & Sarah Lambart both of Scituate were married Nov(1759)

Joshua Gardner of Hingham & Mary Totman of Scituate were married Nov(1759)

[8] Joseph Elmes Junr & Mary Linclon both of Scituate were married Novr ye 29th 1759

Seth Tayler of Pembrook & Martha Stutson of Scituate were married Novr 29. 1759

Josiah Litchfield Junr & Abigail Studly both of Scituate were married Decr 24. 1759

Elisha Jacob & Lucy Randall both of Scituate were married may ye 1. 1760

Joseph Bowker & Eliz^a. Cowen both of Scituate were married may ye 26. 1760

Dwelle Clap & Eliz^a. Elmes both of Scituate were married June ye 5. 1760

Capt Israel Vinal Juⁿ & Mrs Marcy Cushing both of Scituate were married Sepr 25. 1760

Lott Silvester of Marshfield & Lydia Ewell of Scituate were married Oct^o 9. 1760

Aaron Clark of Wells & Betty Jones of Scituate were married Oct^o 24. 1760

---

* As the " Intention " was entered Dec. 9, 1758, this date must be Dec. 20, or later.

James Turner & Deborah Linclon both of Scituate were married Oct⁰ 24. 1760

Daniel Thomas of Marshfield & Sarah Ewel of Scituate were married Novʳ 13. 1760

Solomon Bates of Hanoʳ & Equilla Bates of Scituate were married Novʳ 20. 1760

Jonathan Hatch & Lucy Cole both of Scituate were married Novʳ 27. 1760

Willᵐ Perry & Lydia Turner both of Scituate were married Novʳ 27. 1760

Thoˢ Young & Hannah Barker both of Scituate were married Decʳ 11. 1760

Solomon Briggs of Norton & Remember Litchfield of Scituate were married Decʳ 15. 1760

Elijah Crooker of Marshfield & Eggatha Hatch of Scituate were married Decʳ 18. 1760

James Stockbridge of Scituate & Martha Dunbar of Hingham wer married Febʸ 12. 1761

Samˡˡ Tower of Hingham & Hannah Collamer of Scituate were married Febʸ 12. 1761

Ignatius Vinal & Patience Elmes both of Scituate were married April 2ᵈ 1761

(J)ob Cowing Juʳ & Zillah Perry both of Scituate were married may yᵉ 20 1761

Colburn Barrel & Desier Bowker both of Scituate were married may yᵉ 28. 1761

(D)aniel Damon Junʳ & Hannah Bowker both of Scituate were married may 28. 1761

(Thomas) Joslyn of Hano & Patience Barker of Scituate were married June yᵉ 10ᵗʰ 1761

(John St)etson Junʳ & Bathsheba Dunber both of Scituate were married Septemʳ 10. 1761

(Elisha) Laphum & Elizᵃ. Cole both of Scituate were married Oct⁰ yᵉ 15. 1761

(Th)oˢ Roggers Juʳ of Marshfield & Submit Hatch of Scituate were married Novʳ 19. 1761

(Jo)nathan Hatch & Rachel Curtis both of Scituate were married Novʳ yᵉ 25. 1761

(Th)oˢ Southworth of Duxborough & Anna Hatch of Scituate were married Novʳ yᵉ 26. 1761

(Jos)hua Richmond of Dartmouth & Eliz^a. Cushing of Scituate were merried Novr 26. 1761

(Isra)el Cowing of Rochester & Eliz^a. Cudworth of Scituate were married Jany ye 5th 1762

(Jose)ph Bonney of Pembrook & Eliz^a. Dilano of Scituate were married May 15. 1762

(Davi)d Jones of Hingham & Unice Davis of Scituate were married May 27. 1762

(Sam)uel Boo Negro man & Hannah Richards both of Scituate w^{re} married July 15. 1762

(Seth) Byrum of Bridg^r & Sarah Vinal of Scituate were married Augst 12. 1762

(Joseph) Lambart & Hannah Brooks both of Scituate were married Novr 16. 1762

(Stephen) stetson & Experance Palmer both of Scituate were married Decr 19. 1762

(*worn*) fore mentioned Cupples were married at y^e Respective times (*worn*) their names (*worn*) me David Barns of Scituate Minister

(*To be continued.*)

THE BREWSTER BOOK.

(*Continued from page 77.*)

(p. 185, *upside down*)
Lucretia the wife of Jonathan
Brewster deyed in the yere of our
Lord march : 4th : 16$\frac{78}{79}$

Dannell Brewster mareed to Hanna
Gajer the : 23 : of December :1686

Dannell the Son of Dannell
Brewster and Hanna his
wife Borne at Norwich
October the : 11 : 1687

Hannah the Dafter of Dannell
Brewster and Hannah his wife
Borne at preston the : 2 : day of

Decembe 1690
mary the dafter of Dannel
Bewster and Hanna his wife
Borne at preston Jennauary
the 2 : 1692

> The five preceding entries are in the handwriting of Benjamin [3] Brewster (Jonathan [2], Elder William [1]).
>
> The following entry is in a different hand, not identified.

mary the wife of Christophar
huntington departed this life
December the 24 in the year 1749

(p. 184, *upside down*)
John the son of Dannell Brewster
and of Hanna his wife borne
at preston in Juley 18 1695

Jeruca the Dafter of
Dannell Brewster and of Hanna
his wife borne at preston
November 18 in 1697

Ruth the Dafter of Dannell
Brewster and of Hanna his
wife borne at preston
June the 20 in 17(*worn*)

Betheyah the Dafter of
Dannell Brewster and of
Hanna his wife born at
preston the 5 of Aprell
in 1702

Jeruca deyed the 17 day of Aprel(*worn*)
1704

Jonathan is entred in
another plase

> The six preceding entries are in the handwriting of Benjamin [3] Brewster.
>
> The following entry is on the inside margin of the page, and was written by Daniel [4] Brewster (Benjamin [3], Jonathan [2], William [1]).

Jeruca the Dafter of Danl Brwster
and hannah his wife born at preston the
15 day of october 1710

(p. 183, *upside down*)
Adam Pickett sone to
John Pickett & Ruth his wife
was borne at new London Novemb^r ye 15th 1658

Was marryed to Hannah (ye Dafter
of Daniell & Grace Wetherell)
May ye 26th 1680 : it being wednesday.

Adam Pickett sone to ye aboves^d Adam
& Hannah, was borne at N. London septemb^r
ye 7th 1681 : it being wednesday at about
8 of ye Clock in ye Evening :

The following entry was written on the outside margin of the page. This and the three preceding entries are in the handwriting of Daniel Wetherell.

Hannah ye Dafter of Dan^{ll} (*worn*) Grace
(*worn*)etherell was borne March (*worn*)
(*worn*)oq(*worn*) D(*worn*) : 1659.*

Jeruca the dafter of Danill
Brewster and hanna his
wif died in march : 7 : 1711

(*worn*)bneser the son of Daniel
(*worn*)wster and hana his wif
(*worn*)orne at preston
(*worn*)ptember : 19. 1713

The last two entries were made by Daniel^4 Brewster.

(p. 182, *upside down*)
Dannell the son of mathew Coy and
Ann his wife Borne at mohegin June
the : 15th : 1685

Jonathan Coy Son of mathew Coy and
Ann his wife Borne at mohegin the
: 6 : day of may : 1687

* See page 74.

The Brewster Book. 171

Ruth Coy Dafter to mathew Coy
and Ann his wife Borne at mohegin
october : 7th : 1689

<blockquote>The three preceding entries were made by Benjamin [3] Brewster.</blockquote>

Ebenezer Brewster the son
of Daniel Brewster and Hanay

his Wife Borne Preston
September ye 19 day and in the year
of oure Lord God
    1713

<blockquote>The preceding entry was probably made by Ebenezer himself in 1726. The latter date was written, and then was crossed out and 1713 written underneath with the same ink and evidently at the same time.</blockquote>

(p. 180, *upside down*)
Jonathan the son of Dannel Br(*worn*)
and Hanna his wife borne
preston the 6 day of June in 1705

Hanna Brewster the dafter
of Dannell Brewster mareed
to Josiph freeman the 2 day
of December 1708

Josiph the son of Josiph freeman and
hanna his wife borne march the 4
In the yere 1709 In preston

<blockquote>The three preceding entries are in the handwriting of Benjamin [3] Brewster.</blockquote>

Danill the son of
Josiph freeman and hana(*worn*)
wife Borne in prestan
Apral the : 1 : 1712

<blockquote>The preceding entry was written by Daniel [4] Brewster.

The following entry was probably made by Joseph Freeman.</blockquote>

Hannah The Daugh(*worn*)
of Joseph Freeman and Han(*worn*)
his Wife Born in Preston
Febr^a 23th. Anno Domini (*worn*)

(p. 179, *upside down*)
Jonathan Brewster mared to
Judeth Steven the 18 of
December 1690 shee being then
20 yeres of age wanting 7 dayes

Lewcresha the dafter of
Jonathan Brewster and Judeth
his wife Borne at mohegan the
3 : day of November 1691

Jonathan the son of Jonathan
(*worn*)ewster and Judeth his wif born at
mohegin the 2.of Aprell 1694

   The three preceding entries are in the handwriting of Benjamin [3] Brewster.

   The following record was made by Daniel [4] Brewster.

Mare the Dafter of Joseph Freman
and hanah his wife born at
Preston July : 12th : 1728

(p. 178, *upside down*)
Caleb the Son Joseph Freman
and Hannah his wife born
Preston Febuary 27th 1716-17

Phinehas the Son of Joseph Freem(*worn*)
and Hannah his wife born Preston
October 23th 1718

Nathan The Son of Joseph (*worn*)
and Hannah his wife
born at Preston September ye 23. 17(*worn*)

Benjaman ye Son of Joseph F(*worn*)
and Hannah his wife born at (*worn*)
November ye 27. 1723

Samuel ye Son of Joseph Fre(*worn*)
and Hannah his wife born at Pres(*worn*)
June 26. 1726

   The five entries on page 178 were probably written by Joseph Freeman.

(p. 177, *upside down*)
Reuth Brewster marreed to
thomas Adgate the 15 of
June 1692

Ruth the daughter of thomas adgate
and Ruth his wife Borne at Norwich
march the : 27 ano Domne 169$\frac{2}{3}$

mare the Dafter of thomas
adgate and Reuth his wif
born at Norwitch the 27 of
August 1694

<small>The first and third entries on page 177 were made by Benjamin[3] Brewster. The second, fourth and fifth were written by three different persons, not identified.</small>

(*worn*)aniel Freeman the son
(*worn*)f Joseph Freeman and Hannah
His Wife Departed this Life
April 28th day about 6 a
Clock in the after Noon
In the year 1733

Mehetabel Richards
the Dafter of Willam Richards
(*worn*)eadya his Wife Departed this Life
october ye 1 day 1743

(p. 176, *upside down*)
Daniel Brewster Departed
This Life May 7 and in the year 1735

Hanah Brewster The
Wife of Daniel Brewster
Departed this Life September : 25th day 1727

<small>The first two entries on page 176 are in the same hand, not identified.</small>

<small>The last two entries were made by different persons, unknown.</small>

Joseph Freeman Sener Departed thise
May 12th day 1733

Ebenezer Brewster the son
of Daniel Brewster and Hannah

His Wife Departed this Life
October ye 7 Day in the 27
year of his age in the year 1739

(p. 175, *upside down*)
Dannell meeks marreed to
Elisabeth Brewster the
4 : day of July 1706

Jonathan the Son of Dannell
mekes and of Elisabeth his wife
borne the : 18 : day of Aprell 1707

> The two preceding entries are in the handwriting of Benjamin [3] Brewster.
> The two following entries are in an unknown hand.

Daniel Meeks Senor Departed
this Life April 13th day 1733

Elsabeth Mecks ye wife of
Daniel Mecks Departed this
Life march y^e : 9 Day y^e
year : 1744

(To be continued.)

EARLY RECORDS OF PLYMPTON, MASS.

Communicated by SUSAN AUGUSTA SMITH of North Pembroke, Mass.

These early records of Plympton begin in 1695 while it was the Western Precinct of Plymouth, and continue after it was incorporated as a town in 1707. This Precinct was incorporated Nov. 26, 1695, and included the present limits of Plympton, the greater part of Halifax (about three quarters) and a strip of Kingston, on the Northeasterly part of Plympton (1306 acres), also Carver except South Meadows.

After the act of incorporation as recorded in the first book, there follow records of town-meetings to page 101, when the births, marriages and deaths are scattered along through the book, not chronologically, but, as seems to have been the custom of the times, the earlier records were quite as likely to be found in the last part of the book as in the first part.

Lewis Bradford was Town Clerk of Plympton from 1812 to 1851, and while serving in that capacity spent much time and labor in adding data to the original records, as he obtained it from tombstones and other sources, which would assist the future genealogist in tracing ancestry.

In transcribing these records the notes by Lewis Bradford are put in italics, enclosed in parentheses, and the original paging is indicated by numerals enclosed in brackets.

The Book of Records of the West Satiety
in the Western precinct of Plimouth.

At a Great and General Court or assembly begun and held at Boston upon Wednesday the twenty ninth of May 1695 In the seventh yeare of his maiestyes Reign and continued by adjournment unto Wednesday the Twentheth of november following and the next Tuesday
november 26th 1695.
Upon perusal of the Report of a committee of this Court appointed to view the situation of the Remote Inhabitants of the Westerly part of the town of Plimouth with the number of families there residing and to propose a time in order to making a division between them and the body of sd town for setting up the worship of God in said precinct and having Considered of what was offered by the agents for the said town of Plimouth
The court do approve and allow of the divisional Line stated by the sd Committee viz extending from Jones River pond so called unto Jeduthen Robins his present Dwelling with this varation only so as to leave out of sd line the sd Robins Benaja Pratt John Pratt and Eleazer dunham to make a distinct precinct for setting up the worship of God and support of a Laarned and orthodox ministry among themselves being remote from the present place of publick worship in sd town And do grant and order that all the Inhabitants except as

aforesd that are or shall hereafter Settle within the sd Line and their Lands and Estates Lying there shall stand Charged towards the settlement and support of such ministry in manner as the Law Relating to the maintainance and support of ministers doz direct and provide and to be assessed thereto by two or more assessors as shall from time to time be Elected and appointed by the major part of said Inhabitants for that purpose which sd inhabitants may also nominate and apoint a Collector to gather and pay in the same as by order under the hands of such assessors shall be directed provided nevertheless that all Lands Lying within the said precinct belonging to other persons in sd town not Inhabiting there shall be free from all such assessments and not stand charged towards the support of the ministry in sd place nor shall any Lands belonging to any of sd Inhabitants Lying in parts of the town be charged towards the support of the ministry at the Town and that all the wood and timber being or growing within the sd precinct shall remain and continue to the use of the Comoners and proprietors as formerly and do further order that when and so soon as the Inhabitants of sd precinct shall have provided a learned and orthodox minister to preach the word of God among them shall be freed and exempt from paying towards the support of the ministry at the town and for so Long time as thay shall enjoy and have such a ministry continued with them.

    A true Copy of the General Courts grant Copied out of that which the Inhabitants of the Western Precinct of plimouth had from Boston
      By David Bosworth Clark.

[p. 101] David Shaw the son of Jonathan Shaw by Elizabeth his wife was born 20th March 1730–31 and died 28th of the same month.

Benjamin Soul the son of Benjamin Soul by hannah his wife was born February 1th 1731.

Joseph Bryant the son of Ebenezar Bryant by Elizabeth his wife was born Septemer 12th 1731 and died october 8th 1731.

micah Leach the son of giles Leach by Annah his wife was born august 11th 1722.
John Leach was born July 25th 1725.
Elizabeth Leach was born Aprile 28th 1728.

[p. 102] Isaac Boney the son of Isaac Boney by mary his wife was born April 19 1729.
and died December 7th following.
Sarah Boney was born April 5th 1731.
Silas Sturtevant the son of Cornelius Sturtevant by Elizabeth his wife was born June 27th 1730.
Samuel Waterman the son of Sam^{ll} Waterman by mary his wife was born June 27th 1726.
Mary Waterman was born Aprill 29 1730.

[p. 111.] Jabez Fuller died 14th october 1728.
Sam^{ll} Rickard deceased September 7th 1727. *(Aged about 63 yrs taken from his grave stone. Rebekah Rickard widow d. Apr. 4, 1740 ae. ab. 63.)*
Josiah Samson deceased March 29 1730.

[p. 114] Israel Dunham Deceased Augst ye 18th 1726.
Henery Rickard Deceast Sept. 17th 1726 *(ae. ab. 60)*
(Mercy the wife of Henry Rickard d. Jan. 10, 1729–30, in her 67th year.)
Joseph Sampson deceased Octo^r ye 15th 1726 *(ae. 47 yr. 3 m. 1 d.)*
The Widow Bethiah Waterman Relict of Samuel Waterman Deceast Jan^r ye 29th 1726–7 *(in her 59th yr.)*
Sarah wife of Seth fuller dece^t June ye 7th 1726.
Thomas Witon son of John Witon and Bethia his wife Deceased Decr ye 25th 1725.
Peirces Lukas wife of Joseph Lucas deceased June ye 6th 1726. *(She was the daughter of Lt. Jonathan Shaw by Mehetabel his first wife and was b. Mar. 10, 1692.)*
Barnabas Lucas sone of Joseph Lucas Deceased maye ye 20th 1726.
Samuel Cushman son of Samuel Deceast. April ye the 22^d 1727.
Jemima Cushman Deceast maye ye second 1727
Joseph Cushman Deceast Maye ye 10th 1727.

Jerusha Cushman Daughter of Benjamen Cushman Deceased May ye 22^d 1727.

abigail Harlow widow Deceased May ye 13, 1727. (*wid. of Nathl Sen. in 63^d yr. of her age.*)

Elizabeth Sampson wife of Georg Sampson Sen. Deceased maye ye 27th, 1727.

Rebeckah wife of Jabez Newland Deceas^t agust ye 21st 1727.

Rebeckah wife to mr Isaac Cushman Deceased Sep^t. ye 3, 1727 in ye 73^d year of her age.

Deakcon Elcanah Cushman Deceased Sep^t. ye 4th 1727 (*ae 76y. 3m. 3d.*)

Lef^tt Isaac Cushman Dec^d. Sept^er the 4th. 1727. (*in 51st yr. Son Rev. I. Cushman*)

Susanah Cole wife to John Cole Senr deceased Aug^st 26th 1727 (*in her 59th. yr.*)

Edmund Weston Senr deceased Septem^er 23^d 1727 (*in 67th yr*)

Adam wright Senr Deceased Septr. 20th 1724 (*in 79 or 80th. yr*)

Susanah Bosworth wife to Nehemiah Bosworth Deceased Septem^br 10th, 1728

Samuel Fuller Ju^r died april 18th, 1724.

(*To be continued.*)

THE DIARY OF JABEZ FITCH, JR.

(*Continued from page 105.*)

(*March*, 1757.)

ye 17th Brother & I Set out and went to Mr Katterlans then to ye Wid^w Povertys to Peltons Jno Maynors Jno Spicers Dan^ll Whipples then to Pocatanock Where we Parted & I Came Home — this Day I Hered of ye Sudden Death of Jeremiah Tracy

Sund^y March ye 20th I went to Meeting at Noon Hered of ye Death of Abraham Tocomawos and Som thing How He Com by his End I also Went with a Number Down to ye Rever where ye Indion was Murderd — At Night I Came

Home & Had Oppertunity to Do Some Writing alone in ye Evening —

ye 22^d & 23rd there was a Vary Great Storm of Hail I Made a Powder Horn

ye 24th I went over to Town Se Elisha Rockwell — I Lit of Serg^t Peck in Town Se Nath^n Gallup Lieu^t Billings & His Father Lieu^t Fitch & His Brother I also went to Cort Hered Som Considrable Pleading Se Capt Harris there at Night I went Up to Brother Rudds

ye 25th I staid at Rudds all Day we Had a Bundance of Discorce with one John Thos an Irishman at Night Doc^t Huntington & Lieu^t Peck were there

ye 26th I Came Down to Town Se Capt Fitch & Lie^t Durky I Bought Some Dufen at Esqr Jabez Huntington then I Came Home In ye Rain.

ye 28th I went to John Wights Got Me a Jacket & Carried it to Capt. Mixs to Be Made

March 29th I went to Town to Meet ye Company But they Didnot meet So I went to Cort & Staid there all ye rest of ye Day at Night Came Hom in ye Rain again

ye 30th was a Vary Stormy Day &c Dan^ll Deming was mar^d y^s Night

ye 31st I went to Town Rec^d my Bounty £2 : 4 : 5½ at Night Came Home

About this time we Hered a Bundance of News about Fort Wm Henrys Being Beseegd But Nothing Direct So as to be Depended Upon.

Aprill 2nd we Droyd Some Logs To ye Soymill

Sunday Aprill 3rd Was a Nother Tedious Storm

ye 4th I Wrote Some Poems From ye Lyrics &c —

ye 5th I went to Town to Meet ye Company there was a Press in Town this Day there was a Training of Capt Cooks Company — Capt. Cook Pres^d Several Men about this time —

ye 6th was ye Public Fast

ye 7th I went to Groton to Brother Pelatiahs He & His wife was Gon to Ordination Mr Stoddard was there —

ye 8th in ye Morning Brother & I Went to Sam^ll Walworths to Se His Negro where we was Treated Vary Hansomly

Came Back in ye afternoon He & I Set out Some Apple Trees — In ye Evening we went Down to Mr Burrowss —
ye 9th I Had Much Discorce with Mr Stoddard &c : Ab Gard was there — At Night we Had a Dispute Conserning Space — then Upon ye Trinity
Sunday ye 10th Brother and I went over to Mistic to take Cair of an ox — from 1 to 3 oClok — at Night Brother went to Fishing Cosen Frelove was there & Mr Walworths Daughters
ye 11th I Rose Vary Early about 8 oClok I Toock My Leve of My Brother & His Family — Set out for Norwich I Rid about a Mile oftock Sam^{ll} Walworth & Rid with Him to Nathan Alliens Had Much Discorce with Him — then I Crosd ye River & Rid Alone in to Town where ye Company was Imbodyd — Before Night I Set out to Go Home Helpd a Drunken Man Down to ye Landing and over ye Bridg Then I Bought Several Things Nessary for ye Expadition — Reuben Mix Listed this Day
ye 12th It Raind I went To Town again it was Traning Day In Town at Night I went Up to Brother Rudds
ye 13th In ye Morning I was Not well But about 11 oClok I Grew Better & Set out to Go to Town I went to Lothrops & there Lit of ye Officers & Plaid Hundreds Most of ye afternoon Toard Night Part of Capt. Gallups Cumpany Marchd out of Town — I Came Down to ye Landing and Lit of a Chains to Ride Home on a Hors of Mr Coits
ye 14th Brother Elisha and I Made Fens at Night I went Down to Uncle Haskels &c.
Memorandum : Lieu^t Billings was Married Aprill 12th 1757 and Doct^r Lee ye 14th
ye 15th was a Lowery Day I went to Town again Lt Waterman Set of for Hartford at Night I Came Home in ye Rain
ye 16th I went to Town again Rec^d ye Remainder of My Bounty & First Months wages Which is (*) at Night I Came Home Cald in at John Prides &c —
Sunday ye 17th I went to Meeting Hered Mr Wight from Psalm 102nd 16th this Psalm was Sung & ye 132nd — at Night Yong Roger Haskill was Here —

* The amount was not filled in.

The Diary of Jabez Fitch, Jr.

y̆ᵉ 18ᵗʰ I went over to Town We Contluded to March yᵉ Next Day at Night I Got a Berth to Ride Home Behinde John Choat we went in at Prides there was a Company of my Mates there —

yᵉ 19ᵗʰ I Toock My Leave of Home in yᵉ Morning and went to Brother Elishas Bid Fairwell to Them & Then I went to Mʳ Wights Spent Some time with Him then went over to Town Toock My Snapᵏ & Blanᵗ & Soon Marchᵈ we was Pesterd Extreamly with our Indians Being Drunk we Marchᵈ to Land Lord Huntingtons where we Got Some Diner for our Men — I Toock My Leave of My Father & Sister Rudd and Marchd in yᵉ Front — at yᵉ Widdᵒ Fitchs I Toock My Pack we Got to Aldens in Lebanon — there I Lodgd in a Good Beed with Lieuᵗ Durky — This evening I Had Some Conversation with Som old acquaintants &c

Aprill 20ᵗʰ we Set out from Aldens Early in yᵉ Morning I Marchd in yᵉ Front to Clarks in yᵉ Crank Before Breakfast &c. about 10 oClok we Set out from there I Got Thoˢ Andrus to Carry My Pack I Brought up yᵉ Rear & was Plagued with our Indians Some of em was Drunk About Noon we Got to Houss in Andover where we Rested Some time then Marchd Up to Bolton and I Got Some Dinʳ at Pitkins — then Sent of al yᵉ men and Marchᵈ in yᵉ Rear Down to Websters where Thoˢ Andrus Mad us Som Sport with Some Yong Women &c — then Marchd to Chenees Sent all our Men of from there and we Got to Olcutts Just Before Sunset — Got Som Supper and Lodgd with Lᵗ Durky and Silˢ Waterman in a Vary Good Bead Slep well &c —

Aprill 21ˢᵗ 1757 at Olcutts we Had Tea for Breakfast then we Set out I Had Got Half a Mile and forgot my Powder Horn & went Back again after it — about a Mile from Olcutts I Got Up on Lᵗ Durkys Hors and Rid Into Hartford — we went Down yᵉ Bank and Wated by yᵉ Flood Some time for orders at Last went over to Capt. Marsas and Got Some Dinʳ on My own Cost — then Crossd yᵉ ferry and went Up to yᵉ State Hous where I Toock charge of yᵉ Company and Then Marchᵈ them forward to Mʳ Bentens and Got em Billited out there & among His Neighbors with Much Dificulty — I Got Quarters My Self at Mʳ Bentnes at Night Lodgd In a Bead with Thoˢ Andrus &c —

ye 22nd In ye Morning I Hered that Atwell one of our Men was Sick I went to Se Him and ye Rest of our Men — A Great Deal of Fiddleing and Dansing we Had This Day In ye afternoon I Turnd out Part of our Men & Exercised them — Doc^t Bull Com to Se Atwel our Two Lieu^{ts} Com to Se Us we Drinkd Mothegalan and Plaid Hundreds &c — Then I went in to ye Chamber allone write ye Forgoing Lines Fiddleing & Dansing Going on Below &c — at Night Lodgd with Andrus again

ye 23rd was a Lowery Day we Had Fiddleing & Dansing Going on I Helpd ye Land Lady &c. Thos Andrus Set out to Go Home — In the After Noon Maj^r Pasons Company Marchd By Here Lt Huntley Came to Se us we Plaid a Little at Cards So He went Home to His Quarters — At Night I Lodgd With Serj^t Mack &c —

Sunday ye 24th I Ralied What men I Could and went to Meeting with Mr Seymer Set with Him Hered Mr Whitman from Psalm 44th (*)th and 119th at Noon I was at Land Lord Butlars & was Treated Vary Handsom ye River was Vary Deep — In ye after Noon I Set In ye Gallery &c — At Night Came to our Quarters And Sung Some Hymns — Roger Bissel was there

Memmorandum our Land Ld Has a daughter 6 Years old with 2 Thums on one Hand

(*To be continued.*)

REPORTS FROM STATE SOCIETIES.

MASSACHUSETTS SOCIETY.

On Tuesday evening, May 16, 1899, a meeting of the Society was held at the Hotel Vendome, Boston. The Secretary reported the death, March 24, 1899, of Mrs. Mehitable (Parker) Smith, of Barnstable, Mass., aged ninety-three years, six months and twenty-four days. Mrs. Smith was seventh in descent from John Howland, and was elected a member of the Society September 2, 1899, her State Number being 397, and General Number, 1131. Mrs. Smith's twin sister,

* Illegible.

Mrs. Deborah (Parker) Hall, of Barnstable (also a member of the Society), survives her.

The Secretary announced the election of Mrs. Alonzo Butler Bray, whose record of twenty different lines of descent from nine Mayflower passengers is a remarkable one. The record is as follows: —

Seventh in descent (8 lines) from William Bradford.
Ninth in descent (4 lines) from William and Alice Mullins.
Eighth in descent (4 lines) from John and Priscilla (Mullins) Alden.
Ninth in descent (4 lines) from William and Mary Brewster.
Eighth in descent (4 lines) from Love Brewster.
Ninth in descent (4 lines) from Richard Warren.

The net membership of the Society is now 491, a gain of 92 members in the six months since the annual meeting.

The business meeting was followed by a reception.

Donations to the Library.

" Members and Ascendants of the Massachusetts Society of Colonial Dames of America, 1898," from Mrs. George S. Hale.

" Pilgrims of Boston," from Cyrus A. Hawes.

" Pilgrim Memoranda," from Morton Dexter.

" New England's Memorial " and " Guide to Plymouth and Recollections of the Pilgrims," both from Mrs. Henry E. Raymond.

" The First Parish in Brighton," from Edward B. Kellogg, M.D.

" Noyes Pedigree " and " Adams Pedigree," both from the compiler, James Atkins Noyes.

Members Elected.

April 12, 1899.

472. Mrs. William Henry Drury, Waltham, eighth from John Howland.
473. Miss Zeruah Soule, Duxbury, sixth from George Soule.
474. Mrs. Lindsley Loring, Chestnut Hill, ninth from John Howland.
475. Mrs. William Hill Young, Brookline, ninth from Richard Warren.
476. Nathaniel Cushing Nash, Cambridge, ninth from William Brewster.
477. Herbert Nash, Boston, ninth from William Brewster.
478. Thomas Francis Richardson, Cohasset, eighth from Francis Cooke.

479. Miss Mary Smith Clark, Medford, seventh from John Alden.
480. Miss Sarah Louisa Clark, Medford, seventh from John Alden.
481. Allston Porter Joyce, Medford, seventh from Edward Doty.
482. Dudley Richards Child, Boston, ninth from Isaac Allerton, eighth from Mary Allerton.
483. Miss Edith Child, Boston, ninth from Isaac Allerton, eighth from Mary Allerton.
484. David William Noyes, Boston, ninth from John Alden.
485. William Leonard Benedict, Boston, ninth from Richard Warren.
486. Mrs. Albert Stokes Apsey, Cambridge, seventh from George Soule.
487. Mrs. Fred Eugene Jones, Brookline, eighth from John Howland.
488. Mrs. Britton Davis, El Paso, Texas, seventh from William Bradford.

May 16, 1899.

489. Francis Otis Nash, Boston, ninth from William Brewster.
490. Mrs. Alonzo Butler Bray, Boston, seventh from William Bradford.
491. Mrs. Dole Wadley, Portsmouth, N. H., ninth from William Brewster.
492. Mrs. George William Downing, Lynn, eighth from William Brewster, seventh from Love Brewster.
493. Mrs. Edmund Anthony, Jr., Fairhaven, eighth from Samuel Fuller.
494. Alvin Page Johnson, Boston, tenth from William Brewster.
495. Mrs. Charles Andrew Clark, Newton Centre, eighth from Richard Warren.
496. Mrs. George Henry Whitney Bates, Boston, seventh from John Howland.
497. Henry Nathaniel Fairbanks, Bangor, Me., seventh from John Howland.
498. Mrs. Henry Nathaniel Fairbanks, Bangor, Me., eighth from William Bradford.
499. John Damon, Boston, ninth from Richard Warren.
500. Mrs. George Hiram Walker, Boston, ninth from William Brewster.
501. Elijah Austin Keith, Boston, eighth from John Alden.
502. Mrs. William Bond Way, Milwaukee, Wis., eighth from Francis Cooke.

Reports from State Societies. 185

503. Miss Lillian Minnie Way, Milwaukee, Wis., ninth from Francis Cooke.
504. Mrs. Edmund Cropper Gray, Milwaukee, Wis., ninth from Francis Cooke.

SUPPLEMENTAL LINES FILED.

March, 1899.
43. Horace S. Bacon, ninth from John Alden.
153. Henry C. Yergason, ninth from Stephen Hopkins, eighth from Constance Hopkins.
327. Harry C. Philbrick, tenth from William Brewster, ninth from Love Brewster.
452. Mrs. George Agry, Jr., ninth from John Billington, eighth from Francis Billington; eighth (2 lines) from Edward Doty; eighth from Richard Warren; eighth from Edward Winslow.
459. Mrs. Charles W. Underhill, eighth from Francis Cooke.
460. Mrs. William T. Curtis, eighth from John Alden; eighth from Stephen Hopkins; eighth from Myles Standish.
463. Mrs. Caleb M. Saville, eighth from Edward Doty.
469. Mrs. Walter M. Farwell, tenth from William Brewster; eighth (2 lines) from John Howland.

April, 1899.
468. L. Foster Morse, ninth from William Brewster; seventh (2 lines) from John Howland.
470. Miss Annie C. Morse, tenth from William Brewster; eighth (2 lines) from John Howland.

May, 1899.
278. Mrs. Earl A. Mower, ninth from William Brewster.
395. Mrs. Joshua Bates, eighth from Isaac Allerton, seventh from Mary Allerton; ninth from Richard Warren.
430. Mrs. Edward E. Capehart, tenth from William Brewster; eighth from John Howland.
432. Mrs. George W. Percy, ninth from James Chilton, eighth from Mary Chilton; ninth from Francis Cooke.
490. Mrs. Alonzo B. Bray, eighth (4 lines) from John Alden; seventh (7 lines) from William Bradford; ninth (4 lines) from William Brewster, eighth (4 lines) from Love Brewster; ninth (4 lines) from Richard Warren.
494. Alvin P. Johnson, tenth from William Brewster; tenth from Stephen Hopkins, ninth from Constance Hopkins.
498. Mrs. Henry N. Fairbanks, eighth from John Howland.

NEW YORK SOCIETY.

Members Elected.

April 5, 1899.
523. Henry Trowbridge Allen, New York, ninth from William Bradford.
524. Mrs. Charles Bliss Boynton, East Orange, N. J., eighth from John Alden.
525. Thomas Redfield Proctor, Utica, eighth from John Alden.
526. William Parker Jewett, St. Paul, Minn., eighth from William Bradford.
527. Mrs. Theron George Strong, New York, eighth from Francis Cooke.
528. Mrs. Lewis W. Cherry, Little Rock, Ark., eighth from John Howland.
529. Mrs. Walter Phelps Warren, Troy, eighth from Stephen Hopkins, seventh from Gyles Hopkins.
530. Mrs. Samuel Milford Blatchford, New York, seventh from Richard Warren.
531. Mrs. Charles Dwight Sabin, New York, seventh from Richard Warren.

May 3, 1899.
532. Mrs. Edwin H. Wootton, New York, eighth from John Alden.
533. Mrs. Simeon B. Chittenden, Brooklyn, ninth from John Howland.
534. Miss Edith Warren Sterling, East Orange, N. J., ninth from John Howland.
535. Miss Eleanor Augusta Sterling, East Orange, N. J., ninth from John Howland.
536. Mrs. J. W. Bubb, Fort Sheridan, Ill., seventh from William Bradford.
537. Mrs. Augustus J. Stephenson, Lockport, ninth from John Alden.
538. Mrs. Francis Perkins Furnald, Jr., New York, eighth from John Howland.

May 22, 1899.
539. Jedediah E. Adams, New York, eighth from William Bradford.
540. Charles Appleton Terry, New York, eighth from William Bradford.
541. Cyrus Fay Paine, Rochester, eighth from Stephen Hopkins, seventh from Constance Hopkins.

CONNECTICUT SOCIETY.

MEMBER ELECTED.

April 17, 1899.
195. William Newton Parker, New Haven, ninth from William Bradford.

PENNSYLVANIA SOCIETY.

MEMBERS ELECTED.

March 1, 1899.
108. Mrs. Henry Carney Register, Ardmore, seventh from George Soule.
109. Mrs. Joseph Harrison Brazier, Philadelphia, seventh from George Soule.
110. Jay Bucknell Lippincott, Philadelphia, ninth from William Bradford.
111. Henry Thomas Kent, Clifton Heights, seventh from Francis Cooke.
112. Louise Leonard Kent, Clifton Heights, eighth from John Alden.

SUPPLEMENTAL LINE FILED.

March, 1899.
93. Mrs. J. Bolton Winpenny, tenth from Thomas Rogers.

ILLINOIS SOCIETY.

MEMBERS ELECTED.

March 8, 1899.
63. Solon Tenney French, Chicago, seventh from John Alden.

May 10, 1899.
64. Mrs. Cyrus Bentley, Elmhurst, ninth from William Bradford.
65. Mrs. Joseph Robie Putnam, Chicago, seventh from William Bradford.
66. Mrs. Christine King Pomeroy, Chicago, ninth from William Bradford.

67. Mrs. Charles Bailey Sawyer, Chicago, eighth from Francis Cooke.

May 31, 1899.
68. Hempstead Washburne, Chicago, ninth from Francis Cooke.
69. Paul Blatchford, Oak Park, eighth from William Bradford.

SUPPLEMENTAL LINES FILED.

March, 1899.
46. Hubert C. Downs, ninth from William Brewster, eighth from Love Brewster.
57. Isaac B. Snow, ninth from William Brewster.

April, 1899.
31. Henry V. Freeman, ninth from William Brewster, tenth from William Brewster; ninth (2 lines) from Stephen Hopkins, eighth from Constance Hopkins, eighth from Gyles Hopkins.
52. Fredrik H. Gade, eighth from John Alden, ninth from John Alden; ninth from Thomas Rogers.
62. Miss Cornelia G. Lunt, tenth from Richard Warren.

May, 1899.
38. John McG. Adams, ninth from Stephen Hopkins, eighth from Constance Hopkins.
46. Hubert C. Downs, ninth from William Brewster, eighth from Love Brewster.
48. George Butters, ninth from John Alden; seventh from Edward Doty; eighth from Henry Samson; eighth from George Soule; seventh from Richard Warren, ninth from Richard Warren.
65. Mrs. Joseph R. Putnam, eighth from John Alden; eighth from Thomas Rogers.

OHIO SOCIETY.

MEMBERS ELECTED.

March 7, 1899.
26. Mrs. H. H. H. Crapo Smith, Detroit, Mich., eighth from William White, seventh from Resolved White.

March 28, 1899.
27. William Howard Doane, Cincinnati, ninth from Stephen Hopkins, eighth from Constance Hopkins.

28. Mrs. William Howard Doane, Cincinnati, ninth from John Howland.
29. Miss Ida Frances Doane, Cincinnati, tenth from John Howland.
30. Miss Marguerite Treat Doane, Cincinnati, tenth from Stephen Hopkins, ninth from Constance Hopkins.

DISTRICT OF COLUMBIA SOCIETY.

At the regular meeting held April 11, 1899, Rev. John Louis Ewell, D.D., the Elder of the Society, read a paper on the "Life and Works of John Robinson." Other speakers were Mr. William W. Case, Miss Hattie L. Alden, Mr. Edwin A. Hill, Mr. Thomas S. Hopkins and Mr. Solomon E. Faunce.

On Thursday evening, May 11, 1899, the Society was entertained at the residence of Mrs. George Rochford Stetson. During the evening Mr. Stetson read a paper on the history of Puritan hymnology, illustrating it by frequent selections on the piano.

The following Standing Committees were appointed by the Board of Assistants, April 11, 1899: —

Membership: Thomas Snell Hopkins, William Wallace Case, Jerome Fletcher Johnson, Frank Birge Smith, Edwin Allston Hill.

Publication: Harry Weston Van Dyke, Mrs. Jane S. (Owen) Keim, Miss Hattie L. Alden.

Auditing: William Park Metcalf, George Congdon Gorham, Sherburne Gillette Hopkins.

Room and Property: Rev. John Louis Ewell, D.D., Nathaniel Emmons Robinson, Alonzo Howard Clark, Thomas Blagden, Algernon Aikin Aspinwall.

Entertainment: Dr. Marcus Benjamin, Henry Peter Renouf Holt, Mrs. George Rochford Stetson, Miss Emily Eliza Robinson, Miss Isabel Sargent Chamberlin.

DONATION TO THE LIBRARY.

"The Portland, Conn., Burying Ground Association and its Cemetery," from John Henry Hall.

MEMBERS ELECTED.

February 21, 1899.
47. Benjamin Prentis Watrous, ninth from William Brewster.

March 14, 1899.
44. Mrs. Irving Williamson, Washington, eighth from William Bradford.
45. Mrs. William Wesley Karr, Washington, seventh from George Soule.
46. Miss Carlie Emeline Marsh, Washington, eighth from William Bradford.

April 11, 1899.
48. Mrs. Horace Gedney Young, Albany, N. Y., tenth from John Alden.

May 9, 1899.
49. Howard Wilson Blanchard, Herndon, Va., eighth from John Alden.

SUPPLEMENTAL LINES FILED.

March, 1899.
19. Harry W. Van Dyke, ninth from John Alden; eighth from Peter Brown; ninth from Francis Cooke; eighth from George Soule.
20. William P. Metcalf, ninth from William Brewster, eighth from Love Brewster; ninth from Richard Warren.
21. Edwin A. Hill, ninth from John Howland.
23. Mrs. George R. Stetson, ninth from John Alden; ninth from Thomas Rogers.
34. Caleb R. Stetson, tenth from John Alden; tenth from Thomas Rogers.
35. Mrs. Frank F. Fletcher, tenth from John Alden; tenth from Thomas Rogers.
36. Mrs. William H. Claflin, tenth from John Alden; tenth from Thomas Rogers.

PILGRIM NOTES AND QUERIES.

NOTES.

FOREIGN RESEARCH FUND (see pp. 61, 62). — The Committee on Historical Research will make arrangements for beginning the examination of the English records as soon as sufficient funds are in hand. If those who have promised to contribute will do so promptly it will be of great assistance to the Committee. Subscriptions not acknowledged: Nathaniel C. Nash, $100; L. Emery Holden, $25; John E. Alden, $5; Mrs. Henry C. Purmort, $5; H. Curtis Rowley, $5.

Pilgrim Notes and Queries. 191

MAYFLOWER GENEALOGIES (see pp. 124, 125). — The Committee on Historical Research is perfecting plans for carrying on the work of compiling these genealogies, and expects to be able to announce them in the October issue.

BRADFORD MEERSTEAD. — This name has been selected by the Committee on Marking Historic Sites for the portion of Governor Bradford's estate at Kingston, which was presented to the Massachusetts Society by some of his descendants.

The Committee has been receiving subscriptions for the purpose of marking the spot, by a handsome bronze tablet inserted in the face of a massive bowlder, and properly caring for the grounds. The treasurer has received $414 from the following named descendants : Mrs. Martha B. Stone, Mrs. Ellen H. Hudson, Mrs. Charles Taintor Baker, Mrs. A. L. Gilkey, Francis Olcott Allen, Arthur Orr, J. M. Adams, Mrs. F. A. Barker, Eben Barker, Frederick Alden Barker, Mrs. Titus B. Meigs, Frederick C. Fairbanks, Isabella Eldridge, Mrs. Henry Gay, Mrs. C. A. Nicola, Belle M. Torrey, Mrs. Charles F. Bradford, Edward C. James, Miss H. L. Robbins, Marion Bradford Willard, Bradford Holt Willard, Alden S. Bradford, Frederick Sheldon Parker, Henry Talmadge, Edwin S. Crandon, Mrs. Oliver Ditson, Mrs. Burr Porter, Hannah S. Davis, Mrs. John Crosby Brown, Gardner C. Leonard, Mrs. Timothy Dwight, Mrs. Mary Reed Smith, Charles Healy Ditson, William C. Donnell, Mrs. J. Bolton Winpenny, Miss C. A. Hamilton, Mrs. Mary E. Kountze, Chandler Robbins, Captain R. B. Bradford, Mrs. Lindsay Fairfax, Mrs. Henry W. Wilkinson, Mrs. Amelia Stone Quinton, Mrs. Stephen M. Whipple, Mrs. Zilpha Bradford Shaw, Mrs. Ella Bradford Burnham, Benjamin Delano Sweet, Guilford Smith, Mrs. Guilford Smith, Mrs. Alfred H. Belo, Pamelia Keith Wright, Mrs. Almeric Paget, Mrs. R. M. Newport, Mrs. John F. Lewis, Mrs. George Agry, Jr., Miss Josephine Lippincott, Mrs. Britton Davis, Walter P. Warren, Mrs. Henry N. Fairbanks.

After a long search the Committee has found a suitable bowlder in the town of Plympton, and the owner, Mr. William Perkins, a Bradford descendant, has presented it to the Society.

It is proposed to place in a recess in the bowlder, back of the tablet, a sealed box containing lists of the donors of the land and the memorial, lists of members of each of the State Societies, the names of all Bradford descendants who are members of the Societies, copies of THE MAYFLOWER DESCENDANT, etc.

QUERIES.

[*This department is limited to subjects connected with Pilgrim genealogy and history. Queries can be inserted for subscribers only.*]

10. THOMSON — REED. Lieut. John Thomson of Middleboro mentions in his will, dated 23 April, 1696, his daughter Esther Reed. What was the given name of her husband? Where did he live? Were there any descendants? C. B. R.

11. ROGERS — RICHMOND. Was Abigail[3] Rogers (John[2], Thomas[1]) the first or the second wife of John[2] Richmond (John[1])? Is there any deposition or other record than her gravestone which gives a clue to the date of her birth? Was she the mother of John's first four children? A. B. C.

12. WINSLOW — BROOKS. Did Elizabeth[2] Winslow (Governor Edward[1]) marry Gilbert Brooks of Scituate? H. I. S.

[*Elizabeth[2] Winslow married, first, Robert Brooks, by whom she had one son, John. She married, second, Captain George Corwin of Salem. An article in preparation for the October issue will present conclusive proofs of these marriages.* — EDITOR.]

13. BUCK — CUSHMAN. Who were the parents of Mary Buck, who married, 11 January, 1710-11, Allerton[4] Cushman (Elkanah[3], Thomas[2], Robert[1]), of Plympton? H. C. W.

BOOK NOTES.

Historia. A Magazine of Local History. Vol. I, No. 1, November, 1898; No. 2, February, 1899; No. 3, April, 1899. Edited and published by George C. Turner, Norwell, Mass. Bi-monthly, 8vo, 8 pp. $1 per year. Single numbers, 20 cents.

The town of Norwell was formerly South Scituate, and here was organized, in 1645, the Second Church in Scituate, with Rev. William Wetherell as its pastor. Mr. Wetherell's record of the children baptized by him [among whom were the children of Resolved White and of John and Mary (Brewster) Turner] has been preserved, and its publication was begun in the April issue of *Historia*. Another valuable feature is the copy of the gravestone inscriptions in the old cemeteries.

It is to be hoped that the success of this magazine will be such that others will imitate the good example set by Mr. Turner and start similar publications for the preservation of local records.

THE MAYFLOWER DESCENDANT

THE BREWSTER BOOK.
(Continued from page 174.)

An account of the illustration accompanying this article will be found on pages 3 and 4 of the January issue.

(p. 174, *upside down*)

The entries on page 174 were made by Benjamin[4] Brewster (Benjamin[3], Jonathan[2], Elder William[1]), the first two being made at one time, after the birth of his son Benjamin[5].

Benjmin Brewster marred to
mary smith the 17 of desember
1696

Benjmin Brewster the sonn
of Benjmin Brewster and
mary his wif born at mohegin the
24 of september 1697

John Brewster the son
of Benjamin Brewster and
mary his wif born at
lebonan may 25 1701

mary the dafter of Benja(*worn*)
Brewster and mary his w(*worn*)
born at lebonan aprl
the 24 174*

(p. 173, *upside down*)
Sarah Brewster Dafter of John
Brewster and Dorothy His Wife
born at Preston May the 25 day 1733

This entry is in an unknown hand.

* 1704.

(p. 155, *upside down*)

The entries on this page were probably made by John Brewster himself.

John Brewster Married to
Dorothy Treat Septembar ye 20 1725

Olevour the Son of John Brewster
and Dorothy his wife born at Preston
July ye 20. 1726

Dorothy ye Daughter of John Brewster
and Dorothy his wife born at Preston
Jenuary ye 22 1727–28

Hannah ye Daughter of John Brewster
& Dorothy his wife born at Preston
Sepr ye 26th 1729

Daniel ye son of John Brewster
& of Dorothy his wife born at Preston
April ye 12. 1731

(p. 146, *upside down*)
Daniell Brewster sun to
Daniell Brewster mareed
to Elisebeth fremen Daftear
to Josef freman agest the : 8 : 1710

The preceding entry was made by Daniel[4] Brewster (Benjamin[3], Jonathan[2], Elder William[1]).

The next three entries are in an unknown hand.

Ebnerzer Brewster sone to
Daniel Brewster mared
Susana Smith agesthe
the 28 1735

On the outside margin opposite the preceding entry is written "hannh Brewser his wife."

Benamon the Son of Ebnezer Brewser
Susana his wife borne unto hem
at prason april 15 1736

Ebenezar Brewster the Son
of Ebenezar Brewster Susana
his Wife borne unto them
of preston april 25 1740

(p. 144, *upside down*)
    The handwriting of the entries on this page has not been identified.

Willam parrish mared unto
Betia Brewstr May 23 1738

Bethia Parrish The Daughter
of Willam Parrish and Bethia His
Wife Born at Windham September
26 in The year 1739

Bethiah Parrish the Wife of
Wilian Parrish Desceast febuary
the 8 1741

(p. 138, *upside down*)
    The three entries on this page are in the handwriting of Daniel[4] Brewster, son of " Beniemen " and Ann.

Ann Brewster the wif of
Beniemen Brewster
Departed this Lif may the : 9 : 1709

Beniemen Brewster
Departed this Lif
In September the : 14 : 1710

Daniel Brewster marred to
Dorthy Witter December 19th 17(*worn*)

(p. 99, *right side up*)
wilom wedg the son of
Joshua wedg and rebeckea
his wif Born the Dsember(*worn*)
                    17(*worn*)
    The preceding entry is in an unknown hand.

(p. 118, *right side up*)
    The entries on pages 118, 119, 120 and 129 were made by Nathan Freeman.

Nathan Freeman Maried to Lucy Bloggett
In the year : 1748

(p. 119, *right side up*)
Ruth Freeman the Daughter
of Nathan Freeman and Lucy His

wife was Born october y^e : 24 : Day
In ye year : 1749.

Preston April the : 24 : Day in
The year : 1750 : Ruth Freeman
the Daughter of Nathan Freeman
and Lucy Freeman His wife Departed
this Life and in y^e : 2 : year of Her age

(p. 120, *right side up*)
Preston November : y^e : 2 : Day
In the year : 1753 : Then Lucy
Freeman the wife
of Nathan Freeman Departed
this Life and in the : 25 : year
of Her age.

Nathan Freeman Married to Lucy
Barns February the : 14 : in the year 1753

Preston June the 29th Day 1756
Daniel Freeman Son of
Nathan Freeman and Lcey his
Wife Born June 29th Day

Lucey freeman the Daughter
of Nathan freeman and
Lucey his wife Born November
the tenth Day 1756

(p. 129, *right side up*)
March : y^e : 28 Day in the year 1753
The Nathan Freeman moved to
Mr Daniel Brewsters to
Live With Him

Nathan Freeman
And Lucey Freeman his
Wife

(p. 136, *right side up*)
(*worn*)eruca the Dafter of Jonhn fobes

(*worn*) Ruth his wif departed this lief
february the : 25 1727

<small>The preceding entry was probably made by Daniel [4] Brewster. The following entry is in an unknown hand.</small>

John Fobes Departed
This Life Febry 18 in the year 17(*)

(p. 137, *right side up*)

<small>The first two entries on this page are in an unknown hand. The remaining entries were probably made by Daniel [4] Brewster.</small>

John Fobes Marred to Ruth (*worn*)
ster Jenuary 14th 1718–19

Simeon the Son of John Fobes and R(*worn*)
his wife was born Jenuary 14th 171(*worn*)

marey the Dafter of John Fobes (*worn*)
Ruth his wife was born at preston Jenuary 19 (*worn*)

Jeruca the Dafter of John fobes an(*worn*)
Ruth his wife was born at preston Decem(*worn*)
the 19 1724

hanah the Dafter of John fobes
and Ruth his wife was born at preston
may the 29 1727

Ebnesar the son to John Fobes and Ruth his
wife was born in preston october
the : 22 day at mednith 1728

(*To be continued.*)

PLYMOUTH COLONY WILLS AND INVENTORIES.

(*Continued from page 161.*)

[17] Plym. WYNSLOW GOV
1633
 An Inventory of the goods & Chattels of ffr
Eaton Carpenter of Plymouth as it was

<small>* Illegible.</small>

taken by James Hurst, ffrancs Cooke & Phineas Prat the 8th of November & presented in Court upon Oath the 25th of the same An⁰. 9⁰. Regni Dom. nri. Carol &c.

Inpr one Cow	20	00	00
It one Cow calfe	12	00	00
It 2 young barrow hoggs	01	00	00
It ffifty bushels of Corne			
It 1 Coate	01	12	00
It 1 Cloake	01	10	00
It 1 black sute of cloathes	01	00	00
It 1 white hatt	00	08	00
It 1 black hatt	00	04	00
It 1 doublet	00	05	00
It 1 doublet	00	12	00
It 1 Cushen	00	01	00
It 4 pewter platters	00	12	00
It 1 pewter salt	00	04	00
It 3 sawsers & a cuppe	00	01	00
It 1 Cheese presse	00	03	00
It 1 Chest	00	08	00
It 1 box	00	02	00
It 1 Toole box	00	02	06
It 1 Table	00	15	00
It 1 Cheere	00	13	00
It 1 old bedsteed & fforme	00	02	00
It 2 Curtaines & a Rod	00	02	00
It 1 quart pot & 1 brasse frying pan	00	02	00
	41	18	6
It 1 pcell of salve	00	01	00
It 1 thwart saw	00	04	00
It 1 handsaw	00	01	04
It 1 Rownd adds	00	01	00
It 1 great hamer	00	00	10
It 1 Adds	00	01	04
It 1 holdfast	00	01	08

It 1 Gouge	00 00 02	
It 1 fishing leade & a ffurmer	00 00 06	
It a pcell of old Iron	00 00 10	
It one shovell	00 00 08	
It 1 pistoll one powder horne & one shott purse	00 09 00	
It one peece	01 14 00	
It 6 planes	00 03 00	
It 2 gowges & a chisell	00 00 06	
It A broken holdfast & a bench hooke	00 01 00	
It 2 Awgers an handsaw & a bitt	00 04 00	
It 1 Iron square	00 02 00	
It 1 adds	00 02 06	
It 1 adds	00 02 06	
It 3 Awgers	00 01 06	
It 1 Bevell square	00 01 06	
It 2 fformers & an hedding chisell	00 00 06	
It 1 yron Rule	00 01 00	
It 3 Chake lines	00 01 00	
It 2 herring tubbs	00 03 00	
	04 00 04	
[18] It one pr of bootes	00 05 00	
It one case for bottles	00 02 00	
It one lathar	00 08 00	
It The frame	09 00 00	
It the ware	06 06 09	
It bords	02 08 00	
	18 09 09	

See w^t became of his estate by an order in Court novbr 25th. *1633 — in another Book.**

The debts off ffr Eaton

Inpr debtor to Joh. Barnes pr bill	11 00 00	
It To ffr Billington for worke	01 10 00	
It To Rich Sparrow for worke in the wier & his grane	01 01 00	

* The words in italics are in a later hand.

It To m^r Abr. Shurt	05	09	00
It To m^r Heeks	01	15	00
It To Willam lathan	01	08	00
It To him for worke as it was estimated pr Tho Prence & Kanelm Wynslow being pd & the work undone	05	00	00
It To m^r ffogge	00	11	11
It To m^{rs} ffuller for phisick	00	10	00
It To Samuel Eedy	02	00	00
It To Web for 12 daies worke about him in sicknes	00	12	00
To will wilkes for a kilderkin of butter	02	00	00
To m^r Peirce	00	05	09
To W. Bradford & ptners	21	11	08
To m^r hatharly	04	00	00
To m^r Isack Allerton	105		
To Tho : Prence for 19 days worke	02	07	00
To Joh Doane	02	15	11

more ffranes Eattones Debtts

To Joh Shawe	00	18	00
To m^r Smith	00	11	00
To Thomas Coachman	00	9	00
To His Maidservant	01	1	00
To m^r Hicx	01	00	00
To Joh Barnes	00	14	00

[19] New Plym.   WYNSLOW GOV^R.

> The last will & Testam^t of Will Wright late of Plymoth deceased as it was proved in Court the 2^d of Jan. in the ninth yeare of the raigne of our Soveraigne Lord Charles by the grace of God King of Engl. Scotl. ffr. & Irel. Defend of the ffaith &c.

In the name of God Amen. I Will Wright of new Plymouth in new Engl in America being sick & weake at this prnt, yet by the mercy of God in sownd & pfect strength of memory, calling to minde the weake & fraile estate of man how that he is but a shadow & is suddainly gone. And also I being at this prnt in a speciall manner sensible of the stroake of God thought good & most exspedient for the better setling of my estate, And also for the better establishing of peace & good agreem^t amongst my posterity & those that shall survive me to cause this prnt writing to be made declaring heerby this to be my last will & Test irremoveable, And all former wills & Testam^ts gifts grants legacies or any other conveyancs whatsoever heretofore made by me to any pson or psons w^tsoever to be utterly void & of none effect. And this my last will & Test to be in full force strength & vertue.

Inpr therefore I give & bequeath my body to the dust, & my sowle into the hands of God that gave it. being pswaded in my selfe that although my body shall be laid in the earth there to returne to dust from whence it came, yet at the last day when all flesh shall appeare before the tribunall bar of Gods justice that then my sowle & body shall be reunited, & that both sowle & body shall receive recompence of reward. And whereas I am sensible of the wrath of God wch I have incurred to my selfe by reason of my manifold faylings & disobedience to my God, whereby he hath just cause to appear to me an angry judge, yet I doe beleeve that Jesus Christ pfect God & pfect man hath fully & sufficiently satisfied to God his ffather for all my sins, & that by his bloud alone I stand freely justified before God, & not by any desert merit or worthines of mine owne, for in me dwelleth nothing that is good, & all my righteousnes is filthy & abominable, & that this death is but a passage to life eternall. And I doe desire my God to give me patience that I may beare his hand, & that all the daies of mine appointed time I may wait untill my change shall come, for I know my Redeemer liveth & that I shall shortly see him wth these eies, And I am willing to leave this fraile & troublesom life. & to be wth Christ my Saviour wch is best of all. Secondly whereas God of his great mercy & goodness hath made me ptaker of that great favor affourded to man in the begining I meane in calling me to the estate of marriage & hath given me a faithfull & loving wife wch hath lived wth me to this prnt time to our mutuall joy

& comfort, Therefore my will is, And heereby I doe freely give & bequeath unto Prisilla Wright my loving & lawfull wife all that my mansion or dwelling howse scituate lying & being in new Plymouth in new Engl aforesaid as it now standeth scituate & being neer unto a certaine lane or street comonly called the new street lying upon the one end of the said howse southward, & the other end butting in or upon mine owne ground or garden plot northward together wth all that pcell of ground or garden or garden plott that adjoyneth to my mansion or dwelling howse as it now lieth inclosed & fenced about wth a pale or palisado togeather wth all barnes stables beasthowses wth all their severall appurtenances priviledges & imunities any waies belonging & appertayning to her & her heires forever, To have hold occupie & enjoy the same freely wthout any let or molestacon whatsoever. Also I give & bequeath to Prisilla my loving wife all manner of right title interest & authority to all such moyety pt or pcell of lands or grounds that is or any way may appre to apprtaine or belong to me the said Will Wright when the same shall be assigned & lotted unto me according to the custome & maner of the place now being, To have hold occupie & enjoy the same wth all manner of easem^{ts} priviledges & appurtenances whatsoever to her & her heires for ever. Also I give & bequeath to Prisilla my wife all manner of goods & chattels whatsoever that is or may any way appre to be or belong unto me, either moveable or unmoveable to have hold [20] occupie & enjoy the same to her & her heires forever. Also I give & bequeath to Prisilla my wife full licence leave liberty & authority to aske gather receive & take all manner of debts recconings legacies dues demands w^{t}soev^{r} that is was or any waies may appeare to apprtaine or belong unto me from any prson or prsons w^{t}soever. And also my will & pleasure is that my wife shall have hold occupie & enjoy the same to her & her heires for ever. Also I give & bequeath unto Prisilla my faithfull & loving wife one Cow togeather wth one calfe or young bullock, & also to old melch goats together wth one ewe lamb. Moreover I give & bequeath unto Prisilla my wife all manner of Swine males & ffemales that now doe or any way may appre to belong unto me, to have hold occupie

& enjoy the same to her & her heires forever. Also my will & pleasure is that Prisilla my wife shall give unto the Church at Plymouth w^th^in one yeare after my death one ewe lamb when it hath been weaned one moneth to the only propr use of the said Church to have & hold the same for ever. Also my will & pleasure is that Prisilla my wife do give unto my reverend & respected ffriend m^r^ Will Brewster of Plymouth Elder that cloath sute of apprell wch were given me by my brother ffuller w^th^in two moneths after my death. Also my will & pleasure is, & heereby I doe entreat & desire my trusty & beloved ffriend & brother Will Bradford Gent. to be the suprvisor of this my will & Testam^t^. And my will is that my wife give unto him for his paines five shillings And my will is that my wife shall repaire unto him upon all occasions for advice. Also hereby I make Prisilla my wife full and sole executrix to this my last will & Testm^t^. And heerunto I have set my hand & seale the 16th of Septr. in the yeare of our Lord 1633.

Sealed & dd in the presence of   Will Wright
    Will Bradford
    Christopher Wadsworth.

New Plymouth   WYNSLOW GOVR.
1633

      An Inventory of the goods & Chattels of Will Wright late of Plym. deceased as it was taken by Manasseh Kempton & Joh. ffans the sixth of Novbr 1633 & presented in Court the 2^d^ of January 1633.

In the first Roome.

Inpr one chest wth one sad coloured sute & cloake, one other sute the brieches being w^th^out lining, one red bay wastcoate & one white cotten wastcoate one old black stuffe doublet, 2 hats, a black one & a white one, 1 peece of loome-work. 4   06 00 00
knots of white tape.   2 pre of boothose & 2 paprs

of hookes & eies 2 lb of colored thried, 2 doz. of lases, & 2 pr of old knit stockins wth some other smale things at 6£

It one smale Table wth a carpet, one Cupboard & a chaire wth a sifting trough   01 10 00

It six kettles 3 yron potts & a dripping panne   02 03 00

It 7 pewter platters 3 great ones & 4 little ones. 1 smale brasse morter & pestle 2 pint potts & one pewter candlestick. 1 pewter flaggon 2 pewter cups, 1 wine & one other beere bowle. 1 beaker & one Cadle cup. 1 dram cup & a little bottle 2 salt sellers 3 porrengers. $\frac{1}{2}$ doz. old spoones, 3 pr   02 00 00
of pot hookes. 1 old pr of tongues & an old fireshovell. 1 pr of pot hangers. 2 smale old yron hookes. 1 pr of andyrons. 2 old yron Candlesticks, & a pressing yron. 2 basons 1 smale one & another great one all at 2 £

It one fowling peece   02 10 00

It 2 pr of boot brieches an old pr of Cotten drawers an old blew coate. 2 pr of old yrish stockins. 2 pr of cloath stockins 1 pr of wadmore stockins.   01 10 00
1 old red wastcoate an old black Coate

[21] It one little old fflock bed & an old fether bolster, wth a pre of worne sheets, an old greene   00 15 00
Rugge

In the Buttery

Two old barrels one full of salt, the other halfe full, 1 bucking tub, 1 washing tub & 2 empty   01 00 00
runlets wth smale trifling things.

In the loft over the first roome.

One old halfe headed bedsteed. 1 old bagge of ffeathers. 1 old white Rugge 2 hogsheads & a   00 16 00
barrell

In the bedchamber

One bedsteed one warming pan. 1 fether bed & bolster. 2 pillowes, wth 2 Rugges 1 green one & one white one. 1 truncke & a little chaire table, wth a small carpet & a curtaine & valence for the bed. 1 smale cushen five pr of sheets 4 pr of pillowbeers 2 table cloathes & 15 napkins. 4 towels & 7 shirts. 3 pr of linnen drawers & 2 wrought silke caps & one white holland cap & one dymety wastcoat 3 bands & 4 pr of linnen stockins 13 08 00

It one great Bible & a little bible. 1 Greenhams works. 1 salme booke wth 17 other smale books 01 03 00

In the loft over the bedchamber

One broade axe & 2 felling axes & 2 hand sawes. 1 thwart saw wth a wrest to it. 3 augurs 2 chisels 1 gouge. 1 drawing knife. 1 prser 1 gimlet. 2 hamers. 1 pr of old hinges. 2 chest locks. 1 padlocke. 1 splitting knife 1 old spade. 2 old howes. 2 fishing lines 1 old hogshead. 1 smale runlet halfe full of powder. 1 garden rake. 1 pitch forke. 1 tiller of a whipsaw. 3 yron wedges wth some smale implem^ts & other luber of smale value 02 07 00

It the howse & garden	10 00 00
It the Cattle being one Cow & a steere calfe	20 00 00
It 2 Ewe goates & 1 ewe lamb	07 10 00
It one old Sow. 1 hogg. 1 young sow of 1 yeere old. 1 shote. 1 bore 1 Canoe & a churne	07 00 00
Debts due unto him as apprs pr booke	20 00 00
Suma	99 12 00

Prisilla Wright allowed the Executrix & Administratrix of her deceased husband.

Mr Will Bradford bound wth her in an hundred & ninty pownds for discharge of the Court.

(*To be continued.*)

PLYMOUTH BIRTHS, MARRIAGES AND DEATHS.
(Continued from page 148.)

[p. 13] The Children of m^er William Clarke and of mrs: Hannah Clarke his Wife
Sarah born the 19th of June 1678
William born the 7th of June 1682
Nathaniel born the first day of June 1684 *
Samuel born the 8th of december 1687   Deceas^d Ap. 2nd 1763
The Child of M^er William Clark and Mrs Abia Clarke his wife
Hannah Borne August 2d 1697

The Children of Eleazer Churchell & Mary his Wife †
1 Hannah Churchell born
2. Joannah Churchell born
3 Abigail Churchell born
4. Eleazer Churchell born
5. Stephen Churchell born Feb^ry 1684–5
6. Jedidah Churchell born
7. Mary Churchell born
8. Elkanah Churchell born
9. Nath^ll Churchell born
10. Josiah Churchell born
11. Jonathan Churchell born

The Children of Samuel Lucos & patience Lucos his Wife
1 John Borne on the 24th of January 168$\frac{7}{8}$ deceased January 31st 169$\frac{6}{7}$
2 Joseph Borne on the 26th ‡ october 1689
3 William Borne on the 19th of october 1692
    Patience Borne on the 2d of January 1696

The Children of John dotey senior and Sarah dotey his wife
1 Sarah Borne on the 19th of february 169$\frac{5}{6}$
2 patience born on the 3d of July 1697
3 desire born on y^e 19th of Aprill 1699

---
* The 4 was written over a 3.
† This family was entered in the same hand as that of Ebenezer and Marcy Churchell on the next page.
‡ The 6 was written over a 4.

[p. 14] The Children of William Harlow Junior and of lidiah his Wife
1 Elizabeth born in the 3^d Weke of february 1683
2 Thomas born the 17th of march 1686
3 A daughter born the 5th of february 1687
   Shee dyed the 5th of march following 168$\frac{7}{8}$

The Children of Ebenezer Churchell & Marcy his Wife
1. Ebenezer Churchell Born, June 20th. 1749
2. Branch Churchell Born, Decemb^r 17. 1751
3. Bethiah Churchell Born, Septr. 13. 1753   Decea^d. Decr. 28th 1753
4. Bethiah Churchell Born Novr. 24th 1754
5. Rebeckah Churchell Born Novr 1. 1756 Deceas^d. Augst. 12th 1760.
6. Marcy Churchell Born April 19th. 1759 Deceas^d. Sep^t. 9. 1760
7. George Churchell Born April. 18th. 1761.
8. Marcy Churchell Born Novr. y^e 10th 1763

The Children of Samuel dunham Junior & mary his Wif(*worn*)
1 Samuel borne the 19th of July 1681
2 Wiliam born the 2^d of february 1684
3 Mary born the 13th of october 1687
4 Ebenazer born the 24th of february 169$\frac{1}{2}$
5 Nathaniell born the 12th of May 1698

The Children of thomas Lazell and Mary his Wife
1 Elizabeth borne the 17th of november 1687
2 Joshua borne the 18th february 16$\frac{88}{89}$
3 Thomas borne Aprill 28th 1691
4 Mary borne on the 3^d day of march 1693
5 Hannah Born the 18th of august 1696
6 Sarah Born on the 14th of March 1699
7 John born August 9th 1701

[p. 15] The Children of Eleazar Ring and mary Ring his Wife
1 Eleazar Borne The 7th of November 1688.
   he dyed on the 3^d of december 1688.
2 Andrew born on the 14th of November 1689

3 phebe born on the 26th of January 1691
4 Samuel born on the 12th of March 1694
5 Andrew born ye 28th of March 1696
6 deborah born on the 10th of July 1698
7 Mary borne on the 9 of December 1700
8 Jonathan born on ye 23d of December 1702
9 Suzannah born on ye 9th of Aprill 1705
10 Elkanan born on ye the 19th of octobor 1706

The Children of James Warren and of Sarah Warren his Wife
1 John Borne the 27th of November 1688
   he deceased the first of March 1689
2 Edward borne on the 14th of September 1690
   he deceased on the 28th day of february 1690 or 91
3 Sarah borne the 27th of May 1692
4 Alse borne on the 3d of September 1695
5 Patience born on the 13 of January 169$\frac{8}{7}$
6 James born Aprill the 14th 1700   Deceas^d July 1757
7 Hope born august 2th 1702 died May 3. 1728
8 Marcy born on the 21 of March 170$\frac{4}{5}$
9 Mary born January 14 1707 Deceas^d Feb^{ry} 4th 1795
10 Elizabeth born on the 17 January 17$\frac{10}{11}$ died Novr 5. 1744

[p. 16] The Children of Josiah ffinney and Elizabeth his Wife
1 Josiah borne the 29 January 168$\frac{7}{8}$ he deceased September the 19th 1696
2 Elizabeth borne on the 8th of february 1690
3 Robert borne october 21th 1693
4 pricila born on ye 9th of March 169$\frac{3}{4}$
5 Josiah born on ye 9th of october 1698
6 John born on ye 13th of december 1701
7 phebee born on the 21 of ffebruary 170$\frac{4}{5}$
8 Joshua born on ye 20 of July 1708

The Children of Elaxander Cannedy and Elizabeth his wif(*worn*)
1 hannah borne the 27th of September 1678
2 Elizabeth borne the 6th of Agust 1682
3 Jean born the 19th of Aprill 1685

4 William borne the 8th of march 1689
5 Sarah borne November ye 11th 1693
6 Annable born May 8th 1698
7 John born the 23 Aprill 1703

The Children of Robert barrows and Lydiah his Wife
1 Elisha borne the 19 of march 1686
    he deceased on the 19th of January 1689 or 90
2 Robert borne on the 8th of November 1689
3 Thankfull born desember 8th 1692
4 Elisha born on the 16th of June 1695
5 Thomas born on the 14th of february 1697
6 Lidiah born on the 19th of march 1699

[p. 17] The Children of William Shirtlif and of Suzannah Shirtlef his Wife
Jabiz born the 22d of Aprill 1684
Thomas born the 16th of March 1687
William born the 4th of Aprill 1689
John born About the middle of June 1693
Barnabas born the 17th of March $169\frac{5}{6}$
Ichabod borne November the 8th 1697
Elizabeth Shurtlif born May 28 1699
Mary born december 22d 1700
Sarah born June 8th 1702

The Children of John Morton & phebe his Wife
1 Joannah born some time in february in the yeare 1682
2 phebe born on the 7th of July 1685

The Children of John Morton and Mary his Wife
1 Mary born on the 15th of desember 1689
2 hannah Born on the first of September 1694
3 John borne About the Middle of June 1693
4 Ebenazar born october 19th 1696
5 Deborah born on The 15th day of September 1698
6 persis born November 27th 1700

The Children of Leiut John Bryant & of Abigail Bryant his Wife.
1 Mary Born September ye 11th 1666

2 Hannah Born December ye 2^d 1668
3 Bethiah Born July ye 25 1670
4 Samuel Born february ye 3^d 1673
5 Jonathan Born March ye 23 1677
6 Abigaill Born^e December 30th 1682
7 Beniamin Born^e December 16th 1688

[p. 18] The Children Isaac Cushman and Rebekah Cushman his Wife
1 Rebekah born on the 30th of November 1678
2 Isaac born on the 15th of November 1676 this should have ben first set dow(*worn*)
3 Mary born on the 12th of october 1682
4 Sarah born on the 17th of aprill 1684
5 Icabod born october 30th 1686
6 fear born March the 10th 1689

The Children of John Nelson and Lidiah Nelson his Wife
1 Samuel born on the 4th of July 1683
2 Joanah born on the 9th of may 1689

The Children of John Nelson & patience Nelson his Wife
1 Liddiah borne february y^e 5th 169$\frac{3}{4}$
2 Sarah borne May the 5th 1695 Deceas^d Jan^ry 25th 1767 y^e Widd^o of Thos Spoon(*worn*)

The Children of Samuel Rider & Lidiah Rider his Wife
1 hannah borne June y^e 1 1680 Deceas^d June 29th 1763 y^e Widdow of Jere Jack(*worn*)
2 Sarah borne on the 26th March 1682. Dyed Novr 19. 1778 *w of Joshua Bramhall* *
3 William borne on the 18th of June 1684
4 Lidiah borne october 11th 1686 *w of Elisha Cobb* *
5 Samuel borne on the 26 July 1688
6 Elizabeth borne on the 26th March 1690 She deceased on the 11th of december 1695
7 Joseph born in ye Middle of July 1691
8 Benjamine born in June 1693
9 Mary born on the 10 of october 1694
10 Elizabeth born on ye 16 of March 1695

* The entries in italics are in a very modern hand.

Plymouth Births, Marriages and Deaths. 211

11 Josiah born about the Middle of May 1696
12 Abigaiel born on y^e 29 of January 1700

[p. 19] The Children of Samuel Recard and Rebekah Rickard his Wife
1 Rebekah born on the 9th of february 16$\frac{90}{91}$
2 hannah born the 25th of September 1693

The Children of Robert Harlow Junr & Jean his Wife
1 Sarah Harlow born April 6th 1751. Deceas^d April y^e 27th 1754
2 Jean Harlow born July 19. 1753
3 Robert Harlow born July 14. 1755
4 Sarah Harlow born Decr 12. 1757

The Children of Stephen Bryant & Mehittabel Bryant his Wife
1 Stephen Born on the first day of May 1684
2 daved Born on the 16th of february 1687
3 William born on the 22^d of february 169$\frac{1}{2}$
4 hannah born
5 Ichabod born on y^e 5th of July 1699
6 Timothy born on y^e 25th of August 1702

Abigaill Ransom the daughter of Robert Ransom Junior and Ann his
1 Wife was Born on the 7th day of June 1691
2 Robert born on y^e 15th of September 1695
3 Lidiah born on y^e 26 of ffebruary 1700
4 Ebenazar born on ye 6th of September 1702
5 Mary born on ye 9th of June 1705

The Children of Thomas Bumpas & Marcy his Wife
2 Joanna Bumpas born June 23rd 1752.
1 A Son not named born April 26. 1751 & Dyed the Same day
3 Samuel Bumpas born March 14. 1754. Deceased May 5th 1755
4 A Daughter Born, Named Marcy, May. 2. 1756. Deceased May 6. 1756.

[p. 20] The Children of Eliazar Cushman and Elizabeth Cushman his his Wife

1 Lidiah borne the 13th of december 1687
2 John born on the 13th of August 1690
(3 *deborah born on the* 10th *of July* 1698) *

The Children of Phineas Swift & Rebeckah his Wife
1 Jedidah Swift born June 5. 1753.
2 Abiah Swift born March 7. 1756.

The Children of John Pratt & of Margeret his Wife
1 Benijah borne on the 8th of desember 1686 deceased december 4th 90
2 Ebenazar born on the 29th of Aprill 1688
3 Joannah born on the 26th of october 1690
4 Benijah born May the 6th 1692 deceased August 12th 1692
5 Samuel born september 12th 1693
6 John born March 10th : 1696
7 A daughter born November 17th 1697 deceased december 3^d 169(*worn*)
8 Margeret born July 29th 1700
9 Patience born December ye 4: 1701
10 Thomas born September 23^d 1703
11 Mehittable born ffebruary 24 1705

The Children of Robert Bartlet and Sarah his Wife
1 hannah borne february 21th 1691
2 Thomas borne february the 9th 169¾
3 John born Aprill ye 13th 1696
4 A son borne february ye 16 1698 he deceased february 20th 169(*worn*)
5 Sarah borne Aprill 9th 1699
6 James born on the 7th of August 1701 Deceased Janury 13 1722–23
7 Joseph born ffebruary 22^d 170¾
8 Elizabeth born March 2^d 170⁶⁄₇
9 William born August 2^d 1709 Deceased March 24 1710
10 Ebenazar born Desember 5th 1710
11 Robert born Aprill 30 1713
12 Samuel born Desember 9th 1715

(*To be continued.*)

* This entry has been erased.

PLYMOUTH COLONY DEEDS.

(Continued from page 139.)

[25] 1652   BRADFORD GOVN^R

Memorand; the eleventh of January 1652
That Edmond Weston of the towne of Duxburrow in the Jurisdiction of New Plymouth in new England in america planter doth acknowlidg that for and in consideracon of the full summe of fourteen pounds and ten shillings to him alreddy paied and three pounds and fiveteen shillings to bee paied unto him hee hath freely and absolutly barganed allianated and sold (as administrator of the estate of Thomas howell Deceased) a certaine pcell of upland and meddow which was somtimes the Lands of the said howell unto Robert Waterman of Marshfeild the said Lands lying and being att the North River in the Township of Marshfeild aforsaid videlecet all the one part of foure of the lot of Land there; which was somtimes the Land of Mr Jonathan Brewster being bounded on the one side with the land of Jeremiah Borrowes and on the other side with the Lands of John Barker; To have and to hold the said pcell of upland and meddow belonging therunto soe bounded as abovesaid with all and singulare the appurtenances belonging therunto or unto any pte or pcell therof unto the onely p^rper use and behoofe of him the said Robert Waterman his heires and assignes for ever the said p^rmises with all and singulare the appurtenances privilidges and emunities appertaining therunto to belong unto the onely p^rper use and behoof of him the said Robert Waterman his heires and assignes for ever;

this sale was made to Robert Waterman anno 1649 but acknowlidged the Day and yeare above mencioned

Before such time as the abovesaid Edmond Weston; Did acknowlidge and avouch the sale of the abovesaid Lands Mr Thomas Bourne of Marshfeild did engage before Mr Willam Bradford Governor to pay unto the said Edmond Weston the abovesaid summe of three pounds and fiveteen shillin*(worn)* Remayning due to him from Robert Waterman for the said Lands

[27] 1652   BRADFORD GOVN[R]

These p[r]sents Witnesseth That George Soule of Duxburrow hath covenanted with M[r] John Winslow of Plymouth That ; Mary Soule his Daughter shall Dwell abide and continew with him the said M[r] John Winslow the full tearme of seaven yeares begining from the first day of this p[r]sent month called January and from the said Day fully and compleatly to bee ended ; And in case the said Mary Soule Doe not change her condicon by marriage shee is to Dwell and abide with him the full tearme of eight yeares begining from the first of this p[r]sent month as aforsaid and from thence fully to bee ended   acknowlidged before
    Captaine Thomas Willet
asistant and by him appointe(*worn*) to bee Recorded

Memorand the 15[th] January That
Nathaniell Morton Doth acknowlidge that for and in conside(*worn*)tio(*worn*) of the summe of three pounds and ten shillings to him alreddy paied by Experience Michell of Duxburrow hee hath freely and absolutly barganed allianated and sold unto the said Experience michell a pcell of mersh meddow Lying on Duxburrow side att the end of the Land of the said Experience commonly called and knowne by the name of the long point   To have and to hold the said pcell of Mersh meddow at the mouth of blewfish River called the long point at Duxburrow to him the said Experience Michell his heires and assignes for ever unto the onely pper use and behoofe of the said Experience Michell his heires and assignes forever
    acknowlidged before
    M[r] John Alden asistante.

[29] 1652   BRADFORD GOVN[R]
    A Deed appointed to bee Recorded

Bee it knowne by these p[r]sents that Thomas Shreeve of Plymouth of New England ; for and in consideracon of the summe of six pound to bee paied by John Reyner of Plymouth in New England in good countrey pay wherof three pounds to bee payed the 29[th] of the seaventh called September knowne by the name of Michaelm : Day 1652 the other three pounds to bee paied the same Day twelve month 1653 hath freely and absolutely brganed & sold and by these p^rsents doe bargan & sell unto the said John Reyner his house and garden place somtimes bought by him of Josias Cooke of Eastham and lying between the mill and prison brooke over against John Wood(*worn*) house and garden; excepting that pte which hee sold to Adey Webb as alsoe 4 acres of upland lying to the new feild next to Andrew Rings Lott, bee it more or lesse which the said Thomas Shreeve bought of henery Atkins of Plymouth; and all and singulare the appurtenances therunto belonging and all his Right title and enterest of and to the same and every pte and pcell therof with all the fencing To have and to hold the said house and garden place and upland with all and every the appurtenances unto the said John Reyner his heires and assignes forever and to the onely proper use and behoofe of him the said John Reyner his heires and assignes forever and with warrantice from him his heires and assignes; In Witnesse wherof the said Thomas Shreeve hath heerunto sett his hand the Day and yeare above Written;

In the p^rsence of us   Thomas Shreeve
    John Bower   his T marke
    Josepth Bradford

likewise Martha Shreeve the wife of the abovesaid Thomas Shreeve hath given her free and full consent unto the sale her husband hath made of the house garden plott upland and theire appurtenances unto Mr John Reyner of Plymouth and unto his heires and assignes forever according to the tearmes and condicions above expressed;

[32]   March the tenth 1652
Wheras Mr Edmond ffreeman of Sandwidge in New England Received order by Letters of atorney to Receive of Mr Bradford Mr Winslow Mr Prence and the rest of the pteners att Plymouth all such moneys as were due from them to him and alsoe from M^r hatherley as mencioned in the court booke folio 214 and wheras Mr Edmond ffreeman and Mr Willam Paddy being Joyned with him; were to make Returne

to England all the estate of Mr Beachampe; and haveing made Returne of the estate all that wee can; wee have Joyntly requested of Mr Bradford Govn^r to have the estate Recorded in the court booke and is as followeth

    The 10th of the first month 1652
Willam Paddy of Plymouth being by letter from Mr Beachamp Joyned in comission with M^r ffreeman; both of them have sold and Desposed of the estate as followeth

	£	s	d
Mr Beachamps account of his Land and houses sold as followeth			
To Mr Bradfords Land att Secunke	12	00	00
To Mr Winslows house at Plymouth sold to Willam Paddy of Plymouth	26	10	00
To Mr Prences house at Plymouth and five acres of land at second brooke sold to Mr Willett	32	00	00
Sold to Mr Willett Mr Allertons house att Plymouth att the Rate of	07	00	00
Mr Prences ffarme att Joaneses River sold to Mr Willett and Willam Paddy for Thomas Coachman	75	00	00
To Ephraim hickes att Plymouth the eleven acres of Land by John Barnes	12	00	00
Mr Alden and captaine Standish land att south river the one halfe sold to Arther howland att	21	00	00
The other halfe sold to Thomas Chillingsworth at	25	00	00
	210	10	00
To a Debt att Sandwidge Received by M^r ffreeman	16	19	00
To the Debt of Thomas Dexter Received by M^r ffreeman	20	00	00
To the Debt of M^r hatherley Received in pte by my father	05	00	00
To the Debt of Willam Paddy	04	00	00
To M^r hatherley	11	04	09
To Receive of the Govr and companie	30	00	00
To Rent Received of Mr Prences farme by Willam Paddy	04	00	00

Plymouth Colony Deeds. 217

[33] To Money Mr Edmond ffreeman of what
hee Received of M^r hatherley two oxen £32
and wheat £4 but the oxen sold at £15–10   19 10 00
More to money Received for Land sold to M^r
hatherley   30 00 00
M^r ffreeman   01 18 00
                                             ─────────
                               Summe   353 01 09

Mr Beachampe Debetor
To moneyes Received of Mr Cuddington as by
his letters mencions the 20^{zh} of July 1649
and the 21 of March 1649 which was by
order of Mr Edmond ffreeman and Willam
Paddy the one summe is £196–10s   196 10 00
More as by the same letters   24 00 00
To charges expended by Mr Edmond for viewing
the Lands and houses and expences of sales
and hier of men driveing of cattle and seal-
ling Releases   20 00 00
To monies paied by mis Woodman as by a letter
from Mr Beachampe Dated ——   50 00 00
To a hoggshead of suger the eight month 1651
upon M^r ffreemans account   14 10 00
To allowance to John ffreeman to make his pay-
ment Starling Money   22 10 00
To allowance to John Ellis to make his payment
Starling Money   09 00 00
                                             ─────────
                               summe   336 10 00

To lose of two bulls bought of Chillingsworth 01 00 00
To allowance to a pcell of cattle to John ffreeman 01 00 00
More which is in the hands of Samuell hickes
not yet Received   07 16 00
                                             ─────────
                          summe Totalis   346 06 00

Wheras Mr Strange hath attornied mee Edmond ffreeman
sen(*worn*) for the selling of certaine goods coming to forty
pounds in New England as alsoe for the disposing of a house
which hee had att Concord in New England; Now these may

certify for the Discharge of such goods as hee hath Intrusted mee as aforsaid I have Returned him 38 pound of Beaver the which was Delivered to Mr Strange as appeereth by Mr Doghed his letter Dated the 23^d of the 3^d month; Alsoe paied ten pound to Mr Ward a Minnester and ten pounds to M^r hurst; And for the house at Concord It is not Disposed of by mee; I sent my sonne Paddy to look on It and being not finnished Wee could Doe nothing in It, And since I heare Mr Strange hath given It away;

[34]   A letter from Mr Beachampe to Mr Paddy
London the 20th July 1649
Cozen Willam Paddy
Loveing Cozen youer health Desired with youer wife & all youers with the Rest of our frinds; Cozen my sonn Dogged sent som cloth and bibles to you and Desires you to put to sale and to make Returne in corn as wheat Rye pease barly & oates att as Reasonable a Rate as you can gett it by the first Cozen I pray you tell youer father my brother ffreeman that I have Received the box of writtings hee sent with the letter of atorney; and other writtings to give to my brother Coddington for his Discharge which I have gave him and my brother Willam ffreeman Did make his account and hee paied as followeth; first he paied for goods sent you about five years sence as I Remember   11 10 0
about five yeares sence hee paied for a bill of exchange   12 00 0
and hee hath paied to mee in moneyes   196 10 0
More hee is to pay and Doth promise to pay September next   24 00 0
    244 00 0

This is his Reconing Now as for the other I meane mis Woodmans I can not as yett make any end with them I pray you Remember my love to youer wife and all the Rest; Wee are all in health still blessed bee god my wifes mother is in good health and lives with mee att Ryegate the shipp was goeing from gravesend and by chaunce I mett with one goeing Downe to gravesend which makes mee to write in hast att a shop wher I mett with him in London and have write in great hast I end and Rest

      Youer Loveing Cozen
        John Beachampe
    Subscribed Thuse
    To his Loveing Cozen
    Mr Willam Paddy
    Marchant; in Plymouth
      These
     (*To be continued.*)

MIDDLEBOROUGH, MASS., BIRTHS, MARRIAGES AND DEATHS.

Literally transcribed from the Original Records,

BY GEORGE ERNEST BOWMAN.

The oldest records of Middleborough are in a pigskin covered volume which is not numbered, but is labelled "Early Records." Some of the leaves of this book are in a very bad condition, and it should be preserved by the Emery process.

The book contains the earliest Proprietors' Records, many records of Town Meetings, etc., and a few pages of vital records.

On the inside of the front cover is written "John Soule bult his hous In yere 1700," "William Thomas Son was born in the yeare 1700."

[Early Records, Part I, page 1]

MARRIGES

Joseph Vaughan: maried the Seventh of May 1680

John Haskall was married to Patience Sole some time in January 1666

David Wood was married to Mary Combs widdow y^e 5 of March 168$\frac{4}{5}$

Jerimiah Thomas was married To Lyddia Howland y^e 25 february 1684

John holms was married To Sarah Tommas the 13 febuar (*worn*)

Ebenezer Edy was maried to Sarah Harding the 17 : June one thousand seaven hundred and one in providence by m^r william Hopkins assistant

march 2 : 1699 John Hascall Juni^r was maried to Mary Squire of Cambridg the second marc(*worn*) one thousand six hundred ninty and nine

Dacember 8th : 1701 John Sole was maried to martha Tincom on the eighth day december one thousand seaven hundred and one by Justice Brett

february 12 : 1701 : 2 : John miller was maried to Lidia Combs by Justice Brett febru(*worn*) 12 : 17(*worn*)

Abiel Wood was married to Abijah Bowin in the month of December in t(*worn*) year of our lord : 1683 : By major william Bradford

Nehemiah Bennet the Son of John Bennet Was born the 10th of nov(*worn*)

William Bennet the Son of John Bennet Was born the 21st of April (*worn*)

Lydia Bennet the Daughter of John Bennet was born the 15th of Ap(*worn*)

Ebenezer Bennet the Son of John Bennet was born the 20th of Februa(*worn*)

Elizabeth Bennet the Daughter of Peter Bennet was born the 28th of mar(*worn*)

Isaac Bennet the Son of Peter Bennet was born the 7th of January 17 (*worn*)

Joseph Bennet the Son of Peter Bennet was born the : 16 : day of novembe(*worn*) : 1704

John Bennet the Son of John Bennet was born the day of September 1702

Deborah Bennet the daughter of John Bennet was Born the 25 day of January 170$\frac{4}{5}$

[p. 2]   BIRTHS OF CHILDREN

Seth howland was Born the 28 of November 1677
Isack howland was Born the : 6 : of march 1678 : 79 :
mehetable nelson was Born the fift o Aperil 1670

Lidea Combs was Borne the 8 of may 1679
John Tinkcom the sonn of Epharim Tinkcum was Born the twenty s^d of agust in the yeare 1680
Debarak* Combs was Borne at middlebery in the yeare 73 About the middle of my
Marsy Combs borne at middlebery in the yeare 1674 the thir Jenewary
Epharim Wood the son of Samuell Wood was borne sometime in January in ye yeer 1679.
Rebecca Wood was borne ye 9th of Aprill 1682.
Precilla Howland ye daughter of Isack Howland was borne the 22th Agust 1681.
Jonathan Thomas the Son of David Thomas was born november the 18 1678
Ebenezer Tinkcum was borne march 23 . 1679
Jerimiah Tinkcum was borne August 7 1681
Epharim Tinckum ye son of Eph : Tinckum was borne ye 7 octob : 1682
Peter Tinckum ye son of Ebenezer Tinckum was borne the twentieth of Aprill in ye year 1683.
Elisha Vaughan ye son of Joseph Vaughan was borne 7 february 1680
Jabez Vaughan was borne ye 30 Aprill in ye yeer 1682.
Frances Combes ye daughter of m^r francis Combes was borne ye sixth day of January in ye yeer 1682.
Samuel Nelson ye son of John Nelson was born ye 4 July 1683.
Edward Thomas ye son of David Thomas senio^r was borne ye sixth day of ffebruary in ye year 1669.
Elyzabeth Howland ye daughter of Isaack Howland was borne the second day of December in ye yeer 1682.
Mary Tomson ye daughter of John Tomson Junio^r was borne the second day of may in ye yeer 1681
1682. John Tomson ye son of John Tomson Juni^r was borne ye ninth day of August in ye yeere 1682.
Epharim Tomson ye son of John Tomson Juni^r was borne ye sixteenth of October in ye yeere 1683.

* Deborah.

John Haskall ye son of John Haskall was borne ye eleaventh of June 1670 :

Elizabeth Haskall ye daughter of John Haskall was borne ye 2nd July 1672.

William Haskall ye son of John Haskall was borne ye 11th of June 1674 :

Patience Haskall ye daughter of John Haskall was borne ye 1 day february 1679 :

Bethyah Haskall ye daughter of John Haskall was borne ye 15th January 1681.

Mary Haskall ye daughter of John Haskall was borne ye 4 July 1684

Samuell Wood ye son of Samuel Wood was borne ye 19 september 1684

1683. Hanah Allyn ye daughter of John Allyn was borne ye 27 decemb^r 1683

1684. Thomas Allyn ye son of John Allyn was borne ye 6 of february 1684

1685. Isaac Tinckum ye son of Epharim Tinckum was borne ye last June 1685

1686 Josiah Haskall ye son of John Haskall was borne ye 18th June 1686

Ebenezer howard the son of John howard was borne the 12 (*worn*)

[p. 3] DEATH AND BURIALS

Mercy Allyn the child of John Allyn aged 14 monthes departed this life ye 6 Aprill 1683.

m^r ffrancis Combs departed this life the last day of december 1682.

Elizabeth Howland ye daughter of Isaac Howland departed this life Aprill ye first. 1685.

Samuell Cutbird aged about 42 yeares departed this Life Aprill the seav(*worn*)teenth one Thousand six hundred ninetty and nine (1699)

Mr Samuel Fuller Pastour of the church in Middleborough deceased some time in the month of August in the year one thousand six hundred ninety and five

Francis Billington aged 80 years : Deceased on the third

day of December in the year one thousand six hundred eighty and four

Isaac Billington deceased December the eleventh one thousand seven hundred and nine in the sixty sixth year of his age

[p. 8]   BIRTHES OF CHILDREN:

1687 : Nathan Howland ye son of Isaack Howland was borne ye 17th January 1687 :

      Mathew Allyn ye son of John Allyn was borne ye 8th of October. 1687:

1687 Ane wood the dauter of Samuell Wood was born the 20 of January 1687

1686 Susanna reed the dautter of James reed was born the 10 of march 1686

1688 william reed the Son of James reed was born the 10 of march 1688

      Jabez Wood the Son of Samuel Wood : was borne (*) the twenty ninth 1690

1688 Jeall howLand the dautter of Isaak howLand was born the 13 of october 1688

1689 Jabez Allyn was born the 2 of february 1689

1687 Samuel Tinkom the son of Epharim Tinkom was born the nineteen of march 1687

      Gorg vaughan the son of Josepth vaughan was borne october the third 1683

      Ebenezer vaughan the son of Josepth vaughan was borne February the twenty Seacond 1684

1686 ELezabeth vaughan the dauthter of Josepth vaughan was borne the Seaventh of march 1686

1688 hannah vaughan the dauthter Josepth vaughan was borne november the eighteen 1688

1690 Josepth vaughan the son of Josepth vaughan was borne October the Seacond 1690

1690 Susannah Howland the daughter of Isaac Howland was born october ye fourteenth 1690

1693 Johannah Tomas the daughter of William Tomas was born may the tenth 1693.

* The month was omitted.

1681 Ruth Combs the daughter of francis Combs was born the march the 12th 1681

John wood the son of david wood was born the 19th march 1686

david wood the son of david wood was born the 29 of march 1688

Jabez wood the son of david wood was born the 1 July 1691

Hannah Howland the Daughter of Isaac Howland was born : october the : 6 : 1694

1699 Mary Renolds the daughter of Electious Renolds was born this twelveth day of September 1699

Benjamine Renolds the son of Electious Renolds born august y^e 4th : 1693

Sarah Hascall the daughter of John Hascall junior born the 22 day of march 1700 :

Elinor Bennet the Daughter of John Bennet was Borne the 18th day of december 1689 :

Mary Hascall the daughter of John Hascall Junr was born the 11th day of January $170\frac{1}{2}$

[p. 9]

Josiah meeds the adopted sonne of Daniell Vaughan given to s^d Danie(*worn*)Vaughan and his wife by his mother hester meeds given before John Be(*worn*) and his wife Deborah witnesses to this (*worn*) said Josiah meeds born the 24th July 169(*worn*)

witnesses   The mark 7 of hester me(*worn*)
the mark 0 of deborah
Bennet
John Bennet

(*To be continued.*)

HANNAH (BREWSTER) STARR.

Communicated by MRS. LUCY HALL GREENLAW, of Cambridge, Mass.

Two conflicting statements have long been in print concerning the marriage of Hannah, daughter of Jonathan and Lucretia (Oldham) Brewster and granddaughter of Elder

William Brewster. One of these statements first appeared in Miss Caulkins' "History of New London, Conn." It makes her the wife of Samuel Starr. The other gives her as the wife of John Thompson of Setauket, L. I. (afterwards called Brookhaven), and was made by Benjamin F. Thompson, Esq., in his "History of Long Island."

The Thompson claim, which rests solely upon the unsupported assertion of Benjamin F. Thompson, Esq., and which was repeated without additional evidence in the New York Genealogical and Biographical Record for January, 1896, in an article that includes Thompson's account of his family in almost his own words, is here quoted from the second edition of his "History of Long Island": —

"John Thompson, son of William, came to Long Island in 1656, and settled at Setauket, being one of the fifty-five original proprietors of the town of Brookhaven. He became, by repeated allotments of land, and by purchase, owner of considerable real estate, which he divided among his children. His wife was Hannah, daughter of Jonathan Brewster, a son of elder William Brewster of Plymouth, one of the pilgrims of the May Flower in 1620, and sister of the Rev. Nathaniel Brewster, afterwards minister of Setauket. She was accompanied to Sctauket by three nephews, sons of her brother last named, John, Timothy and Daniel Brewster." — *Volume II. pages 426, 427.*

"His [Jonathan Brewster's] daughter Hannah, married John Thompson in 1656, and died at Setauket, Oct. 4, 1687."— *Volume I. page 422.*

Thompson's statement that the wife of John Thompson (his great-great-grandfather) was Hannah, the sister of Rev. Nathaniel Brewster, is probably based on family tradition and may be correct. In this connection it is well to bear in mind the fact that his *great-grandfather* married Hannah, the *daughter* of Rev. Nathaniel Brewster. As to his statements about Elder Brewster's family, a glance at the inaccuracies they contain shows their worthlessness. On page 422 of volume one he gives *1560* as the year of Elder Brewster's birth, April *16, 1664,* as the date and *Duxbury* as the place of his death, and includes in the list of his children the names of his *daughter-in-law* Lucretia, and *grand-children* William and Mary. On page 421 of the same volume he reveals his own uncertainty as to the parentage of his ancestress when he says that Rev. Nathaniel Brewster is *supposed* to be son of Jonathan and grandson of Elder William Brewster of Plymouth.

Miss Caulkins wrote as follows: —

"Samuel Starr, died, probably, in 1688. Mr. Starr is not mentioned upon the records of New London, at an earlier date than his marriage with Hannah, daughter of Jonathan Brewster, Dec. 23d, 1664. His wife was aged thirty-seven in 1680. . . . No will, inventory, or record of the settlement of his estate has been found, but a deed was executed Feb. 2d, 1687-8, by Hannah, widow of Samuel Starr, and it is probable that her husband had, then recently deceased." — *History of New London, 1852, pp. 318, 319.*

The proof of Miss Caulkins' assertion that Samuel Starr married Hannah, daughter of Jonathan Brewster, I found, while gathering data for the "Early Generations of the Brewster Family," in the following entry on page thirty-nine of the first volume of New London town records: —

"Samuell Starr married Hannah ye daughter of Jon^{on} Brewster 23^d of December 1664."

This entry was made by Obadiah Bruen who was town "recorder" at that time. Some years later Hannah Brewster's brother-in-law, Daniel Wetherell, was elected recorder, which office he held for many years. If this entry in the town records had been wrong he would have noticed it. We are not dependent on this record alone for proof that Jonathan Brewster's daughter Hannah did not marry John Thompson. On page seven of the fifth volume of New London deeds is recorded a conveyance from John Picket and Benjamin Brewster to their "sisters" Grace Wetherell and Hannah *Brewster*, dated 14 February 1661-2. In this deed she is called "Brewster" by her brother and her brother-in-law six years after Thompson is said to have married her. As she was living at New London in February, 1687-8, as

Starr's widow,* and was in full communion with the First Church there at the time of Mr. Saltonstall's ordination, November 25, 1691,† it is certain that she was not even a second wife of John Thompson, who died October 14, 1688, and whose wife, Hannah, died at Brookhaven, October 4, 1687.

THE DIVISION OF LAND.

As the record of the division of the lands in 1623 is of interest to every Mayflower Descendant, it seems best to put it within reach of all. The text given follows that in Volume XII of the "Records of the Colony of New Plymouth," published in 1861, by the Commonwealth of Massachusetts. The paging of the *original record* is indicated in the margin.

[p. 1] The meersteads & garden plotes of (*worn*) which came first layd out 1620.

The north side		The south side
		Peeter Brown
		John Goodman
		Mr Wm Brewster
		high way
	the streete	John Billington
		Mr Isaak Allerton
		Francies Cooke
		Edward Winslow.

[p. 4] The Falles of their grounds which came first over in the May-Floure, according as thier lotes were cast .1623.

Robart Cochman	1	the number
Mr William Brewster	6	(*worn*) akers
William Bradford	3	to (*worn*) one

* New London Deeds, Vol. V., p. 111.   † New London First Church Records ,p.7.

228   *The Division of Land.*

these lye on the South side of the brooke to the baywards.	Richard Gardener	1
	Frances Cooke	2
	George Soule	1
	Mr Isaak Alerton	7
	John Billington	3
	Peter Browen	1
	Samuell ffuller	2
	Joseph Rogers	2

these containe .29. akers.

These lye one the South side of the brook to the woodward opposite to the former.	John Howland	4
	Steven Hobkins	6
	Edward	1
	Edward	1
	Gilbard Winslow	1
	Samuell ffuller Juneor	3

these containe .16. akers besids Hobamaks ground which lyeth betwene Jo: Howlands & Hobkinses.

this .5. akers lyeth behind the forte to the litle ponde.	William White	5
these lye one the north side of the towne next adjoyning to their gardens which came in the Fortune.	Edward Winslow	4
	Richard Warren	(*worn*)
	John Goodman	(*worn*)
	John Crackston	(*worn*)
	John Alden	(*worn*)
	Marie Chilton	(*worn*)

[p. 5]	Captin Myles Standish	2
	Francis Eaton	4
	Henerie Samson	1
	Humillitie Cooper	1

[p. 6] The fales of their grounds which came in the Fortune according as their lots were cast 1623.   This ship came Novr 1621.

these lye to the sea, eastward.   These lye beyond the f(*worn*) brook to the wood we(*worn*) ward.

The Division of Land. 229

William Hilton	1	William Wright &	
John Winslow	1	William Pitt	2
William Coner	1	Robart Hickes	1
John Adams	1	Thomas Prence	1
William Tench &		Steven Dean	1
John Cannon	2	Moses Simonson &	
		Philipe de la Noye	2
		Edward Bompass	1
		Clemente Brigges	1
these folowing lye		James Steward	1
beyond the .2. brooke.		William Palmer	2
		Jonathan Brewster	1
Hugh Statie	1	Benet Morgan	1
William Beale &		Thomas Flavell	
Thomas Cushman	2	& his son,	2
Austen Nicolas	1	Thomas Morton	1
Widow Foord	4	William Bassite	2
15. akers.		19. akers.	

[p. 10] The fales of their grounds which came over in the shipe called the Anne according as their were cast .1623.

	Akers	these to the sea eastward.	ak(*worn*)
James Rande	1	Francis Spragge	3

these following lye beyond the brooke to Strawberie-hill.

Edmond Flood	1	Edward Burcher	2
Christopher Connant	1	John Jenings	5
Francis Cooke	4	goodwife Flavell	1
		Manasseh & John Fance	2
these but against the swampe & reed-ponde		this goeth in wth a corner by ye ponde.	
George Morton &		Allice Bradford	1
Experience Michell	8	Robart Hickes his wife & children	4
Christian Penn	1		
Thomas Morton Junior	1	Brigett Fuller	1
William Hiltons wife & .2. children	3	Ellen Newton	1
		Pacience & Fear Brewster wth Robart Long	3

		William Heard	1
		Mrs Standish	1

These following lye on the other side of the towne towards the eele-river.

Marie Buckett adioyning to Joseph Rogers	1	Robart Rattlife beyonde the swampie & stonie ground	(worn)
Mr Ouldom & those joyned with him	10	These butt against Hobes Hole.	
Cudbart Cudbartsone	6	Nicolas Snow	(worn)
Anthony Anable	4	Anthony Dixe	(worn)
Thomas Tilden	3	Mr Perces .2. Ser :	(worn)
Richard Waren	5	Ralfe Walen	(worn)
Bangs	4		

[p. 11] South side		North side.	
Steph : Tracy three acres	3	Edw : Holman 1. acre	.1
Tho. Clarke one acre	1	ffrances wife to Wil Palmer	.1. acre
Robt. Bartlet one acre	1	Josuah Prat & Phineas Prat	2

THE WILL OF WILLIAM MULLINS.

WITH NOTES BY GEORGE ERNEST BOWMAN.

The will of William Mullins was communicated to the New England Historical and Genealogical Register (Vol. XLII, p. 62) by Henry F. Waters, A.M., in his "Genealogical Gleanings in England," and the text there given has been followed.

The will was made after the arrival of the Pilgrims in New England (then considered a part of Virginia), otherwise the words "Allsoe if my sonne William will come to Virginia" could not have been used, and, as it was evidently a nuncupative will, it was probably written 21 February, 1620, old style, the day of William Mullins' death. The day "2 : April 1621" must therefore refer to the day on which was made the copy carried back to England on the Mayflower. This date is of especial interest, as it establishes beyond question the fact that the Mayflower did not leave Plymouth, on the return voyage, until 2 April 1621 (old style), or later.

The probate record, made 23 July 1621, proves that the former residence of William Mullins was at Dorking, in the County of Surrey, and that he had left behind, in England, a married daughter, Sarah (Mullins) Blunden, who was appointed administratrix by the court. From the will we learn that his wife's given name was Alice, and that his eldest son, William, was left in England, also that the widow, Alice (——) Mullins, and her son Joseph were alive when the Mayflower sailed, as otherwise Governor Carver, in forwarding the copy of the will to be probated, would have annexed a statement of the death of these two legatees.

The second witness, Giles Heale, was the ship's surgeon and Christopher Jones was probably the captain of the Mayflower.

2 : April 1621.

In the name of God Amen : I comit my soule to God that gave it and my bodie to the earth from whence it came. Alsoe I give my goodes as followeth   That fforty ponndes in the hand of goodman Woodes I give my wife tenn poundes, my sonne Joseph tenn poundes, my daughter Priscilla tenn poundes, and my eldest sonne tenn poundes   Alsoe I give to my eldest sonne all my debtes, bonds, bills (onelye yt forty poundes excepted in the handes of goodman Wood) given as aforesaid wth all the stock in his owne handes. To my eldest daughter I give ten shillinges to be paied out of my sonnes stock   Furthermore that goodes I have in Virginia as followeth   To my wife Alice halfe my goodes & to Joseph and Priscilla the other halfe equallie to be devided betweene them. Alsoe I have xxj dozen of shoes, and thirteene paire of bootes wch I give into the Companies handes for forty poundes at seaven years and if thy like them at that rate. If it be thought to deare as my Overseers shall thinck good   And if they like them at that rate at the divident I shall have nyne shares whereof I give as followeth twoe to my wife, twoe to my sonne William, twoe to my sonne Joseph, twoe to my daughter Priscilla, and one to the Companie. Allsoe if my sonne William will come to Virginia I give him my share of land furdermore I give to my twoe Overseers Mr John Carver and Mr Williamson, twentye shillinges apeece to see this my will performed desiringe them that he would have an eye over my wife and children to be as fathers and freindes to them; Allsoe to have a speciall eye to my man Robert wch hathe not so approved himselfe as I would he should have done.

This is a Coppye of Mr Mullens his Will of all particulars he hathe given. In witnes whereof I have sett my hande
John Carver, Giles Heale, Christopher Joanes.

Vicesimo tertio : die mensis Julii Anno Domini Millesimo sexcentesimo vicesimo primo Emanavit Commissio Sare Blunden als Mullins filie naturali et legitime dicti defuncti ad administrand bona iura et credita eiusdem defuncti iuxta tenorem et effectum testamenti suprascripti eo quod nullum in eodem testamento nominavit executorem de bene etc Jurat.
68, Dale.
Mense Julij An^o Dni 162j.

Vicesimo tertio die emanavit comissio Sare Blunden als Mullens filie nrali et ltime Willmi Mullens nup de Dorking in Com Surr sed in partibus ultra marinis def hentis etc ad administrand bona iura et credita ejusdem def iuxta tenorem et effcum testamenti ipsius defuncti eo quod nullum in eodem nominavit exrem de bene etc iurat.
Probate Act Book, 1621 and 1622.

(Translation of the second Latin record.)

In the month of July Anno Domini 1621. On the 23^d day issued a commission to Sarah Blunden, formerly Mullins, natural and legitimate daughter of William Mullins, late of Dorking in the County of Surrey, but deceased in parts beyond the seas, seized &c., for administering the goods, rights and credits of the said deceased, according to the tenor and effect of the will of the said deceased because in that will he named no executor. In due form &c. swears.

SCITUATE, MASS., BIRTHS, MARRIAGES AND DEATHS.

(Continued from page 168.)

The record of the marriages by Rev. David Barnes is completed with this instalment. The parts in parentheses have been supplied from the records of "Intentions of Marriage."

In the next issue will begin the publication of Part II of Vol. IV, which contains the earliest marriages.

---

[9] Mariages

These may Certifie, whom it may Concern, that whereas Trustrum Daves of Sittuate hath been a Suiter to my daughter Sarah Archer and if they shall Proceed to marry I shall not hinder theire Proceeding : Brantery the 16 of march 1695

| Stephen ffrench | Thomas Holebrook |
| Joseph Polle | Mary Holebrook |

These are to Certifie those whom it may Concern that Trustrum Davis and Sarah Archer hath formerly been Legally Published at Sittuate

Sittuate 12th of march 169$\frac{4}{5}$ pr me Isaac Bucke Town Clerke of Sittuate

These may Certifie all persons whom it may Concern that Trustrum Davis of Sittuate and Sarah Archer of Brantry were maried the 19th of march 169$\frac{4}{5}$

pr me Jeremiah Cushing by vertue of this proviance law Concerning mariages

Seth Hammond & Mary Buck both of Scituate were married February 17. 176(3)

David Merritt & Sarah Curtis both of Scituate were married February 17. 176(3)

John James Ju^r & Hannah Jacob both of Scituate were married March 24. 176(3)

Benj^a Stetson & Mercy Turner both of Scituate were married June 14. 176(3)

The Revd Mr Ebenezer Gay of Suffield and Miss Mary Cushing of Scituate were married together Novr 10. 176(3)

Benj^a Bowker & Hannah Sparhawke both of Scituate were married Novr 10. 17(63)

Israel Chittenden & Abigail Turner both of Scituate were married Novr 24. 17(63)

Capt Elisha Turner & Abigail Foster both of Scituate were married Decr 29. 17(63)

Jihiel Simmons of Duxborough & Rhoda Stetson of Scituate w^r mar^d Apr^l 10 : 176(4)

Seth House of Han^o & Bathsheba Foster of Scituate were marr^d May 31 : 176(4)

John Colman Ju^r & Sarah Hammon both of Scituate were marr^d June 7 : 176(4)

Asher Sprage of Hing^m & Lusanna Buck of Scituate were marr^d July 12 : 176(4)

Willm Stetson & Mary Linclon both of Scituate were married July 19 : 17(64)

Abraham Burbank of Suffield & Bethyah Cushing of Scituate were marr^d Novr 1 : 17(64)

Anth^o Waterman of Hallefax & Sarah Curtis of Scituate were married November 15. (1764)

Willm Gardner of Hing^m & Thankfull Collamer of Scituate were married Decr 5 : (1764)

John Cushing Ju^r & Mary Jacob both of Scituate were married Decr ye 6. (1764)

James Silvester & Anna Brooks both of Scituate were married Decr y^e (1764)

Joseph White of Marshfield & Temperance Clap of Scituate were married Fe(1765)

Samuel Brooks & Elizabeth Gray both of Scituate were married March (1765)

John Foster & Sarah Jacob both of Scituate wer married May y^e (1765)

Jabez Standly & Mary Thrift both of Scituate were married June y^e (1765)

Scituate, Mass. 235

[10] Ezekel Turner & Leah Simmons both of Scituate were married June ye 6. 1765

Joseph Carrel & Tamer Farrow both of Scituate were married October 2^d 1765

Moses Dunber a Transient person & Deborah Prouty of Scituate were Mar^d Oct^o ye 28 : 1765

Benj^a Bass of Hanover & Mercy Tolman of Scituate were married October ye 28th 1765

John Pincin & Judeth Pincin both of Scituate were married January ye 9th 1766

Thomas Jinkins Ju^r & Hannah Clap both of Scituate were married February ye 11 : 1766

Lothrop Litchfield & Rhoda Perry both of Scituate were married Feby ye 11 : 1766

Noah Otis & Phebe Cushing both of Scituate were married May ye 1st 1766

John Dorithy & Mary Murphy both of Scituate were married August 11 : 1766

Elisha Turner & Prudence James both of Scituate were married Sepr ye 18 : 1766

Abiel Turner Ju^r & Lurana Silvester both of Scituate were married Novr 13 : 1766

Jabez Wilder Ju^r of Hingham & Martha Collamer of Hingham were married Novr ye 13 : 1766

Dearing Jones & Hannah Ewell both of Scituate were married Novem^r ye 20: 1766

Seth Peirce & Jemima Turner both of Scituate were married Novr ye 27 : 1766

Thomas Tilden & Abigail Hatch both of Scituate were married Decr ye 4 : 1766

Benj^{ae} Thomas of Duxbo. & Abigail Turner of Scituate wer mar^d Jany ye 6 : 1767

Joshua Linclon & Anna Bryant both of Scituate were married Jany ye 8 : 1767

Peleg Bryant Ju^r & Lydia Collamer both of Scituate were married Novr ye 19: 1767

Aaron Magoon of Pembrook & Mary Church of Scituate were married Jany ye 21 : 1768

Constant Clap & Rebecca Bailey both of Scituate were married March ye 3^d 1768

Nehemiah Randall & Rebecca Collamer both of Scituate were married April the 21st 1768

Silvenus Clap & Elizabeth Brooks both of Scituate were married June ye 9th 1768

Benjamin Clap & Sarah Ruggles both of Scituate were married June ye 23^d 1768

Gethelus Cowing & Lucy Hatch both of Scituate were married July ye 11th 1768

Nehemiah Palmer & Abigail Barriel both of Scituate were married July ye 14 : 1768

Israel Damon & Lydia Roggers both of Scituate were married August ye 8 : 1768

David Foster of Pembrook & Christian Farrow of Scituate were merried Decr ye 29 : 1768

(Lieut E)lijah Curtis & Zipporah Randall both of Scituate were merried January ye 5 : 1769

(J)ohn Rite & Molly Woodard both of Scituate were married Febru^y ye 2 : 1769

(Jos)iah Cushing Ju^r of Pembrook & Deborah Cushing of Scituate were married Feby 16 : 1769

(S)amuel Dunber of Hingham & Rhoda Corthiel of Scituate were married may 29 : 1769

(Jo)seph Brooks of Hanover & Lydia Stetson of Scituate were married July 27 : 1769

(Sh)earjashub Bourn & Sarah Woodard both of Scituate were married Octobr ye 19 : 1769

( )rill 1639, Will Parker marryed to Mary the daughter of Tho : Rawlings in Aprill 1639.

(Willia)m Gorham of Barnstable & ye Wid^o Temporance White of Scituate were married Oct^o 26 : 1769

(Benjam)an Dilino & Mary Brooks both of Scituate were married Novem^r the 2^d 1769

(Adam) Hunt of Brantree & Hannah Stetson of Scituate were married March ye 29 : 1770

(Abner) Pincin & Hannah Cowing both of Scituate were married April ye 22 : 1770

(Isaiah Win)g of Hanover & Elizabeth Rose of Scituate were married June ye 12 : 1770

(Simeon Pr)outy & Sarah Griffin both of Scituate were married July the 19 : 1770

(Gershom) Farrow of Abington & Jemime Farrow of Scituate were married Sepr ye 13 : 1770

(Israel Sil)vester Ju^r & Margreat Bowker both of Scituate were married Novem^r ye 15 : 1770

( ) Cupples Save one were married together by David Barns Minister.

[11] Joseph Benson & Susanna Clap both of Scituate were married Decr ye 5th 1770

Benjamin Simmons of Marshfield to Sarah Damon of Scituate were mar^d Decr ye 20 : 1770

Issacher Cato Negro & Dinah Compsit Indian both of Scituate were marr^d Jany ye 3^d 1771

Knight Brown & Priscilla Beals both of Scituate were married Jany ye 17 : 1771

Hezekiah Stodder Ju^r & Lydia Farrow both of Scituate were married Jany ye 31 : 1771

Charles Curtis & Lydia James both of Scituate were married February ye 7 : 1771

Amos Sprague of Hingham & Desier Stodder of Scituate were married Feby ye 21 : 1771

John Damon & Eunice Bowker both of Scituate were married April ye 11 : 1771

Isaac Collier and Tamson Hayden both of Scituate were married April ye 11 : 1771

Zephaniah Hatch & Mary Vinall both of Scituate were married May ye 7 : 1771

Solomon Linclon & Deborah Randall both of Scituate were married May ye 26 : 1771

George Cushing & Lydia Cushing both of Scituate were married June ye 19 : 1771

Samuel Damon & Anna Bowker both of Scituate were married Sepr ye 5 : 1771

David Jorden & Lydia Nickolson both of Scituate were married Sepr ye 8 : 1771

Joseph Tolman Ju^r & Bethyah Turner both of Scituate were married Novr ye 4: 1771

Thomas Totman & Sarah Carman both of Scituate were married June ye 15: 1772

Lemuel Mayho of Marshfield & Anna Mott of Scituate were married June ye 18: 1772

John Beals of Hingham & Rhoda James of Scituate were married July ye 1st 1772

Joshua Turner & Eunice James both of Scituate were married July ye 2^d 1772

James Barrell & Martha Farrow both of Scituate were married Decr the 10: 1772

Thomas Silvester Ju^r & Relief Jorden both of Scituate were married Jany ye 18: 1773

David Farrow Ju^r of Hingham & Judith Stodder of Scituate were married Jany ye 28: 1773

David Kent & Lydia Damon both of Scituate were married Feby ye 1st 1773

Garshum Bowker & Elizabeth Stetson both of Scituate were married Feby ye 18: 1773

John Humphris & Mary Palmer both of Scituate were married March ye 9th 1773

Francis Cushing & Temperance Foster both of Scituate were married April ye 8: 1773

The above have been carried to ye Clark of ye Sessions. all the above Copples were married by David Barns Minister

(To be continued.)

ELIZABETH (WINSLOW) (BROOKS) CORWIN.

By George Ernest Bowman.

In Deane's History of Scituate, Mass., it is said that Gilbert Brooks of that town married Elizabeth, the daughter of Governor Edward Winslow, and had children born in 1645, 1646, 1649, 1650, etc. But an examination of the original records shows that this statement is not correct, and that

Elizabeth Winslow married, first, Robert Brooks (by whom she had at least one son, John), and in 1669 became the second wife of Captain George Corwin, of Salem, whom she survived about thirteen years.

It is evident that Elizabeth was unmarried in 1651, as Bradford's History tells us that Governor Winslow then had but two children living, and calls them both "marigable." These two children were Josiah, who afterwards became governor of Plymouth Colony, and Elizabeth. If the latter were then married and the mother of four children, Bradford could not have called her "marigable."

In his will, dated 2 July 1675, Governor Josiah Winslow mentions his sister Elizabeth as follows : " Item I give to my loveing sister Elyzabeth Corwin my pockett watch, that was sometimes our honored fathers
Item   I doe hereby Confirme unto my Kinsman John Brook (son to my said sister) all those my lands that are on pachaeg neck in the Township of Middlebery . . . . . . one hundred pounds in good and currant pay (viz) fifty ponds to my sisters son John Brooke if then living. . . . . . . And if John Brooke dye without issue the said fifty pounds not paid, that then it be paid to my sister Elyzabeth Corwin if liveing, or otherwise to some child of hers by Captaine Georg Corwin her present husband "

In the first book of the Salem records we find the marriage, 22 September 1669, of Capt. George Corwin and " Mrs. Elizabeth Brooks, widow."

In the first book of the Charlestown records we find recorded the death, 25 December, 1687, of " M[r] John Brookes, sonne of M[rs] Curwin of Salem," and his gravestone gives his age as thirty one, fixing the date of his birth as about 1656.

Capt. George Corwin died at Salem, 3 January 1684–5, and among the original documents relating to the settlement of his estate, and on file in the Essex County Court Papers (Vol. XLIV, June to September, 1685), is one beginning : " A Liste of Severall, Things Inventoried wth the Estate of Cap[t] Geo: Corwine, w[ch] in Right belong to Elizabeth, his Relict Widdow, being Either reserved before, or Given to her, After Marriage."

After naming a dozen or more articles, the "Liste" continues :

"To a Large Tankerd, plate, y^t was my form^r Husbands m^r Robt Brookes. wth o^r Armes
To a plate sug^r box. Given me pr Govr Winslow pr a porring^r d^{to} sent Jno Brook, pr ditto
To a smale hand silv^r Candestick Given ditto Brook. pr m^r Herbert Pelham
B R E 6 of y^m & E B 6 ,, } To 12. Silver spoones : 6 of y^m Gilt & knubd
To .1. ditto Given pr ye Lr^d Mayor
ye above 12. Given pr m^r Jno Brook Uncle to R
To a large quarto bible, wth bezas Notes
To a silver watch "

This document bears the autograph signature, " Eliz : Corwin."

As Gilbert Brooks was living at the date of the marriage of " Mrs. Elizabeth Brooks, widow," and she signs her name to a document in which her former husband is said to have been Robert Brook, it is clear that Deane's statement, like so many others relating to Pilgrim genealogy, was the result of a careless confusion of similar names.

In the Suffolk County Probate Records (Vol. VIII, p. 140) we find that Edward Lyde of Boston, Merchant, was appointed 23 April, 1698, administrator "on the Estate of his Mother in Law Elizabeth Corwin late of s^d Boston Widow dece^d." It is probable that she had removed to Boston to live with her daughter Susanna (Corwin) Lyde, and died shortly before the date of the probate record.

THE DIARY OF JABEZ FITCH, JR.

(Continued from page 182.)

(*April*, 1757.)
ye 25th Captn Kent was Here I Drink^d Tea with Him & Serj^t Mack — 11 oClok I Exercisd ye Comp^y when we Had Don Several of them Fired their Guns Down Just By My Feet & Hurt My face — In ye Afternoon ye Divel Got Into our

Indians they Had Light to Kild Several of our Men we was Oblidg^d To Fix a Guard & Confine Two of them — we Here y^t Capt. Fitch Had Got into Town &c. Some of ye White Men Fought — Atwell Holds Vary Poor — Near Night Part of Capt. Slaps Company March^d By Here — Serj^t Mack

ye 26th In ye Morning we Drinkt Tea Tried our (*) &c — then Set of to Go to Town Got into Town at 10 oClok — Capt. Waterbarry & Capt. Wards Company March^d into Town &c — Our Comp^y was Dismist for an Hour I went To Esqr Buckinghams To Diner with Serj^t Comstick Corp^l Nord(*) P Pride &c — about 3 oClok we were Dismist & orderd to our Quarters while tomorow Then we went Home In ye Evening we Had a Tarable Clammer with our Solders and old Waller after that was over Two Jentlemen was in who Made Us a Considrable Sport &c — then we went to Bead Had Two Hours Laugh & Talk then We went to Sleep

ye 27th I arose Vary Early In ye Morning went to Se Attwell After Considrable Time went to Breakfast Then Serj^t Mack & I Set out for Town about 10 oClok Got to Bulls where we Se our Officers they Soon went after there Money &c — Gen^ll Lyman & Maj^r Pason Rid out of Town Then Mr Waterman & I went Up to Esqr Talents Bid Ins^n Butlar Farwell Then Came Down to Bulls where Joseph Kellog was Sick &c — Then I Came Home alone Eat Some Baket Veal — This Day Thos Andrus Came Back Brought Me a Letter from Father — In ye Eening we Had Considrable Dansing Then we Had a Toot at Drinking wine Huntley and Wintworth Had a Fight &c about 12 oClok Serj^t Thos Andrus and I went to Bead Slept Vary Sound —

ye 28th In ye Morning I went to Se Atwell — Found Him Some Better Came Back Drinkd a Dish of Tea then we went Down to Town where I Rec^d 4 Dol^rs of Capt Fitch Se Capt Whiting I Toock a Gun at Maj^r Pasons For a Negro in Genl Lymans Comp^y about 12 oCk We March^d out of Town and Up to Land Lord Bentonss — I Went to Se Atwell Then Got Some Din^r Capt Slap Came Up with our officers — Then ye Land Lord Treted Me with a Bottle of wine — about 3 oClok Toock Leave of ye Land Lord and His Famaly and

* Illegible.

went of with Lt Huntley Being In ye Rear we Had Got about Half a Mile & I Lit of a Chains To Get My Pack Carried we went Into ye Tavern Next to Farmingtown Drinkd Some Sider — Then ye offi^r went along & Left Me To Carry along Some Indins I Traveld Then with Mr Woodroff ye Man y^t Car^d my Pack — Before I Got Into Town I over Toock old Murfa & was Plagd with Him However about Sunset I Got to Land Lord Lewises In Farmingtown where I Lodgd with Jo^s Kellog after Supper —

Aprill 29th 1757 Farmington &c
In ye Morning I Got Up and Eat Some Milk For Breakfast Capt Slap Got Up While I was Eating Complaind of Being Dry Becaus He Did not Drink anought Yesterday Then we Soon Got Togather Down at ye Loer End of town Cald over ye Role & Got Ready for a March We Had a Cart Provided to Carry Part of our Packs &c when ye Company Marchd of I was Sent Back after John Robens I Lookd all over Town for Him at Last Found Him and went out of Town about 9 oClok Before I Got Up to Strongs I over Toock Capt. Slap & Lt Niccols we Got Up to Strongs and Drinkd Some Punch Capt Slap Paid His Ecknowlegment for Being Drunk ye Day Befor as He Said — Then I Went with ye Teem Up to Wiers ye next Tavern where I Bought Some Din^r &c — Then Ins^n Tracy & I Came To Land Lord Katterlands Where I am Now and Expect to Lodg this Night ye officers are all Gon Allong — we Left Solomon Chebucks about 2 Mile Back — our Cart is Gon Forward at Night I Lodgd in a Bead with Silas Waterman —

ye 30th I Got Up Early in ye Morning Wated Some Time for Breakfast at Last Got Some Bread & Milk Then I Found a Nother Mans Pack and Set out after ye Land Lord Had Treted Us With a Glas of Mothegalen — we Stopd at ye Widd^o Phelpss Then Set of & went To ye Tavern where ye Fool Lives Then I Traveld with Hopkins & Talkd about old Affairs In to Lichfield to Mgr Marshes — Then I Se Esqr Shelden overtoock our officers Eat Some Pork & Pees after a While our Teem was changed & I Set of with it we Cald in at Every Tavern I was of ye Mind to Stay at Woddams However we went To Nashes ye Next Tavern where

Waterman & I Lodgd In a Vary Good Bead in a Dark Room on our own Cost

Now Col. Lyman & Maj^r Pason are ordered to Claverick with 9 Companies of ye Reg^t & Col. Whiting with ye Other 5 to N° 4 &c —

Sunday May 1st was a Vary Sower Cold Morning — after we Had Eat Som Milk we Set out Soon Traveld Down into ye Desolate woods after a while Came by a Pond then to a Tavern Drinkd a Dram and Set of again in ye Rain after So Long a time Came to ye widd^w Seggecks where our Teem Left us Then I Set out with a Small Party Forward & Traveld To Capt. Collis in Canaan Drinkd a Dram Then went To Mr Fanals Thinking it To Have been ye Tavern there we Got Some Directions and Found ye Tavern — There I Se Doc^r Lee He Told me y^t Mr Stanton Had Movd away Into Sheffield — after Some time our Comp^y came Up I Got Some Victals and Set out & went to Major Whitnies there Lit of Capt. Fitch & Lt Huntly Eat Some Supper & went to Bead Lodgd Alone Slept Vary Comfortable —

ye 2nd In ye Morning we Rec^d our Arms Eat Some Breakfast and our Men went off Then Capt. Fitch & I staid & Drinkd a Dish of Tea and Had Some Discorce with ye Maj^{rs} Family and we Came away I went in at Mr Fanels & Got My Pack y^t I Left there ye Last Night — This Day My Back Felt Like Some old Hors y^t Had Ben Gauld with a Saddle &c — Now we Came to Robenss & Had a Waggon Provided to Help Us along Then Pride & I Drinkd a Mug of Flip & went of Soon Crosd ye River and went into Salsberry I went with ye waggon up to Reeds in Salsberry where I went to Din^r with ye Officers Eat Some fried Meet & Eggs Then Set out and went Down to ye Read Hous where Capt. Slap Se Somany Garls —

Then we went according to our Directions by ye Red Hous then By the Barn then about 10 Rods and over a Small Bridg then By a Little Hous & by a Stake & out of Connecticutt into ye Oblong Then we went about 2 Mile To Smiths a Tavern & Set Them to Fidl^n & Dansing In ye Evening I went Down to Edwardss and Lodgd in His Barn with Pride it was a Cold Night ye First of my Lodging in y^t

Form We Talkd about ye Choras that our Mates were then upon at Home Being Training Day Night &c —

ye 3rd we Set of in ye Morning Went By Several Houses where the Small Pox Had Lately Ben we Traveld about 5 Mile Came to a Small Tavern There Got Some Refreshment & I Traveld with Capt. Slap 5 Mile Further we Discorsd about old Times & Espacily about Pocatanok Then we Came to Anchrum where Levingstons Furnis is Toock a View of y^t and Got Some Fried Bacon & Eggs of an old Dutch woman Then we Set out to Go 8 Miles Furder Sun 2 Hours High arivd I Got Some Cake & Sider which Seemed Vary Good There I Se a Daughter of Capt. Coulvers &c — Then we Toock our Lodging In Churchs Barn about These Day I Thought of ye Anuel of y^s Time &c —

May 4th In ye Morning I Got Some Milk then we Set of Tho we Mad Several Stops, In Special where Hopkins Mad us So much Sport Playing with a Dutch Garl at Hendrick Musicks about 11 oClok arriv^d at Claverick Tavern there Rec^d Directions For our Quarters about 2 Miles furder — We Soon Got there & Divided our Comp^y Got Some Din^r and went to ye Stors and Get Some Part of our Allowance Came Back — Lt Billings Lt Waterman & Ins^n Minor Came Down to Se Us at Night I Eat Some Suppoon & Sweet Millok & went to Beed in ye Barn — Something Not well

ye 5th I Eat Bread & Butter & Drinkd Tea at Mr Vandwozers in ye morning Then Pride & I Got Some Sope & Washed Some of our Cloths I wrote considrable in My Jurnal — In ye after Noon I Hered of Lt Billings Going Home I wrote to Father & Brother Pelatiah also wrote For Andrus & Pride — I Got a Young woman to worsh My Hankerchif &c —

ye 6th In ye Morning I Felt Vary well ye Land Lady asked me to Drink a Dish of Tea with Her — Then I went & Se ye Dutch Plowing with 3 Horses a Brest — Capt Fitch & Lt Durky went to Se ye Gen^ll we went To Exercising Directed By ye Ins^n Then Eat Some Din^r This Day I Eat Some Bisket that I Brought From Home — In ye afternoon we Exercised again Capt Gallups Men Some of em Came To Se Us we Plaid Ball Serj^t Mack Hurt His Ancle — I Helped M^r

Vondwozer Plant Corn then I Bought Some apples and Eat em

ye 7th Pride and I Eat a Breakfast of Fresh Fish Then we Exercised a Spell Then I Dind with ye L^t & Ins^n Afternoon Pride Undertuck to Bake a Batch of Bread — Doc^r Lord Came Here — This Day We Began Roll Caling According to ye Gen^{lls} orders In y^e Evening I Eat a Supper of Fresh Fish with Lieu^t Durky & Ins^n Tracy

Claverick May 7th 1757

(*To be continued.*)

EARLY RECORDS OF PLYMPTON, MASS.

(*Continued from page 178.*)

[p. 115] The Children of Ignatious Loring by Sarah his wife.
Caleb Loring was born March y^e 9th 172$\frac{4}{5}$ &
Died March y^e 26th 1725.
Mary Loring was born feb^r y^e first 172$\frac{5}{6}$

James fuller's Child by Judeth his wife
Eleanah fuller was born feb^r y^e 9th 172$\frac{5}{6}$

The Children of william Samson by Joanna his wife
Zeruiah Samson was born march 18th 172$\frac{5}{6}$
william Samson was born Nov^{er} 25th 1727.

the Children of John Brigs by Sarah his wife
Hannah Brigs was born Feb^r y^e 27th 17$\frac{15}{16}$
John Brigs was born June y^e 15th 1718
Barnabas Brigs was born august y^e 15 1720
(*Ebenezer Briggs was the youngest child of this family.*)

The Children of Nathan weston by desier his wife
Nathan weston was born July the 11th 1723
Isaac weston was born June y^e 14th 1725.
(*Mrs. Rebekah Weston wife of Mr. Edmund Weston died November* 18, 1732 *in the* 76th *year of her age. She was a member of the Church in Plympton and the daughter of Mr. John Soule of Duxbury by Rebekah his first wife*)

The Children of Israel may by Elisabeth his wife.
Moses maye was born octo^r y^e 2^d 1708.
Edward maye was born march 22^d 17$\frac{11}{12}$
Elisabeth may was born feb^r the 28th 17$\frac{14}{15}$
Marcy maye was born y^e 12th daye of Sep^t 1717.
Sarah maye was born octo^r y^e 2^d 1720.

[p. 116] Thankful dwelley the daughter of Richard dwelly and margeret his wife was born January 5th 172$\frac{6}{7}$

Jacob Weston a son of nathan weston by desire his wife was born may 14th 1727.

Desier Weston was born aprill 4–1730

Deborah Fuller the daughter of Jabez Fuller by patience his wife was born novem^{or} 23^d 1727.

(*Priscilla his wife.*)*

David Churchill the son of David Churchill by Mary his wife was born august 9th. 1729.

Alice Bosworth the daughter of Jonathan Bosworth and Ruth his wife was born Sept^{or} 30th 1727.

Jonathan Bosworth was born April 8th 1730.

Sarah bent daughter of Joseph Bent by his wife that now is, born Jannuary 27th 1730.

[p. 117] James Briant was maried to Dorkas whipple maye ye 12th 1725.

James ffuller was maried to Judeth Rickard maye ye nineteenth 1725.

moses Shaw was maried to Mary Darling November the 4th 1725 by Mr. Isaac Cushman.

Jonathan Bosworth was maried to Ruth Tilson Septr the 30th 1725 by m^r Isaac Cushman.

Thomas Darling was maried to Rebeckah Weston Novem^r the 18th 1725.

Isaac Waterman was maried to Elizabeth Briant Dec. y^e 23– 1725 by m^r Isaac Cushman.

Nehemiah Bosworth was maried to Susanah Ring Janeway y^e 27th 1725.

John Robbins was maried to Elisabeth Tomas March y^e 16th 172$\frac{5}{6}$ mr Isaac Cushman minister in Plimpton

* See marriage of Jabez Fuller on next page.

Early Records of Plympton, Mass. 247

Barnabas wood of Middleborough was maried to Hanah Robbins March y^e 30th 1726

Benjamen Eaton was maried to Mary Sturtivant July y^e 7th 1726 by Mr. Isaac Cushman.

Ebenezer Raiment was maried to Marcy Fuller July ye 28th 1726 by Mr. Isaac Cushman.

Allerton Cushman was maried to Elizabeth Sampson Sept. the 15th 1726 by Mr. Isaac Cushman.

James Barrows was maried to Tabitha Rickard november the 3^d 1726.

Jabez Newland was maried to Rebeckah Cushman Decem^{br} the 8th by Mr. Isaac Cushman.

Elcanah Shaw was maried to Mehetable Churchel Janewary y^e 11th 172$\frac{6}{7}$ by Mr. Isaac Cushman minister

Jabez fuller was maried to Priscilla Sampson Janewary y^e 12th 172$\frac{6}{7}$ by Mr. Isaac Cushman minister.

Seth fuller was maried to Debrah Cole widow and relect to Samuel Cole march y^e 8–172$\frac{6}{7}$ by Mr. Isaac Cushman

[p. 118] John Shurtlef was maried to the widow Sarah Carver relect of John Carver Junr march y^e 23^d–172$\frac{6}{7}$ by Mr. Isaac Cushman

Thomas Coal was married to Mary Ripley March the 23–172$\frac{6}{7}$ by Mr. Isaac Cushman minister

John Lovewell and Lidia Churchell was married november 8th 1727 by Mr. Isaac Cushman

Joseph Chard and Rebecca bears was married nov^{er} 30th 1727 by Mr. Isaac Cushman

Isaac Bonney and Mary Horrel was married february 22^d 172$\frac{7}{8}$ by Mr. Isaac Cushman

William Morss and Hannah Waterman was maryed may 22^d 1728 by Mr. Isaac Cushman

Thomas Waterman and mercy freeman were married June 12th 1728 by Mr. Isaac Cushman

Jabez Newland and Sarah Standish were marryed Septem^{br} 23^d 1728 by Mr. Isaac Cushman

Nath^{ll} Fisher and bula Edy were maryed Sepember 26th 1728.

Elisha Whitton and Joanna dunham were marryed october 10th 1728 by Mr. Isaac Cushman

(*She was the widow of Israel Dunham*)

Joseph bent and Jemima Billington were marryed october 17th 1728 by Mr. Isaac Cushman.

Barnabas Sampson and Experience adkins were marryed November 6th 1728 by Mr. Isaac Cushman

Ephraim Sampson & Abigail Horrel were marryed Novemer 15th 1728 by Mr. Isaac Cushman

Samuel Benson and Keziah Barrows were marryed Nover 21th 1728 by Mr. Isaac Cushman

Benjamin prat & Margeret Rickard ware marryed February 27th $172\frac{8}{9}$ by Mr. Isaac Cushman.

(*To be continued.*)

REPORTS FROM STATE SOCIETIES.

MASSACHUSETTS SOCIETY.

On Saturday, June 17, 1899, the Society met at Squantum, where Captain Myles Standish and his companions landed when the Pilgrims first visited what is now Boston Harbor. After a shore dinner at Squantum Inn and a brief business meeting, about seventy-five members and guests visited the Monument, the Spring, and Squaw Rock.

A meeting of the Society was held at the Hotel Vendome, Boston, on Thursday evening, September 28, 1899, the two hundred and seventy-eighth anniversary of the setting out of the first expedition to Massachusetts Bay, under command of Captain Standish.

The Secretary reported the death, on August 27, 1899, of Mrs. Mary Russell (Winslow) Bradford, aged 106 years, 2 months, and 18 days. Mrs. Bradford was sixth in descent from James Chilton and fifth in descent from Mary Chilton. She was elected to membership on June 9, 1898, at a meeting of the Board of Assistants held on her one hundred and fifth birthday.

Rev. George Hodges, D.D., read a very interesting paper giving an account of his ancestor, Captain Myles Standish, and the expedition to Massachusetts Bay.

After the exercises refreshments were served.

DONATIONS TO THE LIBRARY AND CABINET.

Photograph of the Barker Garrison House, framed in oak from the house, from Mrs. William Lawrie.

Reports from State Societies. 249

"Church and Cemetery Records of Hanover, Mass.," from Arthur I. Nash.

Photograph of Deed made by Daniel and Mercy (Fuller) Cole in 1700, from Mrs. Godfrey Ryder.

"The Barker Family," from Edward T. Barker.

"Foundations of Genealogy," from the author, William S. Mills.

Year Book of Massachusetts Society S. A. R., 1899, from the Society.

"The Portsmouth Book," from Mrs. John W. Parsons.

"Register of the Lynn Historical Society, 1898-99," from Nathan M. Hawkes.

Two photographs of the Monument and of Squaw Rock, at Squantum, from Mrs. Levi Tower, Jr.

Photograph of family entries made by Colonel Seth Washburn in his "Justice of the Peace Book," from Mrs. George B. Parkinson.

MEMBERS ELECTED.

June 17, 1899.
505. Charles Andrew Clark, Newton Centre, eighth from Thomas Rogers.
506. Mrs. William Wallace Lunt, Hingham, ninth from Richard Warren.
507. Mrs. Godfrey Ryder, Medford, seventh from Samuel Fuller.
508. Miss Nora Lucy Fairbanks, Bangor, Me., ninth from William Bradford.
509. Mrs. Amasa Clarke, Brookline, eighth from Richard Warren.
510. Mrs. George Hartwell Peirce, Somerville, eighth from William Bradford.
511. Theodore Studley Lazell, Boston, ninth from William Brewster.
512. James Draper Lazell, Boston, ninth from William Brewster.
513. Mark Lyman Vining, Ypsilanti, Mich., eighth from John Alden.
514. Mrs. William Henry Webster, Ypsilanti, Mich., eighth from John Alden.
515. Rev. George Hodges, D.D., Cambridge, eighth from Myles Standish.

August 30, 1899.
516. Joseph Henry Sears, Brewster, ninth from William Brewster.

250   *Reports from State Societies.*

517. Mrs. Herbert Allen Chapin, Somerville, eighth from Richard Warren.
518. Alfred Stevens Burbank, Plymouth, seventh from William Bradford.
519. Liberty Emery Holden, Cleveland, O., ninth from John Alden.
520. Prof. Wilfred Harold Munro, Providence, R. I., tenth from James Chilton, ninth from Mary Chilton.
521. Miss Edith May Tilley, Newport, R. I., tenth from John Alden.

September 28, 1899.
522. Mrs. John Henry Parks, Duxbury, seventh from John Alden.
523. Miss Marianna Page Smith, Boston, tenth from William Brewster.

SUPPLEMENTAL LINES FILED.
June, 1899.
487. Mrs. Fred E. Jones, ninth from Isaac Allerton, eighth from Mary Allerton.
497. Henry N. Fairbanks, eighth from Isaac Allerton, seventh from Mary Allerton.
507. Mrs. Godfrey Ryder, seventh from John Alden; eighth from John Billington, seventh from Francis Billington; seventh from William Bradford; seventh from Francis Eaton, sixth from Samuel Eaton; seventh from John Howland; seventh from Myles Standish; seventh from Richard Warren.
510. Mrs. George H. Peirce, eighth from John Alden; seventh from William Bradford; ninth from William Brewster, eighth from Love Brewster; eighth from Richard Warren, ninth from Richard Warren.
511. Theodore S. Lazell, ninth from John Billington, eighth from Francis Billington; eighth from Francis Eaton, seventh from Samuel Eaton; eighth from Samuel Fuller; eighth from Stephen Hopkins.
512. James D. Lazell, ninth from John Billington, eighth from Francis Billington; eighth from Francis Eaton, seventh from Samuel Eaton; eighth from Samuel Fuller; eighth from Stephen Hopkins.

July, 1899.
167. J. Weston Allen, ninth from Richard Warren.
404. Rev. Charles A. Brewster, eighth from John Howland.
487. Mrs. Fred E. Jones, eighth from George Soule.

August, 1899.
498. Mrs. Henry N. Fairbanks, eighth from Richard Warren.

September, 1899.
297. Archie L. Talbot, ninth from Degory Priest.

NEW YORK SOCIETY.

Members Elected.

June 7, 1899.
542. Mrs. James Junius Goodwin, New York, ninth from William Bradford.
543. Mrs. Luther D. Eddy, Sparkill, seventh from Myles Standish.
544. Mrs. Ralph W. Cutler, Hartford, Conn., ninth from William Bradford.

August 24, 1899.
545. Henry Whitney Tyler, New York, eighth from John Howland.
546. Mrs. Lucius Duncan Bulkley, New York, tenth from Edward Fuller, ninth from Samuel Fuller.
547. Edward Willard Brown, New York, eighth from John Howland.
548. Mrs. Henry Joseph Speck, Troy, tenth from John Alden.
549. Mrs. Amos H. Fowler, Denver, Col., ninth from Francis Cooke.
550. Russell Blakeley, St. Paul, Minn., seventh from Myles Standish.

CONNECTICUT SOCIETY.

Donations to the Library.

"The Averys of Groton," from John D. Rockefeller.

"History of the Primitive Yankees, or Pilgrim Fathers," "Account of the Pilgrim Celebration at Plymouth, 1853," Stowell and Wilson's "History of the Puritans and Pilgrim Fathers," all from Edwin A. Hill.

"The Foundations of Genealogy," from the author, William Stowell Mills.

"The Mayflower Fuller Genealogy," from the compiler, F. A. Fuller.

Eleven photographs of Scrooby, Austerfield, Delft Haven, and Leyden, taken by W. S. Case, and presented by him.

MEMBERS ELECTED.

June 26, 1899.
196. Mrs. William Edward Halligan, Bridgeport, eighth from William Bradford.
197. Mrs. Gardner Morse, New Haven, eighth from Francis Cooke.
198. John Henry Hall, Hartford, seventh from Edward Doty.
199. Miss Grace Loines Hall, Hartford, eighth from Edward Doty.
200. Mrs. Sherwood Stratton Thompson, New Haven, eighth from William Bradford.
201. James Brewster Cone, Hartford, eighth from William Brewster, seventh from Love Brewster.
202. Mrs. Henry Stuart House, Hartford, ninth from William Brewster.

August 21, 1899.
203. Dr. Charles Wellman Hitchcock, M.D., Detroit, Mich., eighth from William Bradford.

SUPPLEMENTAL LINES FILED.

February, 1899.
19. Miss Sarah E. Robinson, ninth from William Brewster.
120. Mrs. George J. Bramble, ninth from William Brewster.

PENNSYLVANIA SOCIETY.

MEMBER ELECTED.

June 7, 1899.
114. Mrs. Frank L. Clark, Sewickley, ninth from Francis Cooke.

ILLINOIS SOCIETY.

DONATIONS TO THE LIBRARY.

"Butters' Genealogy," from George Butters.
"The Puritan in England and New England," "History of Gilsum, N. H.," "Bay-Path," "A Shelf of Old Books," "Great Cities of the World," "Sermon on the Mount," "The Queen's Reign and its Commemoration," all from Mrs. Henry C. Purmort.

MEMBERS ELECTED.

July 15, 1899.
70. Mrs. Charles H. Ray, Chicago, eighth from Stephen Hopkins, seventh from Gyles Hopkins.

71. Mrs. Paul Blatchford, Oak Park, tenth from William Brewster.
72. Lawrence Williams, Chicago, eighth from Edward Fuller, seventh from Samuel Fuller.
73. George Edward Wright, Chicago, ninth from William Brewster.

SUPPLEMENTAL LINE FILED.

July, 1899.
21. Walter M. Howland, eighth from Stephen Hopkins, seventh from Gyles Hopkins.

OHIO SOCIETY.

MEMBERS ELECTED.

June 6, 1899.
31. Charles Humphreys Newton, Marietta, ninth from Francis Cooke.
32. Miss Hariette Maria Hinsdale, Cincinnati, ninth from Richard Warren.
33. Edward Wyllys Buell, Cincinnati, ninth from William Bradford.

DISTRICT OF COLUMBIA SOCIETY.

DONATION TO THE LIBRARY.

"The Johnson Memorial," from the estate of the compiler, James Bowen Johnson.

MEMBERS ELECTED.

June 13, 1899.
50. John Parker Lothrop, Washington, seventh from John Howland.
51. Mrs. Preston Heath Bailhache, Washington, seventh from John Howland.
52. Richard Henry Gadd, Washington, ninth from William Brewster.
53. Miss Jessie M. Craig, Washington, ninth from John Alden.
54. Mrs. Charles H. Warner, Milwaukee, Wis., eighth from John Allen.

July 31, 1899.
55. Miss Edith Gifford, Hartland, Wis., eighth from Richard Warren.

56. Miss Jessie Eastman Hopkins, Washington, eighth from Stephen Hopkins, seventh from Gyles Hopkins.
57. Miss Anne Ashmun Vilas, Minneapolis, Minn., ninth from John Howland.
58. Percival Madden Vilas, Minneapolis, Minn., ninth from John Howland.
59. Mrs. Theophilus Levi Haecker, St. Paul, Minn., eighth from John Howland.

PILGRIM NOTES AND QUERIES.

NOTES.

THE MAYFLOWER GENEALOGIES. — The Massachusetts Society has begun the compilation of the genealogies of the Mayflower passengers and all of their descendants, *in all male and female branches.* This work is being done in the most thorough and critical manner. Every page of the original records of Plymouth Colony, and the old Pilgrim towns, will be searched with the greatest care, and every item noted which will assist in fixing relationship or be of interest to descendants of the Pilgrims. All other original records which can supply information will be examined with the same care. The results will be systematically arranged as the work progresses, and published in THE MAYFLOWER DESCENDANT.

This method of research will eventually be extended over the entire period prior to the Revolution. The material for the later generations will be collected in the usual way, on blanks sent out to every person known to be descended from a Mayflower passenger.

This exhaustive research will require a great deal of time, and the expense will be heavy. In order to provide the necessary funds the "Colonial Research Fund" has been started, and all persons interested in Pilgrim genealogy and history are urged to assist in the work by contributions to this fund. All receipts will be acknowledged in THE MAYFLOWER DESCENDANT.

Descent has been traced from twenty-two Mayflower families, and nearly all the records relating to the earlier generations of each of these families are to be found within the limits of the old Plymouth Colony. If the compilation of the genealogy of each of these families should be undertaken separately, it would necessitate the critical examination of these old records twenty-two different times, and the consequent waste of time and money would be great, to say nothing of the disastrous effects of so much entirely unnecessary handling of the records, which are already, in many cases, in a very dilapidated condition.

Moreover, there were numerous intermarriages among the early generations of the Pilgrim families, and there will be much unnecessary duplication of research work if the genealogies are not compiled under one general direction. Descendants of Jacob[2] Cooke (Francis[1]) are also descended from Stephen[1] Hopkins, through his daughter Damaris[2], and both the Cooke and the Hopkins genealogies, if prepared separately, must contain all of the numerous descendants of this couple.

FOREIGN RESEARCH FUND. — Subscriptions not heretofore acknowledged: Miss Emma C. B. Jones, $5; Mrs. William Lawrie, $25; Edward B. Kellogg, M.D., $3; F. Apthorp Foster, $10; Miss Mary Rivers, $5; Alden Freeman, $6; James Atkins Noyes, $5.

BRADFORD MEERSTEAD. — The Treasurer reports the following additional names of contributors to the fund: Alfred S. Burbank, Mrs. W. E. Halligan, Stephen Jewett, Mrs. Arthur Luetchford, Miss Alma Luetchford.

PRESTON, CONN. — The First Congregational Church of Preston, founded in 1698, will publish, if enough advance subscriptions are obtained, a volume of about 200 pages, containing the admissions, dismissals, baptisms, marriages and deaths found on their records. The volume will contain between four and five thousand genealogical entries, and the price to advance subscribers will be $2. Communications may be addressed to Miss Mary E. Morse, Preston City, Conn.

QUERIES.

[*This department is limited to subjects connected with Pilgrim genealogy and history, and Queries can be inserted for subscribers only. Answers should be sent to the Editor for publication in later issues.*]

14. CUSHMAN. What was the maiden name, and who were the parents of Persis, the first wife of Robert[4] Cushman (Thomas[3], Thomas[2], Robert[1])? They were married about 1697, and Persis died before 14 January, 1743-4.
G. E. R.

15. COOMBS — CUSHMAN. Who were the parents of Elizabeth Coombs, who married, 12 January, 1687-8, Eleazer[3] Cushman (Thomas[2], Robert[1]) of Plymouth?   W. R. C.

16. WALKER — WARREN. Who were the parents of Sarah Walker, who married, 19 November, 1645, Nathaniel[2] Warren (Richard[1]) of Plymouth? S. W. W.

ANSWER TO QUERY.

7. COBB. Rachel Cobb was born at Middleborough, 8 December, 1702, and was the daughter of John Cobb and his wife Rachel[3] Soule (John[2], George[1]), who were married at Plymouth, 5 September, 1688. — EDITOR.

THE MAYFLOWER DESCENDANT IN 1900.

The following series of literal transcripts from original records, begun in Volume I, will be continued through the year :
Plymouth Colony Wills and Inventories,
Plymouth Colony Deeds,
Plymouth Births, Marriages and Deaths,
Scituate Births, Marriages and Deaths,
Middleboro Births, Marriages and Deaths,
Early Records of Plympton, Mass.,
The Brewster Book,
The Diary of Jabez Fitch, Jr.

The January number will contain the first instalment of the Marshfield Births, Marriages and Deaths, and the records of other Pilgrim towns will be taken up as rapidly as possible.

In addition to the regular series of Plymouth Colony Wills, each number will contain at least one will of a Mayflower passenger, with the inventory of the estate, if it is found on the records.

A number of private records, from old family Bibles, or other original documents, will be published during the year.

The many conflicting statements relating to Pilgrim genealogy have caused a great deal of confusion, which might have been avoided had the authors taken pains to consult the records. An important feature of the magazine for the coming year will be articles based on a critical study of the original records, which will establish the correct lines of descent in disputed cases.

It is hoped that the publication of the "Mayflower Genealogies" may begin during the year.

Each number will contain at least one illustration of an old document.

The "Reports from State Societies" and "Notes and Queries" will be published as usual.

INDEX OF PERSONS.

Adams, ——, 86
  mrs. Edward Livingston, 48, 114
  Eleanor, 151
  James, 151
  Jedediah E., 186
  John, 151, 157, 158, 229
  John McGregor, 57, 188, 191
  Stephen Jarvis, 57
  William M., 122
Addington, Isa., 68, 69, 71
Adgate, Mary, 173
  Ruth, 173
  Thomas, 173
Adkins, Experience, 248
Adverd, Henry, 93
Agry, mrs. George, Jr., 116, 121, 185, 191
Alden, ——, 181, 216
  Elizabeth, 150, 163
  George Adelbert, 48
  Hattie Lucinda, 60, 189
  John, 11, 13, 15, 16, 50-53, 55, 57, 59, 61, 63, 79, 98, 115-126, 137, 150, 163, 183, 185-188, 190, 214, 228, 249-251, 253
  John E., 190
  Priscilla, 16, 63, 126, 127, 150, 183
  William F., 60
Alderson, Victor Clifton, 48, 57
Allard, mrs. James Ellsworth, 117
Allen, Francis Olcott, 56, 191
  Francis Richmond, 48, 114
  Frederick Baylies, 48
  Henry Trowbridge, 186
  John Weston, 250
  Martha, 45
  mrs William Bradford, 55
Allerton ⎫
Alerton ⎬ Bartholomew, 9, 12, 16, 149
Alderton ⎭
  Fear, 149
  Isaac, 9, 12, 15, 16, 25, 50, 55, 63, 79, 86, 117, 118, 125, 126, 149, 157, 161, 184, 185, 200, 216, 227, 228, 250
  John, 11, 15, 79
  Mary, 9, 12, 50, 55, 117, 118, 149, 184, 185, 250
  Mary (Norris), 63, 88, 126
  Remember, 9, 12, 149
  Sarah, 149
  Walter Scott, 51, 54, 121
Allien, Nathan, 180
Allyn, Hannah, 222
  Jabez, 223
  John, 222, 223
  Matthew, 223
  Mercy, 222
  Thomas, 137-139, 222
  Winnefred, 139
Alverson, Sarah, 64
Ames, Harriet S., 117
  Orilla P., 117
Andrus, ——, 244
  Anna, 37
  David, 41
  John, 101
  sergt., 103
  Thomas, 105, 181, 182, 241
Annable ⎫
Anable ⎬ Anthony, 152, 230
  Hannah, 152
  Jane, 152
  Sarah, 152

Anthony, Arthur Cox, 116, 120
  mrs. Edmund, Jr., 184
  Henrietta Rogers, 115, 120
  mrs. Nathan, 49
  Silas Reed, 48, 50, 118
  mrs. Silas Reed, 116
Appleton, Nathan, 48
Apsey, mrs. Albert Stokes, 184
Archer, Sarah, 233
Arms, mrs. Frank H., 54
Arnold, mrs. George Francis, 48
  mrs. Richard, 48
*Aspinwall, Algernon Aikin, 60, 189
  William Humphrey, 61
Atkins, Henry, 215
Atkinson, Maud L., 49
Attiman, Lydia, 45
Atwel ⎫
Atwell ⎬ ——, 182, 241
Attwell ⎭
Atwood, Barnabas, 142
  mrs. Ebenezer T., 119
  Elizabeth, 142
  Isaac, 142
  Joanna, 142
  John, 142
  Mary, 142
  Nathaniel, 142
Avery, capt., 105
  Joseph, 38, 41

Backus, J. Bayard, 51, 121
Bacon, Horace S., 185
  Leon Brooks, 52
Bailey ⎫
Baily ⎬ ——, 41, 104, 105
Baley ⎪
Baly   ⎭
  Abigail, 45, 46
  Anna, 41
  Benjamin, 45
  Ebenezer, 45
  Elizabeth, 45
  Israel, 44
  Jacob, 43
  John, 38, 40, 41, 104
  Joseph, 45
  Keziah, 44
  Martha, 45
  Mary, 45
  Rachel, 47
  Rebecca, 236
  Ruth, 43, 45
  Sarah, 44
  Seth, 47
  Timothy, 44
  William, 46
Bailhache, mrs. Preston Heath, 253
Baker, mrs. Charles Taintor, 191
  George Fales, 57
  Hannah, 166
  William, 166
Balch, Elizabeth, 43
  Sarah, 44
Baldwin ⎫
Baldwin ⎬ ——, 39, 42
Boldwin, ⎭
  mrs. Charles G., 52
  Hannah, 166
  Samuel, 166

Index of Persons.

Ballard, Jarvis, 71
Ballou ⎫
Bellou ⎬ capt., 103
Bellou ⎭
Bangs ⎫
Banges ⎬ ——, 230
  Edward, 81, 154, 161
Barbour, William E., 59
Barce, John, 115
Barker ⎫
Berker ⎬ Barnabas, 108
  Content, 110
  Eben, 191
  Eben Francis, 56
  Edward T., 118, 249
  Elizabeth, 45
  Frederick Alden, 191
  mrs. Frederick Alden, 49, 191
  Hannah, 167
  John, 213
  Mary, 108
  Mercy, 165
  Patience, 167
Barnes ⎫
Barns ⎬ David, 164, 165, 168, 233, 237, 238
  John, 199, 200, 216
  Marion Oscar, 124
  Lucy, 196
Barnum, mrs. Charles William, 122
Barrell ⎫
Barrel ⎬ Abigail, 236
Barriel ⎭
  Colburn, 167
  Desire, 167
  Hannah, 108
  James, 238
  Lydia, 43
  Martha, 238
Barrows, Elisha, 209
  James, 247
  Keziah, 248
  Lydia, 209
  Robert, 209
  Tabitha, 247
  Thankful, 209
  Thomas, 209
Bartlett ⎫
Bartlet ⎬ Charles, 59
  Ebenezer, 212
  Elizabeth, 212
  Hannah, 212
  James, 212
  John, 212
  Joseph, 212
  Robert, 99, 153, 212, 230
  Samuel, 212
  Sarah, 212
  Thomas, 212
  William, 212
Bartol, George Edward, 57
Bass, Benjamin, 235
  Mercy, 235
Bassett ⎫
Basset ⎬ Elizabeth, 151
Bassite ⎭
  William, 96, 151, 157, 229
Bates, Abigail, 45
  Aquilla, 167
  Deborah, 44
  mrs. George Henry Whitney, 184
  John, 45
  mrs. Joshua, 185
  Solomon, 44, 167
Battles, Joseph, 45
  Susanna, 45
Bayard, Thomas F., 56, 126
Beachamp ⎫
Beachampe ⎬ John, 216–219
Beal ⎫
Beale ⎬ Grace, 107
Beals ⎭
  Jedediah, 107

Beal ⎫
Beale ⎬ John, 238
Beals ⎭
cont'd.
  Priscilla, 237
  Rhoda, 238
  William, 229
Bemon ⎫
Beamont ⎬ John, 3, 5
Bears, Rebecca, 247
Bearse ⎫
Beirce ⎬ Austin, 138
Becket ⎫
Buckett ⎬ Mary, 64, 230
Bell, Jared Weed, 121
Belo, mrs. Alfred H., 191
Benedict, William Leonard, 184
Benjamin, Marcus, 60, 189
Bennett ⎫
Bennet ⎬ Deborah, 220, 224
  Ebenezer, 220
  Elinor, 224
  Elizabeth, 220
  Isaac, 220
  John, 220, 224
  Joseph, 220
  Lydia, 220
  Nehemiah, 220
  Peter, 220
  Repentance, 128
  William, 220
Benson, Joseph, 237
  Keziah, 248
  Samuel, 248
  Susanna, 237
Bent, Jemima, 248
  Joseph, 246, 248
  Sarah, 246
Bentley, mrs. Cyrus, 187
Benten ⎫
Benton ⎬ ——, 181, 241
Billings, lieut., 39, 102, 179, 180, 244
  mrs. Charles K., 53
  Roger, 39
  William, 41
Billington ⎫
Billinton ⎬ Eleanor, 10, 63, 126, 127, 151
  Francis, 10, 16, 63, 127, 151, 160, 185, 199, 222, 250
  Isaac, 223
  Jemima, 248
  John, 10, 14, 63, 79, 125–127, 151, 152, 185, 227, 228, 250
Bingham, Josh., 102
Bishop, mrs. William D., Jr., 122
Bishop of London, 56
Bissell ⎫
Bissel ⎬ James Dougal, 121
  Roger, 182
Black, M. Percy, 54
Blagden, Thomas, 189
Blair, Jane, 106
Blakeley, Russell, 251
Blanchard, Hannah, 36
  Howard Wilson, 190
  Susanna Reed, 115
  Walter E., 119
Blatchford, mrs. Eliphelet Wickes, 58
  Paul, 188
  mrs. Paul, 253
  mrs. Samuel Milford, 186
Bliss, mrs. Cyrus W., 115
Blodgett ⎫
Bloggett ⎬ Lucy, 195
Blossom, Thomas, 31
Blunden, Sarah, 231, 232
Blunt, sergt., 40
Bond, Henry Richardson, Jr., 54
Bonney ⎫
Boney ⎬ Elizabeth, 168
  Isaac, 177, 247

Index of Persons. 259

Bonney ⎫
Boney ⎬ Joseph, 168
cont'd. ⎭
  Mary, 177, 247
  Sarah, 177
Bonum ⎫
Bonan ⎬ Ann, 143
  Ebenezer, 143
  Elizabeth, 143
  George, 132, 143
  Lydia, 143
  Ruth, 143
  Samuel, 143
  Sarah, 143
  Susanna, 143
Boo, Hannah, 168
  Samuel, 168
Booth, Zeruiah, 44
Borcherling, mrs. Charles, 52
Boreman, Thomas, 159
Bosworth, Alice, 246
  David, 176
  Jonathan, 246
  Nehemiah, 178, 246
  Ruth, 246
  Susanna, 178, 246
Bourn ⎫
Bourne ⎬ Margaret, 106
  Richard, 106
  Sarah, 236
  Shearjashub, 43, 236
  Thomas, 213
Bowen ⎫
Bowin ⎬ Abijah, 220
  Henry J., 119
Bower, John, 215
Bowker, Anna, 237
  Benjamin, 108, 234
  Desire, 167
  Edmund, 165
  Elizabeth, 166, 238
  Eunice, 237
  Gershom, 238
  Hannah, 108, 167, 234
  Joanna, 164
  Joseph, 166
  Luke, 164
  Lydia, 165
  Margaret, 237
  Mary, 165
  Ruth, 109
Bowman, George Ernest, 1, 23, 42, 48, 49, 65, 91, 113, 139, 161, 219, 230, 238
Boynton, mrs. Charles Bliss, 186
Braddock, general, 39
Bradford, Abigail, 147
  Alden S., 191
  Alice, 26, 147, 153, 229
  Ann A., 49, 119
  mrs. Charles F., 191
  David, 115
  Dorothy, 9, 87
  Gamaliel, 48, 49, 113
  George L., 49
  Israel, 115
  John, 147
  Joseph, 215
  Joseph Edward, 61
  Levi, 115
  Lewis, 175
  Mary Russell (Winslow), 248
  Mercy, 147, 153
  Polly, 115
  Priscilla, 147
  Royal Bird, 54, 191
  Samuel, 147
  William, 9, 12, 13, 16, 27, 49, 50, 52, 53, 55, 56–59, 61, 79, 91, 96–98, 114–117, 119, 121–125, 127, 131, 133–137, 147, 153, 157, 161–163, 183–188, 190, 191, 200, 205, 213–216, 220, 227, 239, 249–253

Bradley ⎫
Bradly ⎬ Elizabeth, 71–73
Bradle ⎥
Brawly ⎭
  Hannah, 71
  Lucretia, 72
  Peter, 71, 72, 77
Bradstreet, Simon, 68
Bramble, mrs. George J., 54, 252
  Sarah, 38
Bramhall, Joshua, 210
Branch, ——, 104
  Thomas, 38
Bray, mrs. Alonzo Butler, 183–185
Brayman, Mary, 109
Brayton, mrs. Charles Ray, 49, 51, 114
Brazier, mrs. Joseph Harrison, 122, 187
Breed, lieut., 102, 103
Brett, ——, 220
Brewster ⎫
Bruster ⎥
Brewser ⎥
Brester ⎬ ——, 137
Brewste ⎥
Bewster ⎥
Brwster ⎭
  Ann, 72–74, 195
  Benjamin, 2, 4, 7, 8, 41, 72–77, 169, 171–174, 193–195, 226
  Bethiah, 169, 195
  Charles Augustus, 48, 50, 250
  Daniel, 72, 73, 168–173, 194–197, 225
  Dorothy, 193, 194
  Ebenezer, 170, 171, 173, 194
  Elijah, 37
  Elizabeth, 7, 8, 71, 74, 174
  Fear, 229
  Flora L., 114
  Grace, 7, 8, 71, 74
  Hannah, 8, 168–171, 173, 194, 224–226
  Henry Colvin, 121
  Jerusha, 169, 170
  John, 169, 193, 194, 225
  Jonathan, 3–5, 7, 8, 72–74, 81, 148, 150, 168, 169, 171, 172, 193, 194, 213, 224–226, 229
  Josh., 104
  Judith, 172
  Love, 3, 9, 12, 50, 117, 118, 121, 127, 150, 162, 183–185, 188, 190, 250, 252
  Lucretia, 150, 168, 172, 224, 226
  Lyman Dennison, 55
  Mary, 3, 4, 7–9, 35, 63, 72, 75, 127, 148, 150, 169, 183, 193, 226
  Nathaniel, 225, 226
  Oliver, 194
  Patience, 229
  Ruth, 3, 7, 8, 74, 169, 173, 197
  Samuel, 41
  Sarah, 193
  Sarah Crocker, 115
  Susanna, 194
  Timothy, 225
  William, 3, 4, 7–9, 12, 27, 50, 51, 53, 55, 58, 59, 63, 74, 79, 115–122, 125, 127, 150, 158, 162, 183–185, 188–190, 203, 225–227, 249, 250, 252, 253
  Wrestling, 9, 12, 115, 150, 162
Brickel, ——, 37
Briggs ⎫
Brigs ⎬ Barnabas, 245
  Clement, 150, 229
  Cornelius, 46, 165
  Deborah, 45
  Ebenezer, 245
  Hannah, 44, 245
  Jerusha, 165
  John, 47, 245
  Joseph, 44
  Judith, 47
  Leah, 47
  Lydia, 46

Briggs }
Brigs } Mary, 43, 44
cont'd.
  Remember, 167
  Sarah, 44, 245
  Solomon, 167
Brigham, mrs. Loriman S., 49, 119
Brinley, Charles A., 56
Britteridge }
Britterige } Richard, 10, 15, 79, 87
Brooks }
Brookes }
Brook } Anna, 234
Brooke }
  Elizabeth, 234, 236, 239, 240
  Gilbert, 192, 238, 240
  Hannah, 168
  John, 239, 240
  Joseph, 236
  Lydia, 236
  Mary, 109, 236
  Nathaniel, 165
  Patience, 165
  Robert, 192, 239, 240
  Samuel, 234
  Sarah, 165
  William, 109
Brown }
Browne } ——, 39
Browen }
  Edward Willard, 251
  Elizabeth Mussey, 54
  Hannah, 44
  James Crosby, 57
  John, 81, 96
  mrs. John Crosby, 191
  Jonathan, 166
  Judah, 39
  Knight, 237
  Martha, 152
  Mary, 64, 152, 166
  Nathaniel, 40
  Peter, 10, 15, 51, 64, 79, 81, 82, 87, 116, 118, 119, 121, 125, 127, 152, 190, 227, 228
  Priscilla, 237
  Samuel, 44
  mrs. William Liston, 59
Brownell, Silas Brown, 53
Bruen, Obadiah, 226
Bryant }
Briant } Abigail, 209, 210
  Anna, 235
  Anne, 110
  Bathsheba, 107
  Benjamin, 166, 210
  Bethiah, 210
  David, 211
  Dorcas, 246
  Ebenezer, 176
  Elizabeth, 45, 107, 176, 246
  George, 145
  Hannah, 210, 211
  H. W., 64
  Ichabod, 211
  James, 145, 246
  Joanna, 145
  John, 145, 209
  Jonathan, 210
  Joseph, 176
  Lydia, 235
  Mary, 46, 107, 209
  Mehitable, 211
  Peleg, 46, 235
  Ruth, 145
  Ruxby, 166
  Samuel, 210
  Sarah, 145
  Seth, 45
  Stephen, 211
  Timothy, 211
  William, 211

Bubb, mrs. J. W., 186
Buck }
Bucke } Hannah, 43
  Isaac, 233
  Jonathan, 46
  Joseph, 46
  Leah, 46
  Lusanna, 234
  Mary, 192, 233
  Rachel, 46
  Sarah, 44, 109
Buckett }
Becket } Mary, 64, 230
Buckingham, ——, 241
Buell, Edward Wyllys, 253
Bugbee, mrs. Frederick Abroy, 55
Bulkley, mrs. Henry Thorp, 55
  mrs. Lucius Duncan, 251
Bull, ——, 182, 241
  William Lanman, 51, 121
Bumpas }
Bumpasse } Edward, 149, 159, 161, 229
Bompass }
  Joanna, 211
  Mercy, 211
  Samuel, 211
  Thomas, 211
Burbank, Abraham, 234
  Alfred Stevens, 250, 255
  Bethiah, 234
Burcher }
Bircher } Edward, 25, 229
Burnham }
Burnam } mrs. Ella Bradford, 191
  James, 41
Burnit, Jacob, 102
Burrows }
Borrowes } ——, 180
  Amos, 105
  capt., 103
  Jeremiah, 213
  Josh., 105
  Lemuel, 105
  Samuel, 103, 104
Bush, John Standish Foster, 50
Bush-Brown, Henry Kirke, 53
Butler }
Butlar } ——, 182
  Ensign, 241
Butten, William, 9, 86
Butters, George, 58, 188, 252
Button, ——, 105
  Zebulon, 38
Butts, mrs. George Coit, 53
Byram }
Byrum } Sarah, 168
  Seth, 168

Caesar, Julius, emperor, 18
Cahill, Ann, 44
  Martin, 44
Campanella, 3
Canady }
Cannedy } Alexander, 208
  Ann, 107
  Annable, 209
  Elizabeth, 208
  Hannah, 208
  Jean, 208
  John, 209
  Sarah, 209
  William, 209
Cannell, mrs. Thomas E., 51
Cannon, John, 229
Canterbury, archbishop of, 126
Capehart, mrs. Edward Everett, 115, 120, 185
Carlile, Elizabeth, 165
  William, 165
Carman, Sarah, 238
Carpenter, ——, 37
  mrs. John Quincy, 56

Index of Persons.   261

Carrel, Joseph, 235
  Tamar, 235
Carter, ——, 37
  Joseph, 45
  Robert, 9, 232
  Sarah, 45
Carver, John, 9, 11, 79, 88, 231, 232, 247
  Katharine, 9
  Sarah, 247
Case, W. S., 251
  William W., 60
Castle, William Henry, 56
Caswell, Elizabeth, 45
  John, 45
Cato, Dinah, 237
  Issacher, 237
Caulkins, miss, 225, 226
Chamberlin, Isabel Sargent, 60, 189
Chambers, Thomas, 95, 134
Chandler } Edmund, 6, 157
Chandeler }
  Samuel, 160
  Theophilus Parsons, 56
  Zebedee, 128
Chapin, mrs. Herbert Allen, 250
Chapman, ——, 40
Chard, Joseph, 247
  Rebecca, 247
Charles, capt., 102
Chatfield, mrs. Albert Hayden, 123
Cheney } ——, 181
Chenee }
  Charles Edward, 57
Cherry, mrs. Lewis W., 186
Chester, capt., 103
Chew } John, 29
Cheew }
Child, Dudley Richards, 184
  Edith, 184
Chillingsworth, ——, 217
  Thomas, 216
Chilton, James, 10, 14, 52, 53, 63, 79, 87, 89, 116–120, 123, 125, 127, 185, 248, 250
  Mary, 10, 15, 52, 53, 116–120, 123, 185, 228, 248, 250
Chittenden, Abigail, 234
  Deborah, 46
  Elizabeth, 44
  Israel, 46, 234
  Mary, 46
  Mehitable, 43
  Sarah, 46
  mrs. Simeon B., 186
Choat, John, 181
Christopher } Christopher, 77
Christophers }
  Elizabeth, 77
  John, 77
  Mary, 77
Chubbuck } Solomon, 242
Chebuck }
Church, ——, 110, 244
  Caleb, 108
  Hannah, 110
  Jerusha, 165
  Mary, 166, 235
  Nathaniel, 166
  Richard, 86
  Sarah, 108
Churchill }
Churchel } Abigail, 206
Churchell }
  Bethiah, 207
  Branch, 207
  David, 246
  Ebenezer, 206, 207
  Eleazer, 206
  Elizabeth, 145
  Elkanah, 206
  George, 207
  Hannah, 145, 206
  James, 148

Churchill }
Churchel } Jedidah, 206
Churchell }
cont'd.
  Joanna, 206
  John, 134, 135, 145
  Jonathan, 206
  Josiah, 148, 206
  Lydia, 147, 148, 247
  Mary, 206, 246
  Mehitable, 247
  Mercy, 206, 207
  Nathaniel, 206
  Rebecca, 145, 207
  Samuel, 148
  Sarah, 145
  Stephen, 206
  William, 147
Claflin, mrs. William Henry, 124, 190
Clap } Abigail, 46
Clapp }
  Anna, 44
  Antoinette, 118
  Arthur W., 119
  Benjamin, 107, 236
  Constant, 236
  Deborah, 45
  Dwelly, 166
  Elizabeth, 165, 166, 236
  Galen, 165
  Grace, 107
  Hannah, 44, 235
  Job, 46
  Joseph, 44, 165
  Mary, 45
  Michael, 166
  Patience, 165
  Rachel, 164
  Rebecca, 236
  Sarah, 44, 166, 236
  Susanna, 46, 237
  Sylvanus, 236
  Temperance, 234
Clark }
Clarke } ——, 181
Clerk }
  Aaron, 166
  Abia, 206
  Abigail, 141
  Alonzo Howard, 60, 121, 189
  mrs. Amasa, 249
  Anna, 141
  Betty, 166
  Charles Andrew, 249
  mrs. Charles Andrew, 184
  Elizabeth, 141
  mrs. Frank L., 252
  Hannah, 206
  Josiah, 141
  Mary Smith, 184
  Mary Stimson, 50, 118
  Nathaniel, 206
  Rebecca, 141
  Richard, 10, 15, 79
  Samuel, 206
  Sarah, 141, 206
  Sarah Louisa, 184
  Susan, 29, 30
  Susanna, 141
  Thomas, 81, 141, 150, 230
  William, 206
Cleare, ——, 66
Cleaveland, Livingston W., 49
Coates, Alice Nicholson, 122
Cobb, Ebenezer, 141
  Elisha, 141, 210
  James, 141
  John, 141, 256
  Martha, 141
  Patience, 141
  Rachel, 128, 256

Index of Persons.

Coddington } —, 217, 218
Cuddington }
Coe, Henry Clark, 121
  Henry Francis, 48
Coggeshall, George Bradford, 52
Coit, —, 180
Cole } Alfred Winslow, 116
Coal }
  Daniel, 249
  David, 44
  Deborah, 247
  Desire, 165
  Elizabeth, 46, 167
  Ensign, 43
  Job, 86
  John, 178
  Jonathan, 44
  Lucy, 167
  Mary, 165, 247
  Mercy (Fuller), 249
  Samuel, 247
  Sarah, 43, 44
  Susanna, 178
  Thomas, 247
Coleman } John, 43, 234
Colman }
  Joseph, 133
  Leah, 43
  Sarah, 234
Collamer } Anthony, 165
Collymore }
  Hannah, 167
  John, 106
  Lydia, 235
  Margaret, 106
  Martha, 235
  Mercy, 165
  Peter, 91-93
  Rebecca, 236
  Sarah, 165
  Thankful, 234
Collier, Isaac, 237
  Tamsen, 237
  William, 82, 157, 162
Collis, capt., 243
Coombs }
Combes } —, 156
Combs }
  Deborah, 221
  Elizabeth, 255
  Frances, 221
  Francis, 221, 222, 224
  Lydia, 220, 221
  Mary, 219
  Mercy, 221
  Ruth, 224
Compsit, Dinah, 237
Comstock } sergt., 241
Comstick }
Cone, James Brewster, 252
Conant } Christopher, 229
Connant }
Coner, William, 229
Conney, John, 71
Converse, Sarah, 25
Cooke } —, 39
Cook }
  capt., 179
  Damaris, 16, 127
  Daniel, 40
  Francis, 10, 14, 16, 51-53, 56, 57, 59, 79, 82, 88, 115, 116, 118-123, 125, 127, 149, 183, 184-188, 190, 198, 227-229, 251-253
  Hester, 149
  Jacob, 149, 255
  James, 103
  Jane, 149
  John, 10, 14, 16, 53, 59, 82, 115, 116, 120, 127, 149
  Josias, 215
  Mary, 149

Cooper } Humility, 10, 14, 151, 228
Coper }
Copeland, Elizabeth, 108
  Joseph, 108
Corning, Samuel, 38
Corthiel, Rhoda, 236
Corwin }
Corwine } —, 239
Curwin }
  Elizabeth, 239, 240
  George, 192, 239
Cotton, Bowland, 140
  Elizabeth, 140
  Joanna, 140
  John, 140
  Josiah, 140
  Maria, 140
  Samuel, 140
  Sarah, 140
  Theophilus, 141
Cowing } Deborah, 45
Cowen }
  Elizabeth, 166, 168
  Gethelus, 236
  Hannah, 236
  Israel, 168
  Job, 45, 167
  Lucy, 236
  Lydia, 45, 46
  Mary, 166
  Zillah, 167
Cowles, Elizabeth, 25
  Robert, 26
Coy, Ann, 170, 171
  Daniel, 170
  Jonathan, 170
  Matthew, 170, 171
  Ruth, 171
Crackstone }
Crackston } John, 9, 13, 79, 149, 228
Crakstone }
Craig, Jessie M., 253
Crandon, Edwin Sanford, 113, 114, 117, 119, 191
Crane, Frank Warren, 52
  Warren C., 52
Crary } —, 105
Corarie }
Crocker, Sarah Haskell, 50
  William, 138
Crooker, Agatha, 167
  Elijah, 167
Crowell, Asa Clinton, 117
Cudbartson } see Godbertson
Cutbird }
Cudworth, Benjamin, 46
  Elizabeth, 44, 168
  Hannah, 45, 46
  Israel, 45
  James, 47
  John, 44
  Jonathan, 45
  Martha, 45
  Mary, 44-46, 109
  Rachel, 47
  Sarah, 44
Culver } capt., 244
Coulver }
Cunningham, Theodore Bliss, 53
Curloo, Abigail, 44
  Edward, 44
Curtis } Abigail, 165
Curtice }
  Benjamin, 165
  Charles, 237
  Elijah, 165, 236
  Elisha, 46
  mrs. Evelyn Goss, 59, 60
  Lydia, 237
  Mary, 165, 166
  Rachel, 167
  Ruth, 109

Index of Persons.

Curtis
Curtice } Sarah, 46, 233, 234
cont'd.
  mrs. William Theodore, 117, 185
  Zipporah, 236
Cushing, Bethiah, 234
  David, 35
  Deborah, 108, 236
  Elizabeth, 168
  Francis, 238
  George, 237
  Hannah, 35, 166
  Jeremiah, 233
  John, 234
  Joseph, 107, 109
  Josiah, 109, 236
  Lydia, 107, 237
  Mary, 234
  mrs. Matthew, 119
  Mercy, 107, 166
  Phebe, 235
  Rachel (Lewis), 35
  Ruth, 109
  Temperance, 238
Cushman
Coachman } Allerton, 142, 192, 247
Cochman
  Benjamin, 178
  Deborah, 212
  Eleazer, 211, 255
  Elizabeth, 142, 211, 247, 255
  Elkanah, 142, 178
  Fear, 210
  Ichabod, 210
  Isaac, 178, 210, 246-248
  Jabez, 142
  James, 142
  Jemima, 177
  Jerusha, 178
  John, 212
  Joseph, 177
  Josiah, 142
  Lydia, 212
  Mary, 16, 63, 126, 210
  Martha, 142
  Mehitable, 142
  Persis, 255
  Rebecca, 178, 210, 247
  Robert, 227, 255
  Samuel, 177
  Sarah, 210
  Thomas, 153, 200, 216, 229
Cutler, mrs. Ralph W., 251

Damon, Anna, 237
  Daniel, 46, 167
  Eunice, 237
  Hannah, 106, 167
  Israel, 236
  Joanna, 46
  John, 184, 237
  Joseph, 46
  Josiah, 47
  Judith, 46, 47
  Leah, 47
  Lydia, 236, 238
  Mehitable, 43
  Ruth, 46
  Samuel, 237
  Sarah, 44, 237
  Silence, 107
  Thankful, 45
Darling, Mary, 246
  Rebecca, 246
  Thomas, 246
Dart
Darte } Ann, 72
David, mrs. Mary S., 54
Davie, Humphry, 68
Davis
Daves } mrs. Britton, 184, 191

Davis
Daves } mrs. Carrie Rawson, 59
cont'd.
  Elizabeth, 165
  Eunice, 168
  mrs. Frank V., 53
  Hannah S., 191
  Howland, 51, 121
  Samuel, 23, 91
  Sarah, 233
  Serviah, 164
  Tristram, 233
  William, 164
  William T., 129
Davol, mrs. Bradford D., 117
Dean
Deane } Elizabeth, 30
  Stephen, 29-31, 154, 229
Delano
Delanoy
de la Noye } Benjamin, 236
Dilano
Dilino
  Elizabeth, 168
  Mary, 236
  Philip, 97, 137, 149, 229
Dellys
Dellis } Elizabeth, 44
  Mary, 45
Deming, ——, 104
  Daniel, 104, 179
  Lucy, 104
Denison, Avery, 39
  mrs. George B., 55
Devereux, mrs. Clara Anna Rich, 59
Dewey, Edward Wilkins, 51
Dexter, Henry M., 3, 5, 6
  Morton, 48, 49, 113, 183
  Thomas, 138, 216
Dickinson, John, 139
Dimock, Henry Farnam, 121
Ditson, Charles Healy, 191
  mrs. Oliver, 125, 191
Dixe, Anthony, 230
Doane
Done } ——, 161
  Ida Frances, 189
  John, 82, 83, 154, 200
  Marguerite T., 53, 189
  William Howard, 188
  mrs. William Howard, 189
Dogget
Dogged } ——, 218
Doghed
  John, 131
  Thomas, 131
Donnell, William C., 49, 117, 191
Dorby, Jonathan, 164
Dorithy, John, 235
  Mary, 235
Doty
Dotey
Dowty } Benjamin, 143
Dolton
  Desire, 206
  Edward, 10, 16, 79, 117, 119, 123, 125, 127, 143, 144, 150, 161, 184, 185, 188, 252
  Elisha, 144
  Elizabeth, 143, 144
  Hannah, 143
  Isaac, 144
  Jacob, 144
  John, 115, 143, 144, 206
  Josiah, 144
  Martha, 143, 144
  Mary, 143
  Mercy, 143
  Patience, 143, 206
  Samuel, 143, 144
  Sarah, 143, 206
  Thomas, 143

Index of Persons.

Doty
Dotey
Dowty } William H., 121
Dolton
cont'd.
Downing, mrs. George William, 184
  Ichabod, 104
Downs, Hubert Cowles, 58, 188
Drew, Elizabeth, 146
  Hannah, 146
  John, 146
  Lemuel, 146
  Nicholas, 146
  Samuel, 146
  Thomas, 146
Drinkwater, Martha Leach, 36
Drummond, Josiah H., 49, 64
Drury, mrs. William Henry, 183
Dudley, Joseph, 68
Dunbar } Bathsheba, 167
Dunber
  Deborah, 235
  Joanna, 164
  Martha, 167
  Moses, 235
  Rhoda, 236
  Samuel, 236
Dunham } Barshua, 141
Downham
  Bathsheba, 141
  Ebenezer, 207
  Eleazer, 141, 175
  Elisha, 141
  Israel, 141, 177, 247
  Joanna, 247
  John, 82, 134
  Joshua, 141
  Josiah, 141
  Mary, 207
  Mercy, 141
  Nathaniel, 141, 207
  Samuel, 131, 207
  Susanna, 141
  William, 207
Durkee } lieut., 105, 179, 181, 244, 245
Durky
Dwelly } Deborah, 47
Dwelley
  Elizabeth, 43
  Grace, 107
  Jedediah, 43
  Joseph, 43
  Margaret, 246
  Mary, 43
  Mercy, 106
  Richard, 246
  Thankful, 246
  William, 47
Dwight, mrs. Timothy, 191
Dyer } major, 41
Diah
Dymond, Thomas, 73

Eames, Anthony, 165
  Hannah, 165
Earle, George H., 125
Easdell, James, 146
  Rebecca, 146
Eaton
Eeaton } Benjamin, 247
Eatton
  Catherine Swanton, 116
  Christian, 153
  Elizabeth, 128
  Francis, 10, 15, 63, 79, 118, 120, 125, 127, 153, 197, 199, 200, 228, 250
  Lucy Houghton, 116
  Mary, 247
  Rachel, 64, 153
  Samuel, 10, 15, 16, 63, 120, 127, 128, 137, 153, 250
  Sarah, 10, 15, 63, 127

Eddy
Edy } Beulah, 247
Eedy
  Ebenezer, 220
  mrs. Luther D., 251
  Samuel, 200
  Sarah, 220
Edson, Josiah, 45
  Ruth, 45
Edwards, ——, 243
Eells } Abiah, 166
Ells
  Hannah, 165
  Mary, 109
  Mercy, 107
  Nathaniel, 106, 107
Eggleston, Percy Coe, 54
Eldredge } Edric, 119
Eldridge
  Isabella, 191
  Thomas, 103, 105
Ellet, ——, 103
Ellis, George William, 55
  John, 217
  mrs. Mary Rhodes, 59, 60
  Mordecai, 46
  Sarah, 46
Ellsworth, William W., 121
Elms
Elmes } Abigail, 45
Emms
  Betty, 165
  Elizabeth, 44, 166
  John, 165
  Joseph, 44, 166
  Mary, 166
  Patience, 44, 167
  Samuel, 45
  Surviah, 165
  Zibiah, 165
Ely, ——, 11
  John Hugh, 123
Emerson, mrs. Ralph, 59
Endicott } John, 26
Endecott
English } Thomas, 11, 15, 79
Enlish
Ewell } Hannah, 235
Ewel
  John Louis, 60, 189
  Lydia, 166
  Relief, 43
  Sarah, 167

Fairbanks, Frederick C., 191
  Henry Nathaniel, 184, 250
  mrs. Henry Nathaniel, 184, 185, 191, 251
  Nora Lucy, 249
Fairfax, mrs. Lindsay, 191
Fallowell
ffallowell } Gabriel, 132
ffalloway
  Jonathan, 132
  William, 132
Fanal } ——, 243
Fanel
Fanen, John, 105
Farrow, Christian, 236
  David, 238
  Gershom, 237
  Jemima, 237
  Judith, 238
  Lydia, 237
  Martha, 238
  Tamar, 235
Farwell, mrs. Walter Merrick, 117, 185
Faunce
ffaunce
Fance } Benjamin, 143
ffance
ffans
  Eleazer, 142

Index of Persons.

Faunce ⎫
ffaunce ⎪
Fance ⎬ Hannah, 106, 142
ffance ⎪
ffans ⎪
cont'd. ⎭
  Jean, 147
  Joanna, 147
  John, 142, 147, 149, 203, 229
  Joseph, 142
  Judith, 142
  Manasseh, 229
  Martha, 147
  Mary, 142
  Mehitable, 142
  Mercy, 142
  Patience, 147
  Priscilla, 147
  Solomon Elmer, 124, 189
  Thomas, 106, 139, 140, 143, 147
Fellows, mrs. Frank E., 58
Ferguson ⎱ Mary, 107
Forgason ⎰
Fethers, mrs. Ogden H., 53
Field, Deborah, 45
  John, 45
Finney ⎫
ffinney ⎬ Elizabeth, 208
ffenney ⎭
  Jerusha, 144
  John, 208
  Joshua, 208
  Josiah, 208
  Lydia, 144
  Phebe, 208
  Priscilla, 208
  Robert, 132, 144, 208
Fish, lieut., 103
  Jonathan, 47
  Mary, 47
Fisher, ——, 102
  Beulah, 247
  mrs. Charles H., 117, 118
  Nathaniel, 247
  Onesiphorus, 36
Fitch ⎱ ——, 181
ffitch ⎰
  Abigail, 76
  Abijah, 38
  Anna, 76, 77
  Asa, 37-39
  Benjamin, 76
  capt., 104, 179, 241, 243, 244
  Chester, 37
  Cordilla, 4
  Cordilla Walker, 1, 4, 37, 50
  Elisha, 37, 38, 40-42, 102-105, 180, 181
  Elizabeth, 75
  Hezekiah, 75
  Ichabod, 102
  Jabez, 4, 8, 36, 37, 76, 104
  Jabez Deming, 4
  James, 75
  John, 76
  lieut., 179
  Lucy, 37
  Lurene, 37
  Mary, 75, 76
  Pelatiah, 37, 38, 40, 41, 76, 103, 105, 179, 244
  Samuel, 4, 40, 75, 76
  Stephen, 38, 42, 103
  Walter, 42
Flavell, ——, 229
  Thomas, 229
Fletcher, mrs. Frank Friday, 124, 190
  Moses, 10, 15, 79
Fling, Christopher, 106
  Martha, 106
Flood, Edmund, 229
Fobes, Ebenezer, 197
  Hannah, 197

Fobes ⎱ Jerusha, 196, 197
cont'd. ⎰
  John, 45, 196, 197
  Martha, 45
  Mary, 197
  Ruth, 197
  Simeon, 197
Fogg ⎱
ffogge ⎬ ——, 82, 200
ffog ⎰
  Ralph, 157
Foot ⎱ ——, 103
Foote ⎰
  mrs. Edward, 115
  John Crocker, 54
Ford ⎱
Foord ⎬ ——, 229
fford ⎰
  John, 152
  Lemuel, 164
  Martha, 152
  Priscilla, 164
Foster ⎱ Abigail, 43, 234
ffoster ⎰
  Albert Volney, 58
  Asa Lansford, 50
  Bathsheba, 234
  Christian, 236
  David, 236
  Edward, 83, 86
  Eva Cornelia, 58
  Francis Apthorp, 17, 48, 255
  Freeman, 50
  George, 25
  John, 234
  Joseph, 43
  Margaret, 106, 164
  Richard, 98, 99
  Ruth, 108
  Sarah, 234
  Temperance, 238
  Volney William, 58, 116
Fowler, mrs. Amos H., 251
Fox, George Lyman, 60, 61
  John, 38
Francis, David, 45
  Lemuel, 46
  Lydia, 45
  Maria, 46
Franklin, Elizabeth, 45
  Hannah, 110
  Lydia, 45
  Mary, 46
Freeman ⎫
ffreeman ⎬ Alden, 121, 255
Freman ⎪
Fremen ⎭
  Benjamin, 172
  Betsey R., 119
  Caleb, 172
  Daniel, 171, 173, 196
  Edmund, 215-218
  Elizabeth, 194
  Hannah, 171-173
  Henry V., 188
  James, 23, 91
  mrs. James E., 119
  John, 217
  Joseph, 171-173, 194
  Louise, 116, 120
  Lucy, 195, 196
  Mary, 172
  Mercy, 247
  Nathan, 73, 172, 195, 196
  Paulina, 115, 120
  Phineas, 172
  Ruth, 195, 196
  Samuel, 172
  William, 218
French ⎱ Silence, 43
ffrench ⎰
  Solon Tenney, 187

Index of Persons.

French
ffrench } Stephen, 233
cont'd.
Fuller } Bridgett, 63, 82, 86, 152, 157, 160,
ffuller } 200, 229
  Deborah, 246, 247
  Edward, 10, 15, 59, 60, 63, 79, 119, 120, 123, 124, 125, 127, 251, 253
  Eleanor, 245
  F. A., 251
  Jabez, 177, 246, 247
  James, 245, 246
  Jane, 93
  Judith, 245, 246
  Matthew, 137, 138
  Mercy, 24-28, 247
  Priscilla, 246, 247
  Samuel, 9, 10, 13, 15, 16, 24-28, 31, 59, 63, 79, 91-93, 115, 123-125, 127, 137, 138, 152, 178, 184, 203, 222, 228, 249-251, 253
  Sarah, 177
  Seth, 177, 247
Furnald, mrs. Francis Perkins, 186

Gadd, Richard Henry, 253
Gade, Fredrik Herman, 58, 188
Gager } Hannah, 168
Gajer }
Gale, capt., 104
Gallup } ——, 104, 180, 244
Gallep }
  Nathan, 105, 179
Gannett, Deborah, 45
Gard, Ab., 180
Gardiner
Gardner
Gardener } Joshua, 166
Gardenar
Gardinar
  Mary, 166
  Richard, 10, 15, 79, 228
  Thankful, 234
  William, 234
Garner, Nathaniel, 146
  Samuel, 146
  Susanna, 146
Garnet, Abigail, 109
  Samuel, 109
Garrett, Abigail, 45
  Deborah, 45
  Jael, 46
  John, 45
  Richard, 95
Gates, Daniel, 37
Gay, Ebenezer, 234
  mrs. Henry, 191
  Mary, 234
Geer, mrs. Oliver Joseph, 55
Ghiraldi, Lilio, 19
Gidings, capt., 41
Gifford, Edith, 253
Gilkey, mrs. A. L., 191
Gilman, Dorothea Folsom, 89
  John Taylor, 89
Gilson, ——, 81, 86, 161
Godbertson
Godberson
Cudbartsone } Cudbart, 230
Cutbird
  Godbert, 149, 154, 157
  Samuel, 149, 222
  Sarah, 149, 154
Goddard, Lester Orestes, 58
Godding, mrs. Fred Lawson, 50, 118
Goodman, John, 10, 15, 79, 87, 227, 228
Goodspeed, Deborah, 45
  Nathaniel, 45
Goodwin, mrs. James Junius, 251
Gore, capt., 42
Gorham, George Congdon, 60, 189
  John, 49

Gorham } Temperance, 236
cont'd. }
  William, 236
Gould, Mehitable, 44
Graves, mrs. Dwight W., 58
Gray, Abigail, 164
  Ann, 66, 67, 145
  Desire, 145
  mrs. Edmund Cropper, 185
  Edward, 145
  Elizabeth, 234
  Joanna, 145
  John, 145
  Mary, 145
  Mercy, 145
  Samuel, 145
  William, 164
Greeley, Eliphalet, 36
Green } Elizabeth, 146
Greene }
  Richard Henry, 51, 124
  mrs. Richard Henry, 121
  William, 146
Greenlaw, mrs. Lucy Hall, 49, 58, 224
Greenwood, Isaac J., 54
Gregory XIII, pope, 19
Greve, mrs. Harriet Fisher, 59
Griffin, Sarah, 237
Grinnell, mrs. Charles Edward, 48
  William Milne, 51, 121
Gross, Charles Edward, 55
  mrs. Charles Edward, 55
  Edmund, 108
  Olive, 108
Gyles } ——, 30, 34, 105
Giles }
  Edm., 33, 161

Hacker, Frances, 68
Haecker, mrs. Theophilus Levi, 254
Hale, Arthur, 56
  Edward Everett, 122
  mrs. George S., 183
Hall, mrs. Deborah (Parker), 183
  Grace Loines, 252
  John, 138
  John Henry, 189, 252
Halliburton, Abigail, 44
  Andrew, 44
Halligan, mrs. William Edward, 252, 255
Hamilton, C. A., 191
Hammond
Hammon } Agatha, 107
Hamon
  Joseph, 45
  Mary, 233
  Sarah, 46, 234
  Seth, 233
  Thankful, 45, 109
Handy, Edward A., 59, 60
Harding, Martha, 82, 83
  Sarah, 220
Harlow, Abigail, 178
  Elizabeth, 207
  Jean, 211
  Lydia, 207
  Nathaniel, 178
  Robert, 211
  Sarah, 211
  Thomas, 207
  William, 207
Harris, capt., 179
  Mercy, 67
Harwood, mrs. Sydney, 48
Hascy, mrs. Oscar Lawrence, 124
Haskell
Haskill } ——, 38, 41, 180
Haskall
Hascall
  Bethiah, 222
  Elizabeth, 222

Index of Persons.

Haskell
Haskill
Haskall } John, 219, 220, 222, 224
Hascall
cont'd.
  Josiah, 222
  Mary, 220, 222, 224
  Patience, 219, 222
  Roger, 180
  Sarah, 224
  William, 222
Hatch, Abigail, 235
  Agatha, 167
  Anna, 167
  David, 44
  Desire, 106
  Elizabeth, 44, 164
  Frederic Horace, 51, 121
  Grace, 107
  Hezekiah, 44, 109
  Jonathan, 45, 167
  Keziah, 165
  Lucy, 167, 236
  Lydia, 45
  Martha, 45, 106
  Mary, 109, 237
  Mercy, 109
  Nehemiah, 106, 165
  Patience, 44
  Rachel, 167
  Serviah, 164
  Submit, 167
  Thomas, 45
  William, 92
  Zephaniah, 237
Hatherly
Hatherley } Timothy, 93, 95, 161, 200, 215-217
Hatharly
Hawes, Cyrus Alger, 51, 118, 120, 183
Hawkes, Nathan Mortimer, 49, 249
Hayden, Tamsen, 237
Hayward, John, 68
Heale, Giles, 231, 232
Heard, William, 230
Hewes, see Hughes
Hicks
Hickes
Hicx } Ephraim, 154, 216
Heeks
  Lydia, 154
  Margaret, 153
  Phebe, 154
  Robert, 25, 27, 28, 81, 153, 160, 200, 229
  Samuel, 154, 217
Higgins
Higgens } Richard, 157, 160
Hill, Abraham, 101
  Edwin Allston, 54, 60, 189, 190, 251
  Charles, 73
  Jane, 73
  Ruth, 73
Hilton, William, 229
Hinchman, mrs. Charles S., 56
Hinckley, Mary G., 110
  Thomas, 139
Hinsdale, Hariette Maria, 253
Hitchcock, Charles Wellman, 252
Hoar, George F., 126
Hobamak, 228
Hodges, George, 248, 249
Holbeck, William, 10
Holbrook
Holebrook } Bethiah, 45
  Hannah, 44
  Lydia, 46
  Mary, 44, 233
  Priscilla, 46
  Thomas, 233
Holden, Liberty Emery, 190, 250
Hollis, Deborah, 108
  Samuel, 108

Holloway, Mary, 45
  Ward, 45
Holman
Holdman } Edward, 150, 230
  John, 160
Holmes
Holms } Eleazer, 147
  Elisha, 147
  Elizabeth, 147
  Ephraim, 115
  John, 147, 220
  Jonathan, 115
  Levi, 115
  Lydia, 115
  Mercy, 147
  Nathaniel, 147
  Sarah, 147, 220
  William, 159, 161
Holt, Henry Peter Renouf, 60, 189
Hooke, John, 9, 12
Hopkins
Hobkins } ——, 242, 244
  Caleb, 111, 112, 151
  Catharine, 111
  Charles Augustus, 48
  Constance, 10, 14, 58, 59, 119-121, 124, 185, 186, 188, 189
  Damaris, 10, 118-120, 123, 152, 255
  Deborah, 151
  Elizabeth, 10, 127, 151
  Gyles, 10, 13, 16, 50-52, 110, 112, 113, 119, 120, 127, 151, 136, 188, 252-254
  Jessie Eastman, 254
  Joshua, 111, 112
  Oceanus, 10
  Sherburne Gillette, 60, 189
  Stephen, 10, 13, 16, 50-52, 58, 59, 79, 89, 110-112, 116, 118-121, 123-125, 127, 151, 154, 160, 185, 186, 188, 189, 228, 250, 252, 253-255
  Thomas Snell, 48, 60, 189
  William, 111, 112, 220
Horrel, Abigail, 248
  Mary, 247
House, Anne, 107
  Bathsheba, 234
  David, 43, 44
  Elizabeth, 43, 44
  mrs. Henry Stuart, 252
  John, 107
  Mary, 45
  Samuel, 137
  Seth, 234
  Silence, 43
Howard, Ebenezer, 222
  John, 222
Howarth, mrs. John Bradshaw, 115, 118, 120
Howell, Thomas, 213
Howes
Hous } ——, 101, 181
  Abby Christina, 50
Howland, Arthur, 216
  Charles Allen, 48
  Desire, 150
  Elizabeth, 16, 63, 127, 150, 221, 222
  Hannah, 224
  Henry, 81, 97, 98
  Henry E., 51, 122
  Henry R., 121
  Isaac, 220-224
  Jael, 223
  John, 9, 11, 14, 16, 50-53, 55, 57, 61, 63, 79, 114, 116-123, 125, 127, 150, 182-186, 189, 190, 228, 250, 251, 253, 254
  Lydia, 219
  Nathan, 223
  Priscilla, 221
  Seth, 220
  Susanna, 223
  Walter Morton, 48, 57, 123, 253
Hoyt, mrs. Eugene, 115

Hubbard, Hervey N. P., 129
Hudson, mrs. Ellen H., 191
  mrs. Elmer E., 119
Hughes } John, 94
Hewes }
  Nicholas, 35
Huling, Ray Greene, 115, 120
Hull, capt., 104
Humphris, John, 238
  Mary, 238
Hunt, Adam, 236
  Hannah, 236
Huntington, ——, 101, 179, 181
  Christopher, 169
  Jabez, 179
  Mary, 169
Huntley } lieut., 182, 241–243
Huntly }
Hurst, ——, 218
  James, 82, 198
Hutchins, Augustus L., 121
  Waldo, 51, 121
Hutchinson, Elisha, 68, 69
Hyde } ——, 103
Hide }
  James Nevins, 57, 123
  William Waldo, 54
Hyland, Ann, 44
  Benjamin, 46
  James, 43
  Mary, 43
  Sarah, 46

Ilands, John, 68

Jackson } Abraham, 143
Jacson }
  Deborah, 44
  Israel, 143
  Jere, 210
  Jonathan, 44
  Lydia, 143
  Margaret, 143
  Samuel, 143
  Sarah, 44, 143
  Seth, 143
Jacob, Elisha, 166
  Hannah, 166, 233
  John, 166
  Lucy, 166
  Mary, 234
  Sarah, 234
James, Edward C., 191
  Eunice, 238
  Hannah, 44, 233
  John, 233
  Lydia, 237
  Prudence, 235
  Rhoda, 238
  Thomas, 44
Jayne, mrs. Henry La B., 123
Jefferies, mrs. Richard S., 52
Jenkins }
Jenkens } Abigail, 43
Jinkins }
  David, 46
  Edward, 43
  Elizabeth, 46
  Hannah, 235
  Martha, 47
  Mary, 46
  Rebecca, 46
  Samuel, 46
  Sarah, 44, 110
  Thankful, 45
  Thomas, 44, 235
Jennings } mrs. Charles B., 54
Jenings }
  John, 229
Jenney }
Jenny } Abigail, 153
Jene }

Jenney }
Jenny } Herbert, 48, 59, 123
Jene }
cont'd.
  John, 27, 29, 81, 153, 157
  Samuel, 153
  Sarah, 153
Jewett, Stephen, 255
  William Parker, 186
Johnson, Alvin Page, 184, 185
  mrs. Edward Lewis, 116
  Edward Morrill, 52
  mrs. Edward Morrill, 53
  Francis, 28
  general, 39
  James Bowen, 60, 253
  James Gibson, 54
  Jerome Fletcher, 124, 189
Jones } ——, 5
Joanes }
  Betty, 166
  Charles Davies, 59
  Christopher, 231, 232
  David, 168
  Dearing, 235
  Deborah, 47
  Emma C. B., 59, 255
  Eunice, 168
  mrs. Frances Dearing, 59
  mrs. Fred Eugene, 184, 250
  Hannah, 235
  Joseph Davis, 114
  Mary, 109
  Mary Benson, 109
  Ralph, 5
Jordan } David, 237
Jorden }
  Lydia, 237
  Relief, 238
Joslin } Anna, 107
Joslyn }
  Patience, 167
  Thomas, 107, 167
Joyce, Allston Porter, 184
  Mary, 131

Karr, Mrs. William Wesley, 190
Katerlan }
Katerlin } ——, 40, 41, 103, 178, 242
Katterlan }
Katterland }
Keep, Helen Elizabeth, 50
Keim, mrs. de B. Randolph, 61, 189
Keith, Ebenezer, 46
  Elijah Austin, 184
  Horace A., 118
  Mary, 46
  Wallace C., 119
Kellogg } Edward Brinley, 50, 183, 255
Kellog }
  Frederic Rogers, 52
  Joseph, 241, 242
Kempton, ——, 160
  Ephraim, 147
  Julian, 153
  Manasseh, 29, 153, 157, 203
Kendall, E. Otis, 56
Kent, capt., 240
  David, 238
  Henry Thomas, 122, 187
  Louise Leonard, 122, 187
  Lydia, 238
  Mary Augusta, 56
Kerr, Charles, 34
  Mark, 34
Keyes, Rollin Arthur, 58
King, Amariah, 145
  Hannah, 145
  John, 145
  Lydia, 107
  Rebecca, 43
Knowles, Samuel, 112

Index of Persons.   269

Knowlton, ——, 39
  Hosea M., 48
Kountze, mrs. Mary E., 191

Lamb, ensign, 105
Lambert } Hannah, 168
Lambart }
  Joseph, 168
  Lydia, 165
  Mary, 164
  Sarah, 166
Lanckford, Richard, 83, 85, 86
Lane, mrs. Daniel H., 48
Langemore, John, 9
Lanman, ——, 41
Lapham }
Laphum } ——, 110
  Content, 110
  David, 43
  Elisha, 167
  Elizabeth, 167
  Joshua, 108
  Mary, 108
  Rebecca, 43
Latham, Anna Morton, 116, 120
  Chilton, 67
  John, 105
  Susanna, 66, 67
  William, 9, 11, 153, 200
Laurence, Miner, 101
Lawrie, mrs. William, 48, 248, 255
Lazell, Elizabeth, 207
  Hannah, 207
  James Draper, 249, 250
  John, 207
  Joshua, 207
  Mary, 207
  Sarah, 207
  Theodore Studley, 249, 250
  Thomas, 207
Leach, Anna, 177
  Elizabeth, 177
  Giles, 177
  John, 177
  Josiah Granville, 56
  mrs. Josiah Granville, 57
  Micah, 177
Lee, ——, 180, 243
  Edward Clinton, 56
Lefingwell, ——, 102
Lehmer, mrs. James Dunn, 60
Leister } Edward, 10, 16, 79
Litster }
Leonard, Gardner C., 191
  George H., 119
Lewis, ——, 242
  mrs. John Frederick, 56, 191
Lilius, Aloysius, 19
Lincoln }
Linclon } Abiah, 166
  Abigail, 109
  Anna, 235
  Benjamin, 114
  Deborah, 167, 237
  Hannah, 166
  Isaac, 46, 109
  Jacob, 44
  Jael, 46
  Joshua, 106, 235
  Mary, 44, 166, 234
  Mercy, 106
  Mordecai, 166
  Solomon, 237
Linsey, Martha, 106
Lippincott, Craige, 57
  Jay Bucknell, 122, 123, 187
  Josephine, 57, 123, 191
Liscom, Nehemiah, 164
  Rachel, 164
Litchfield, Abigail, 166
  Bathsheba, 44

Litchfield }
cont'd. } Desire, 46
  Eleazer, 46
  Fear, 45
  Isaac, 46
  James, 44
  Josiah, 44, 166
  Judith, 46
  Lothrop, 235
  Lydia, 46
  Nicholas, 45
  Priscilla, 46
  Remember, 167
  Rhoda, 235
  Ruth, 44, 45
  Samuel, 45, 46
  Sarah, 45, 109
  Susanna, 44, 46
Little, Amos Rogers, 56
  Ann, 99
  David, 45
  Deborah, 45
  Elizabeth, 45
  Mary, 46
  Mercy, 46
  Thomas, 98, 99
Livingston }
Levingston } ——, 244
Lobdell, Isaac, 144
  Martha, 144
  Samuel, 144
  Sarah, 144
Lock, Maria, 108
  Scipio, 108
Lombard, Josiah Lewis, 58
London, bishop of, 126
Long, Robert, 229
Longstreet, mrs. Cornelius T., 52
Longworth, mrs. Nicholas, 59, 60
Lord, ——, 42, 245
  mrs. Elizabeth Watson Russell, 59
Loring, Alice (Cushing), 35
  Caleb, 245
  Ignatius, 245
  mrs. Lindsley, 183
  Lydia, 128
  Mary, 245
  Sarah, 245
  Solomon, 35
Lothrop, ——, 180
  John Parker, 253
  Joseph, 112, 113
Lovel }
Lovewell } Desire, 106
  John, 247
  Joseph, 106
  Lydia, 247
Lucas }
Lukas } Barnabas, 177
Lucos }
  John, 206
  Joseph, 177, 206
  Patience, 206
  Persis, 177
  Samuel, 206
  William, 206
Lucy, Charles, 114
Luetchford, Alma, 255
  mrs. Arthur, 255
Lunt, Cornelia Gray, 59, 188
  mrs. William Wallace, 249
Lyde, Edward, 240
  Susanna (Corwin), 240
Lyman, colonel, 243
  general, 243

Mack, sergt., 182, 240, 241, 244
Magoon, Aaron, 235
  Mary, 235
Man, Ensign, 109
  Ruth, 46

Index of Persons.

Man *cont'd.* } Tabitha, 109
Thomas, 46
Manchester, William C., 49
Mansel, John, 47
Leah, 47
Manson, Thomas Lincoln, 121
Margeson, Edmund, 10, 15, 79
Marsa, capt., 181
Marsh, Carlie Emeline, 190
mgr., 242
William Lowrey, 48, 60
Martin, Christopher, 9, 13, 79, 87
mrs. Medad Chattman, 124
Mason } George Champlin, 122
Mayson
John, 2
Samuel, 104
Massasoit, 88, 89
Masterson, Nathaniel, 134-136
Mastick, mrs. Seabury Cone, 52
Maverick, Remember, 16, 126
May } Edward, 246
Maye
Elizabeth, 246
Israel, 246
Mercy, 246
Moses, 246
Sarah, 246
Mayhew, Matthew Allen, 113
Maynor, ——, 38
John, 178
Mayo } Anna, 238
Mayho
Lemuel, 238
Samuel, 139
McCobb, Lois D., 117
McComb, mrs. William E., 53
McConnell, mrs. Benton, 122
McNeely, Mrs. Robert Knox, 57
Meech, Hezekiah, 105
Meeds, Hester, 224
Josiah, 224
Meeks }
Mekes } Daniel, 174
Mecks }
Elizabeth, 174
Jonathan, 174
Meigs, mrs. Titus B., 191
Mellus, Abigail, 109
Merrick } mrs. Frederick Laforest, 58
Merricke
William, 135, 136
Merritt } Abigail, 43
Merrit
David, 108, 233
Deborah, 44
Elisha, 46
Elizabeth, 46
Hannah, 43, 45, 108
James, 46
John, 43
Jonathan, 43, 46
Mary, 45, 47
Mehitable, 43
Penelope, 46
Priscilla, 46
Sarah, 46, 233
Metcalf, William Park, 60, 189, 190
Middlecott } Richard, 65, 68, 69, 71
Meddlecott
Sarah, 66, 67
Miller, Elihu Spencer, 56
John, 220
Lydia, 220
William E., 53
Mills, William Stowell, 249, 251
Miner } Laurence Waterman, 54
Minor
ensign, 244
Minter, Desire, 9, 11
Minton, Henry Brewster, 51

Mitchell }
Michell } Experience, 81, 97, 98, 149, 214, 229
Michaell }
Mix, capt., 102, 179
Reuben, 180
Rufus, 39
Seth, 40
Mixter, Samuel Jason, 48
mrs. William, 49
More, ——, 9
Ellen, 9
Jasper, 9, 11, 87
Richard, 9, 12, 16, 150
Morey, Sarah, 44
Susanna, 44
Morgan, Benet, 229
Henry Augustus, 54
mrs. James L., 122
Josh., 105
Morison, mrs. John Holmes, 49
Morris, John E., 54
Seymour, 58
mrs. Seymour, 57
Morse } Annie Conant, 117, 185
Morss
mrs. Gardner, 252
Hannah, 247
Lemuel Foster, 117, 185
Mary E., 255
William, 247
Morton, Deborah, 209
Ebenezer, 147, 209
Ephraim, 147, 153
George, 47, 229
Hannah, 147, 209
Henry, 145
Joanna, 209
John, 147, 153, 209
Joseph, 147
Josiah, 144
Marcus, 48
Mary, 209
Nathaniel, 77, 133, 134, 153, 157, 214
Patience, 153
Persis, 209
Phebe, 209
Sarah, 47, 153
Susanna, 144, 145
Thomas, 150, 229
Moseley, mrs. Frank, 51, 114, 118, 120
Moses, mrs. James, 125
John, 64
Mott, Anna, 238
Grace, 43
Mower, mrs. Earl A., 185
Mullin, Arthur, 107
Mary, 107
Mullins }
Mullines }
Mullens } Alice, 9, 63, 125-127, 183, 231, 232
Mollines }
Molines }
Joseph, 9, 231, 232
Priscilla, 9, 13, 15, 125, 163, 231, 232
William, 9, 13, 15, 63, 79, 88, 125-127, 163, 183, 230-232
Munro, Benjamin, 115
Wilfred Harold, 250
Murdoch, mrs. Florence Carlisle, 59
Murdock } James, 146
Mordow
John, 146
Jonathan, 146
Lydia, 146
Robert, 146
Thomas, 146
Murphy }
Murphey } ——, 242
Murfa }
Murfie }
Margaret, 45

Index of Persons. 271

Murphy
Murphey
Murfa } Martha, 52
Murfie
cont'd.
Mary, 235
Virginia Hulburt, 52
Musick, Hendrick, 244

Nash, ——, 242
  Arthur Irving, 116, 249
  David, 46
  Deborah, 44
  Francis Otis, 184
  Hannah, 43, 44
  Herbert, 183
  James, 109
  John, 43
  Joseph, 44, 109
  Nathaniel Cushing, 183, 190
  Penelope, 46
  Sarah, 109
  Thankful, 109
Neal, Anne, 107
  James, 106
  Jane, 106
  Mary, 108
Nelson, Joanna, 210
  John, 210, 221
  Lydia, 210
  Mehitable, 141, 220
  Patience, 210
  Samuel, 210, 221
  Sarah, 210
Nevers, mrs. Edward, 58
Newcomb, George Whitefield, 58
Newland, Jabez, 178, 247
  Rebecca, 178, 247
  Sarah, 247
Newman, Samuel, 97
Newport, mrs. Reice Marshall, 53, 191
Newton, Charles Humphreys, 253
  Clara Chipman, 59
  Ellen, 229
  Ellen Huldah, 59
Nichols } Benjamin R., 23, 91
Niccols
  Ichabod, 89
  John Taylor Gilman, 89
  Leah, 43
  lieut., 242
  Willard Atherton, 89
Nickolson, Lydia, 237
Nicola, mrs. C. A., 191
Nicolas, Austin, 229
Noble, ——, 101
Nord-, ——, corporal, 241
Northey, Eleanor, 44
  Joseph, 44
Norton, Edward Loudon, 51, 121
  mrs. Edward Loudon, 121
Noyes, David William, 184
  James Atkins, 48, 49, 183, 255
Numa, emperor, 17

Oakes, Elizabeth, 36
Olcutt, ——, 181
Oldham
Oldam } ——, 230
Ouldom
  Lucretia, 8
Olin, William M., 49
Orcutt, Margaret, 47
  Thankful, 45
  Thomas, 45, 47
Orr, Arthur, 58, 59, 191
Otis, Abigail, 44
  Elizabeth, 45
  Ephraim, 108
  Job, 43
  Joseph, 45, 46

Otis
cont'd. } Mercy, 46
  Noah, 235
  Phebe, 235
  Ruth, 106
  Sarah, 46
  Thankful, 43
Owen, mrs. Frank K., 114

Pabodie, Elizabeth, 163
  Hannah, 163
  John, 163
  Lydia, 163
  Martha, 163
  Mary, 163
  Mercy, 163
  Priscilla, 163
  Rebecca, 163
  Ruth, 163
  Sarah, 163
  William, 163
Packer, Ichabod, 40
Paddy, William, 215–219
Page, mrs. Washburn Eddy, 116
Paget, mrs. Almeric, 121, 191
Paine, Cyrus Fay, 186
  William, 66
Palmer } Abigail, 236
Pallmer
  Bathsheba, 107
  David, 38
  Experience, 168
  Frances, 151, 230
  Jane, 107
  Joseph, 107
  lieut., 105
  Mary, 238
  Nehemiah, 236
  Ruth, 43
  Samuel, 107
  William, 81, 151, 159, 229, 230
Parker, Frederick Sheldon, 52, 191
  Frederick Wesley, 36, 48, 125
  Mary, 236
  William, 236
  William Newton, 187
Parkinson, mrs. George B., 249
Parks, mrs. John Henry, 250
Parrish, Bethiah, 195
  William, 195
Parsons, Charles L., 118
  mrs. John W., 249
Partridge } George, 135, 136
Partrich
  Ralph, 96, 97
Payson } major, 182, 241, 243
Pason
Peaks, Hannah, 43
  Israel, 45
  Leah, 46
  Lydia, 45
  Priscilla, 46
  Rachel, 46
  Sarah, 43
  William, 46
Peame, Mary, 8
Pearmain, Sumner B., 125
Pearson, mrs. Edward Joseph, 122
Pease, mrs. Ella G. S., 34, 36, 117
Peck, mrs. James S., 49
  lieut., 102, 179
  sergt., 102, 103, 179
Peirce
Pierce } ——, 109, 200, 230
Perce
  Abraham, 141, 150
  Bathsheba, 44
  mrs. George Hartwell, 249, 250
  James Oscar, 61
  Jemima, 235
  Jeremiah, 44

272 Index of Persons.

Peirce }
Pierce } mrs. Jonathan F., 49
Perce }
cont'd.
  Martha, 45
  Mary, 46
  Mercy, 109
  Rebecca, 141
  Seth, 235
Perry, Abigail, 164
  Betty, 165
  Elizabeth, 107, 165
  Keziah, 44
  Lydia, 167
  Rhoda, 235
  Ruxby, 166
  Samuel, 107
  Sarah, 45
  William, 167
  Zillah, 167
Pelham, Herbert, 240
Pelton, ——, 178
Penn, Christian, 229
Percy, mrs. George Washington, 115, 120, 185
Perkins, William, 191
Peterson, Mary Louisa, 61
Phelps, ——, 242
Philbrick, Harry C., 119, 185
Phillips, Amos, 115
  Priscilla, 115
Pickett } Adam, 170
Picket }
  Hannah, 170
  John, 8, 170, 226
  Ruth, 73, 170
Pickles, Margaret, 106
  Nathan, 106
Pincin, Abner, 236
  Agatha, 107
  Hannah, 236
  John, 235
  Judith, 235
  Thomas, 107
Pitcher, Ezra, 44
  Lydia, 108
  Nathaniel, 43
  Zeruah, 44
Pitkin, ——, 181
  mrs. Charles L., 48
Pitt, William, 229
Plais, Nathan, 41
Plimpton, Henry Richardson, 117
  mrs. Henry Richardson, 117, 121
Pollard, Mary, 67
Polle, Joseph, 233
Pomeroy, mrs. Christine King, 187
Pond, Virgil C., 51, 119
Pontus, ——, 160
Pope, Thomas, 132, 133
Porter, mrs. Burr, 48, 49, 125, 191
  mrs. Hobart H., 121
Poverty, ——, 178
Powers, ——, 101
  Bethiah, 43
  Nicholas, 43
Pratt } Benajah, 175, 212
Prat }
  Benjamin, 248
  Charles H., 58
  Ebenezer, 212
  Edith F., 118
  E. Leora, 118
  Franklin S., 58
  Hannah, 44
  Joanna, 212
  John, 175, 212
  Jonathan, 44
  Joshua, 83, 149, 159, 230
  Margaret, 212, 248
  Mehitable, 212
  Patience, 212

Pratt }
Prat } Phineas, 149, 198, 230
cont'd.}
  Samuel, 212
  Thomas, 212
Prence, Patience, 151
  Rebecca, 27, 151
  Thomas, 25, 27, 28, 31, 150, 153, 200, 215, 216, 229
Preston, mrs. Carl Weber, 58, 123
Pride, ——, 40, 41, 104, 181, 243-245
  Harbud, 41
  John, 180
  Jonathan, 39
  P., 241
Priest / Degory, 10, 15, 51, 56, 79, 87, 119-121,
Preist \   125, 127, 251
  Mary, 149
  Sarah, 149
Prince, see also Prence
  ——, 12
  Abiel, 35
  Ammi, 35, 36
  Benjamin, 35
  Cushing, 35, 36
  David, 35, 36
  Else, 35, 36
  Hannah, 34-36
  Paul, 34-36
  Pyam, 35, 36
  Rachel, 35, 36
  Ruth, 35, 36
  Sarah, 35, 36
  Thomas, 35, 36
Proctor, Thomas Redfield, 186
Prouty, Deborah, 235
  Edward, 107
  Elizabeth, 107
  Eunice, 107
  Hannah, 108
  Jemima, 107
  Lettice, 164
  Mary, 46
  Nehemiah, 164
  Sarah, 237
  Simeon, 237
  William, 107
Prower, Solomon, 9, 87
Puffer, mrs. Dexter R., 114, 118, 119
Punderson, ——, 38
Purmort, mrs. Henry C., 123, 190, 252
Putnam, mrs. Earl Bill, 57
  mrs. Joseph Robie, 187, 188

Quaintaince, mrs. John, 55
Quincy Charles Frederick, 58
  mrs George H., 36, 118
  Mary Perkins, 50
Quinton, mrs. Amelia Stone, 191

Ramsdell } Daniel, 64
Ramsden }
  John, 95
  Joseph, 64
  Sarah, 64
  Thomas, 64
Rand, James, 229
Randall, Deborah, 237
  Ezra, 164
  Lucy, 166
  Margaret, 164
  Mary, 43
  Nehemiah, 236
  Rebecca, 236
  Ruth, 108
  Zipporah, 236
Ransom, Abigail, 211
  Ann, 211
  Ebenezer, 211
  Lydia, 211

Ransom cont'd. { Mary, 211
  Robert, 211
Rattlife, Robert, 230
Rawlings, Mary, 236
  Thomas, 236
Rawson, mrs. Frances Delphine, 59, 60
Ray, mrs. Charles H., 252
Raymond } Ebenezer, 247
Raiment
Francis Henry, 115
  mrs. Henry Emmons, 48, 114, 183
  Mercy, 247
Reed, ——, 243
  Esther, 192
  James, 223
  Susanna, 223
  William, 223
  mrs. William Edmond, 55
Register, mrs. Henry Carney, 122, 187
Remich, Daniel Clark, 50
Remick, mrs. John Anthony, 48
Renolds, Benjamin, 224
  Electious, 224
  Mary, 224
Requesens, duke of, 21
Reyner, John, 96, 97, 214, 215
Rhodes, Elizabeth McKean, 57
  James Mauran, 56
Rice, mrs. John M., 119
Richards, Benjamin, 41
  Hannah, 168
  Jeremiah, 125
  John, 99, 101
  Lydia, 173
  Mehitable, 173
  William, 93-95, 157, 160, 173
Richardson, Thomas Francis, 183
  William Minard, 48
Richmond, Elizabeth, 168
  John, 128, 192
  Joshua, 168
  Joshua Bailey, 114, 128
Rickard } Esther, 144
Recard
  James, 144
  John, 144
  Judith, 246
  Hannah, 211
  Henry, 177
  Margaret, 248
  Mary, 144
  Mercy, 144, 177
  Rebecca, 177, 211
  Samuel, 177, 211
  Tabitha, 247
Rider, see also Ryder
  Abigail, 211
  Benjamin, 210
  Elizabeth, 210
  Hannah, 210
  Jo., 142
  Joseph, 210
  Josiah, 211
  Lydia, 210
  Mary, 210
  Samuel, 210
  Sarah, 210
  William, 210
Ridgdale } Alice, 10
Rigdale
  John, 10, 14, 79
Ring, Andrew, 28-31, 207, 208, 215
  Deborah, 208
  Eleazer, 207
  Elkanah, 208
  Jonathan, 208
  Mary, 28, 29, 31, 207, 208
  Phebe, 208
  Samuel, 208
  Susanna, 208, 246

Ripley, Hannah, 114
  James Huntington, 116
  Joshua, 114
  Mary, 247
Rite, see Wright
Rivers, Mary, 255
Robbins }
Robens } ——, 243
Roben }
  Chandler, 191
  Elizabeth, 246
  Hannah, 247
  H. L., 191
  Jeduthan, 175
  John, 101, 242, 246
Robinson } Emily Eliza, 60, 189
Robenson
  Isaac, 138
  John, 113, 189
  Mary L., 60
  Nathaniel Emmons, 60, 189
  mrs. Nelson D., 55
  Sarah E., 252
  Silence, 94, 95
  Thomas, 93-95
Rockefeller, John D., 251
Rockwell, Elisha, 40, 179
Rogers } Abigail, 128, 192
Roggers
  John, 49, 64, 128, 161
  Joseph, 10, 14, 16, 52, 119, 123, 127, 153, 228, 230
  Joshua, 43
  Lydia, 236
  Mary, 44
  Mehitable, 43
  Submit, 167
  Thomas, 10, 14, 52, 64, 79, 118, 119, 121, 123, 125, 127, 128, 167, 187, 188, 190, 249
  William Flint, 116
  Winfred Hervey, 50, 120
Romulus, 17
Rosbotham, Joseph, 115
Rose, Elizabeth, 237
  Faith, 106
  Thomas, 106
Rossiter } —— , 40, 105
Rossater
Roth, ——, 38
Rowly } ——, 81
Rowley
  H. Curtis, 190
Rudd, ——, 38-42, 101-105, 179-181
  Jonathan, 102
  Lurene, 38
Ruggles, Grace, 164
  Sarah, 236
Russell } Abigail, 44
Russel
  adjutant, 102
  Joshua, 107
  Silence, 107
Ryder, see also Rider
  mrs. Godfrey, 249, 250

Sabin, mrs. Charles Dwight, 186
Sage, mrs. Russell, 121
Salisbury, Edward E., 54
  mrs. Edward E., 54
Saltonstall, ——, 227
  major, 100
Samoset, 88
Samson } Abigail, 248
Sampson
  Barnabas, 248
  Elizabeth, 178, 247
  Ephraim, 248
  Experience, 248
  George, 178
  Henry, 10, 14, 16, 125, 127, 137, 150, 162, 188

274   *Index of Persons.*

Samson ⎫
Sampson ⎬ Joanna, 245
cont'd. ⎭
  Joseph, 177
  Josiah, 177
  Maria, 108
  Priscilla, 247
  William, 245
  Zeruiah, 245
Sargent, mrs. Dudley A., 49
  John Smith, 57
Savery, Mary, 64
Saville, Caleb Mills, 117
  mrs. Caleb Mills, 117, 185
  George Washington Webb, 117
Sawyer, mrs. Charles Bailey, 188
Schoff, Wilfred Harvey, 57
Seabury, Benjamin, 45
  Frederick C., 121
  Rebecca, 45
Sears, Joseph Henry, 249
Seaver, James Edward, 116
Sedgwick ⎫
Seggeck ⎬ ——, 243
Sewall, Samuel, 114
Seward, mrs. William H., 53
Seymour ⎫
Seymer ⎬ ——, 182
Shaw ⎫
Shawe ⎬ David, 176
Shau ⎭
  Elizabeth, 176
  Elkanah, 247
  Harriet Arline, 117, 121
  Henry S., 118
  John, 151, 200
  Jonathan, 176, 177
  Joseph, 93-95
  Mary, 246
  Mehitable, 177, 247
  Moses, 246
  Nathaniel A., 120
  Thomas, 138
  Zilpha Bradford, 191
Shelden, ——, 242
Shepard, mrs. James Erving, 50, 120
Shreeve, Martha, 215
  Thomas, 214, 215
Shuntup, Henry, 101
Shurt, Abr., 200
Shurtleff ⎫
Shurtlef ⎬ Barnabas, 209
Shirtlef ⎭
Shirtlif
  Elizabeth, 209
  Ichabod, 209
  Jabez, 209
  John, 209, 247
  Mary, 209
  Sarah, 209, 247
  Susanna, 209
  Thomas, 209
  William, 209
Silvester ⎫
Sylvester ⎬ Anna, 234
  Desire, 36
  Elisha, 107, 164
  Elizabeth, 43
  Eunice, 107
  Faith, 106
  Grace, 164
  Israel, 237
  James, 234
  Lot, 166
  Lurana, 235
  Lydia, 166
  Margaret, 237
  Olive, 108
  Relief, 238
  Thomas, 238

Simmons ⎫
Simons ⎬ Abigail, 109
Symons ⎭
Simonson
  Benjamin, 237
  Jihiel, 234
  Leah, 47, 235
  Moses, 149, 229
  Peleg, 109
  Rachel, 47
  Rhoda, 234
  Ruth, 109
  Sarah, 237
  Thomas, 26
Sirkman, Henry, 63
Skerry, Harry Weed, 52
Skinner, William Converse, 55
  mrs. William Converse, 55
Slap, capt., 241-244
Slaughter, mrs. William Dennis, 61
Sloan, Robert Sage, 121
Slocum, Grace Woods, 116, 120
  Joseph Jermain, 51
Smith, ——, 136, 160, 200, 243
  Ellen H., 60
  Ephraim, 105
  Frank Birge, 60, 189
  mrs. Frank Sherman, 124
  Guilford, 191
  mrs. Guilford, 191
  mrs. Henry Martyn, 116
  mrs. H. H. H. Crapo, 188
  Marianna Page, 250
  Mary, 136, 193
  mrs. Mary Reed, 191
  mrs. Mehitable Parker, 182
  Nathan Holt, 55
  Ralph, 136
  mrs. Samuel F., 49
  Susan Augusta, 174
  Susanna, 194
Snow, Constance, 16, 127, 151
  mrs. Daniel Kimball, 116, 120
  Isaac Burrows, 58, 188
  Mark, 113
  Nicholas, 151, 230
Soper, Anna, 46
  John, 46
  Mary, 108
  Oliver, 49
  Sarah, 106
Sosigenes, 18
Soule ⎫
Soul ⎬ Abigail, 165
Sowle ⎭
Sole
  Abner, 49
  Benjamin, 176
  George, 9, 12, 16, 57, 64, 79, 117-119, 122, 125, 127, 152, 183, 184, 187, 188, 190, 214, 228, 250
  Hannah, 176
  Horace Homer, 48
  John, 219, 220, 245
  Martha, 220
  Mary, 152, 214
  Patience, 219
  Rachel, 256
  Rebecca, 245
  Zachariah, 152
  Zeruah, 183
Southworth, Anna, 167
  Constant, 142
  Desire, 142
  Ichabod, 142
  Mary, 142
  Nathaniel, 142
  Rebecca, 45
  Sarah, 36
  Thomas, 167
Sparhawke, Hannah, 234

Sparrow, Jonathan, 112, 113
  Richard, 86, 157, 199
Speck, mrs. Henry Joseph, 251
Spicer, ——, 37, 41
  John, 178
Spooner, Thomas, 210
Sprague)
Sprage } Amos, 237
Spragge)
  Anna, 151
  Asher, 234
  Desire, 237
  Elizabeth, 107
  Francis, 82, 151, 161, 229
  Frank William, 49, 54
  Lusanna, 234
  Mercy, 151
  Samuel, 131
Spur, ——, 101
Squanto, ——, 88, 89
Squire, Mary, 220
Standish, Alexander, 150
  Barbara, 149, 230
  Charles, 150
  James Myles, 48
  John, 150
  Moses, 128
  Myles, 9, 12, 13, 16, 26, 48, 50, 52, 58, 59, 79, 87-89, 96, 98, 115-119, 125, 127, 136, 149, 158, 162, 185, 216, 228, 248-251
  Rose, 9, 88
  Sarah, 247
Standly, Deborah, 108
  Jabez, 108, 234
  Mary, 234
Stanton, ——, 243
Staples, Joshua, 44
  Mary, 44
Stark, William Molthrop, 54
Starkweather, Woodberry, 40
Starr, Hannah Brewster, 224, 226
  Samuel, 225, 226
Statie, Hugh, 229
Stearns, John Goddard, 115
Stedman, Isaac, 93
Steele)
Steel } Abigail, 43
  Frederick Morgan, 57, 59
Stephenson, mrs. Augustus J., 186
Sterling, Edith Warren, 186
  Eleanor Augusta, 186
Stetson)
Stutson } Bathsheba, 167
Studson)
  Benjamin, 165, 234
  Bethiah, 43
  Caleb, 115
  Caleb Rochford, 61, 190
  Deborah, 44, 110
  Elizabeth, 164, 165, 238
  Eunice, 46
  Experience, 168
  George, 46
  George Rochford, 124, 189
  mrs. George Rochford, 60, 189, 190
  Gideon, 108, 165
  Hannah, 236
  Job, 46
  John, 43, 167
  Jonah, 164
  Leah, 106
  Lydia, 108, 236
  Margaret, 106
  Martha, 106, 166
  Mary, 45, 46, 110, 234
  Mercy, 234
  Nathaniel, 45
  Relief, 43
  Rhoda, 234
  Stephen, 168
  William, 234
Stetson)
Stutson } Zibiah, 165
Studson)
cont'd.
Stevens)
Steven } Benjamin Franklin, 48, 114
  George Holley, 116
  John, 109
  Judith, 172
  mrs. Solon W., 51
Steward, James, 229
Stewert, William, 104
Stimson, mrs. Daniel M., 121
Stockbridge)
Stocbridge } Abigail, 109
  Anna, 107
  Benjamin, 106
  David, 108
  Deborah, 108
  James, 167
  Martha, 167
  Mary, 109
  Michael, 109
  Ruth, 106
  Samuel, 45
  Sarah, 45
  William Mauran, 49
Stoddard, ——, 40, 41, 103, 104, 109, 179, 180
  Benjamin, 109
  Mary, 108
  Ruth, 109
  Samuel, 103
Stodder, Desire, 237
  Hezekiah, 237
  Isaiah, 165
  Judith, 238
  Lydia, 46, 237
  Mary, 165
  Sarah, 43
  Tabitha, 43
Stone, mrs. Martha B., 191
  Ralph, 117
Story, ——, 37
  Elias, 9
  Ezekiel, 37
  Jonathan, 37
Stran, mrs. Charles T., 117
Strange, ——, 217, 218
Strong, ——, 101, 242
  mrs. Theron George, 186
  William Ripley, 121
Studley)
Studly } Abigail, 166
  Deborah, 44
  Eliab, 43
  John, 109
  Mary, 43, 45, 109
  Sarah, 45
  Susanna, 45
Sturtevant)
Stirtevant } Cornelius, 177
  Elizabeth, 177
  Hannah, 145
  John, 145
  Mary, 247
  Silas, 177
Sutton, Abigail, 45
  Elizabeth, 44
  Margaret, 47
Sweet, Benjamin Delano, 49, 118, 191
Sweetser, J. B., 35
  Prince, 36
  Salathiel, 36
  William, 36
Swift, Abiah, 212
  Catharine, 166
  Phineas, 212
  Jedidah, 212
  Rebecca, 212
  Simeon, 166

Sylvester, see Silvester
Talbot, Archie Lee, 51, 251
Talent, ——, 241
Talmadge, Henry, 191
Tappin, ——, 66, 67
Taylor }
Tayler } David, 43
Tailer }
  Elizabeth, 43
  George W., 53
  John, 89, 90
  Lettice, 164
  Martha, 166
  Rebecca, 90
  Seth, 166
  William, 65, 67, 68, 90
Taintor }
Tayntar } mrs. James U., 55
  Joseph, 90
  Rebecca, 90
Tench, William, 229
Terry, Charles Appleton, 186
  John Taylor, 51
  Mary Elizabeth, 61
  Roderick, 51, 121
  Wyllys, 121
Thacher, Thomas, 67
Thomas }
Tomas } Abigail, 235
Tommas }
  Benjamin, 235
  Daniel, 167
  David, 116, 120, 221
  Edward, 221
  Elizabeth, 246
  Frank R., 49
  Israel, 115
  James, 115
  Jeremiah, 219
  Joanna, 223
  John, 179
  Jonathan, 221
  Lydia, 219
  Nathaniel, 129, 131
  Ruth, 109
  Sarah, 167, 220
  William, 219, 223
Thomson }
Thompson } Benjamin F., 225
Tomson }
  mrs. David, 52
  Edward, 10, 86
  Ephraim, 221
  Hannah, 225, 227
  John, 192, 221, 225-227
  Josiah, 119
  Mary, 221
  mrs. Sherwood Stratton, 252
  William, 225
Thorp, Alexander, 43
  Alice, 158
  Elizabeth, 43
  John, 158, 160
Thrift, Mary, 234
Tilden, Abigail, 235
  Benjamin, 44
  Grace, 44, 107
  Lettice, 43
  Mary, 43
  Ruth, 44
  Sarah, 45
  Thomas, 43, 230, 235
Tilley }
Tillie } Ann, 10
  Edith May, 250
  Edward, 10, 14, 79
  Elizabeth, 10, 11, 14
  John, 10, 11, 14, 63, 79, 127
Tilson, Ruth, 246

Tinkham }
Tincom }
Tinkom }
Tinckum } Ebenezer, 221
Tinkcum }
Tinkcom }
  Ephraim, 64, 221-223
  Isaac, 222
  Jeremiah, 221
  John, 221
  Martha, 220
  Peter, 221
  Samuel, 223
Tinker, Thomas, 10, 14, 79
Tisdale }
Tisdall } John, 6
Tobey }
Toby } Frank Bassett, 59
  Jane, 107
Tocomawas, Abraham, 178
Tolman }
Tollman } Bethiah, 238
  Elizabeth, 108
  Hannah, 166
  Joseph, 45, 238
  Mary, 45
  Mercy, 235
Tompkins, Hamilton B., 121
Torrey, Belle M., 191
  Caleb, 45
  James, 93, 134
  Keziah, 165
  Mary, 45
Totman, Mary, 166
  Sarah, 238
  Thomas, 238
Tower, Charlemagne, 56
  Deborah, 108
  Hannah, 167
  Jemima, 107
  mrs. Levi, 249
  Samuel, 167
Tracy }
Tracie } ——, 37, 105
  ensign, 242, 245
  Jedediah, 105
  Jeremiah, 178
  John, 40
  Jonathan, 38
  Nathan, 105
  Rebecca, 153
  Samuel, 102, 105
  Sarah, 153
  sergt., 37
  Stephen, 153, 159, 230
  Thomas, 38
  Tryphosa, 153
Treat }
Treet } ——, 40
  Dorothy, 194
Tremere, Deborah, 108
Trevore, William, 11
Troop, ——, 42
Tubbs, Bethiah, 45
  Morris, 45
Turner, ——, 109
  Abiel, 235
  Abiezer, 43
  Abigail, 109, 234, 235
  Amos, 44
  Bethiah, 238
  Catharine, 166
  Deborah, 167
  Elisha, 234, 235
  Elizabeth, 165
  Eunice, 238
  Ezekiel, 108, 235
  Fear, 45
  Frederic Alonzo, 63
  George C., 106, 164, 192
  Grace, 43, 44, 107

Index of Persons.

Turner *cont'd*, Hannah, 44
  James, 107, 167
  Jemima, 235
  Jesse, 107
  John, 3, 8, 10, 15, 35, 79, 192
  Jonathan, 109
  Joshua, 238
  Leah, 235
  Lettice, 43
  Lurana, 235
  Lydia, 46, 167
  Mary, 45, 107, 192
  Mehitable, 44
  Mercy, 234
  Priscilla, 46, 164
  Prudence, 235
  Rachel, 108
  Richard, 108
  Ruth, 35, 108
  Sarah, 109
  Seth, 44
  Thomas, 107
Tuttle, mrs. Elias A., 51
Tyler, Edward Royall, 51
  Henry Whitney, 251
  mrs. John, 115
  Zebulon, 38
Tyng, Edward, 68

Underhill, mrs. Charles William, 117, 185

Vandwozer / Vondwozer \ ——, 244, 245
Van Dyke, Harry Weston, 60, 189, 190
Varney, Carolyn S., 117
Vassall / Varssall \ William, 92
Vaughan, Daniel, 224
  Ebenezer, 223
  Elisha, 221
  Elizabeth, 223
  George, 223
  Hannah, 223
  Jabez, 221
  Joseph, 219, 221, 223
Viall, mrs. Christopher Colson, 55
Vilas, Anne Ashmun, 254
  Percival Madden, 254
Vinal, Deborah, 46
  Desire, 165
  Elizabeth, 45
  Ezekiel, 43
  Hannah, 43
  Ignatius, 167
  Israel, 166
  Issacher, 46
  Jacob, 46
  John, 44
  Joseph, 47
  Lydia, 46
  Martha, 47
  Mary, 46, 237
  Mercy, 166
  Nicholas, 165
  Patience, 167
  Priscilla, 46
  Sarah, 43, 44, 168
  Stephen, 43
  Tabitha, 43, 109
Vining, Mark Lyman, 249
Vinton, Charles Harrod, 56
Vollmer, mrs. Henry, 51

Wade, Elizabeth, 45
  Hannah, 43
  Jacob, 45
  Joseph, 108
  Nathaniel, 43
  Rachel, 108
  Sarah, 46

Wadham / Woddam \ ——, 101, 242
Wadley, mrs. Dole, 184
Wadsworth, Abiah, 115
  Christopher, 203
Walker, mrs. George Hiram, 184
  Sarah, 256
Wallen, Joyce, 24, 153
  Ralph, 153, 230
Waller, ——, 241
Walworth / Wolworth \ ——, 180
  Samuel, 179, 180
  Thomas, 105
Ward, ——, 218
  capt., 241
  mrs. George Arthur, 116, 120
Warner, mrs. Charles H., 253
  Lucien Calvin, 52
Warren / Waren \ Abigail, 152
  Alse, 208
  Anna, 152
  Charles Elliot, 52
  Edward, 208
  Elizabeth, 30, 152, 157, 160, 208
  George Herbert, 121
  Henry Herbert, 121
  Hope, 208
  Jabez, 128
  James, 208
  John, 208
  Joseph, 99, 152
  Mary, 152, 208
  Mercy, 208
  Nathaniel, 99, 152, 256
  Patience, 208
  Pelham Winslow, 121
  Richard, 10, 14, 51-53, 56-58, 79, 113, 115, 116-121, 123, 125, 127, 128, 152, 183-186, 188, 190, 228, 230, 249-251, 253
  Sarah, 152, 208, 256
  Walter P., 191
  mrs. Walter Phelps, 186
  William Watts Jones, 53
  Winslow, 48, 122
Washburn / Washburne / Washbone \ Hempstead, 188
  Ichabod, 115
  John, 6, 96
  Seth, 249
  Sylvia, 115
Wason, Ann, 107
  Thomas, 107
Waterbarry, capt., 241
Waterman, ——, 102, 241, 243
  Anthony, 234
  Bethiah, 177
  David, 102
  Elizabeth, 246
  Ezekiel, 102
  Hannah, 247
  Isaac, 246
  lieut., 41, 180, 244
  Mary, 177
  Mercy, 247
  Robert, 213
  Samuel, 177
  Sarah, 234
  Silas, 181, 242
  Thomas, 247
Waters, Henry F., 230
Watrous, Benjamin Prentis, 189
Way, Lillian Minnie, 185
  mrs. William Bond, 184
Webb / Web \ Adey, 157, 200, 215
Webster, ——, 181
  Ebenezer, 38, 40
  James Reed, 59, 60

278 Index of Persons.

Webster *cont'd.* mrs. } Shadrach, 41
mrs. William Henry, 249
Wedg, Joshua, 195
  Rebecca, 195
  William, 195
Weed, Edward Franklin, 52
Weeks, Andrew Gray, 36, 49, 115
  Ezra, 36
  Nathaniel, 36
  Rachel, 35
Welch, Ashbel, 56
  mrs. Ashbel, 114
  Ashbel Russell, 56
Wendell, mrs. Ten Eyck, 116
Wentworth, ——, 241
West, Pelatiah, 115
Weston, ——, 81, 156
  Desire, 245, 246
  Edmund, 178, 213, 245
  Francis, 86
  Isaac, 245
  Jacob, 246
  Nathan, 245, 246
  Rebecca, 245, 246
  Thomas, 2
Wetherell } Daniel, 2, 71, 72, 74, 75, 170, 226
Withrel
  Grace, 71, 74, 75, 170, 226
  Hannah, 74, 170
  Joseph, 46
  Lydia, 46
  Mary, 74, 75
  William, 74, 192
Whipple, Daniel, 40, 178
  Dorcas, 246
  mrs. Stephen M., 191
Whitcomb, Hannah, 44
  Mary, 46
  Noah, 46
White, Abigail, 45
  Daniel, 130, 131
  Desire, 46
  Elizabeth, 45
  Gowin, 95
  mrs. John Daugherty, 50, 120
  Jonathan, 130
  Joseph, 234
  Mary, 45
  Mercy, 130
  Peregrine, 10, 13, 16, 55, 127, 129-131, 150
  Rebecca, 46
  Resolved, 10, 13, 16, 92, 127, 150, 188, 192
  Sarah, 44, 47, 130
  Susanna, 10, 12, 88, 127
  Temperance, 234, 236
  Timothy, 44
  William, 10, 12, 13, 55, 79, 88, 117, 119, 125, 127, 188, 228
Whiton
Whitton
Witon } Abijah, 164
Whiten
Whitten
  Bethiah, 177
  Deborah, 44
  Elisha, 247
  Enoch, 106
  Jael, 165
  Joanna, 247
  John, 177
  Leah, 106
  Margaret, 106
  Mary, 164
  Thomas, 177
Whitfield, ——, 38
Whiting, capt., 102, 241
  col., 41, 102-104, 243
  mrs. William Sawin, 51
Whittlesey, mrs. George D., 54
Whitman, ——, 182

Whitmore, W. H., 22
Whitney } major, 243
Whitnie
Wier, ——, 242
Wight, ——, 180, 181
  John, 179
Wilder, Jabez, 235
  Martha, 235
  Roger, 9, 11
Wilkes, William, 200
Wilkinson, mrs. Henry W., 49, 191
Willard, Bradford Holt, 191
  James LeBaron, 121
  Marion Bradford, 191
  Susan Barker, 49
Willet, Thomas, 214, 216
Williams, ——, 40
  Joseph, 38
  Lawrence, 253
  Mary, 109
  mrs. Mary Loring, 59
  Roger, 25, 28
  Seth, 109
  Thomas, 10, 15, 79
  William, 39
Williamson, ——, 232
  Sarah, 108
  mrs. Irving, 190
Wills, William, 92
Wilson, mrs. John R., 58
Wing, Ebenezer, 108
  Elizabeth, 237
  Isaiah, 237
  Mary, 108
Winpenny, mrs. J. Bolton, 56, 187, 191
Winslow } Ann, 89, 90
Wynslow
  Edward, 9, 12, 13, 16, 24, 27, 29, 30, 34, 67, 79, 82, 83, 85, 88, 89, 125-127, 150, 154, 157, 158, 185, 197, 200, 203, 215, 216, 227, 228, 238, 239
  Elizabeth, 9, 88, 192, 238, 239
  general, 42
  Gilbert, 10, 15, 79, 228
  John, 27, 28, 65-71, 150, 151, 157, 214, 229
  Joseph, 67, 70
  Josiah, 81, 239, 240
  Kenelm, 82, 200
  Mary, 16, 63, 65, 67-69, 89, 127, 151
  Parnell, 67
  Samuel, 67
  Sarah, 67
  Susanna, 16, 150
  William Copley, 54
Winter, Christopher, 133, 134
  John, 133, 134
Winthrop } John, 26, 28
Wynthrop
Withrow, mrs. Thomas Foster, 59, 123
Witter, Dorothy, 195
Wolcott, Roger, 126
Wood, ——, 231
  Abiel, 220
  Abijah, 220
  Ann, 223
  Barnabas, 247
  David, 219, 224
  Elizabeth, 144
  Ephraim, 221
  Hannah, 247
  Henry, 29
  Jabez, 223, 224
  John, 136, 137, 215, 224
  Mary, 108, 144, 219
  Mary Emma, 50
  Rebecca, 221
  Samuel, 221-223
Woodman, ——, 217, 218
Woodruff } ——, 242
Woodroff
  mrs. James P., 52

Woodward } Molly, 236
Woodard }
 Sarah, 236
 Walter, 92
Woodworth, Anna, 44, 46
 Benjamin, 46
 Eleanor, 44
 Elisha, 44
 Hannah, 46
 James, 106
 Mary, 108
 Robert, 108
 Sarah, 106
Wooster, colonel, 100
Wootton, mrs. Edwin H., 186
Worthington, ——, 39, 102
 Harry Cushman, 58
Wright } Adam, 178
Rite }
 George Edward, 253
 John, 236
 Molly, 236

Wright }
Rite } Pamelia Keith, 191
cont'd. }
 Priscilla, 26, 160, 202, 203, 205
 William, 24-27, 150, 200, 202, 203, 229

Yearington, Peter, 105
Yergason, Henry Christopher, 59, 124, 185
Young, Elizabeth, 44
 Hannah, 167
 mrs. Horace Gedney, 190
 Jael, 165
 Joseph, 43
 Joshua, 44
 Margaret, 45
 Mary, 45
 Lydia, 43
 Robert, 45
 Thomas, 45, 165, 167
 mrs. William Hill, 183

Zabriskie, mrs. N. Lansing, 54

INDEX OF PLACES.

Abington, Mass., 50, 237
Albany, N. Y., 52, 124, 190
Amsterdam, Netherlands, 19
Anchrum, N. Y., 244
Andover, Conn., 101, 181
Ardmore, Penna., 57, 122, 187
Auburn, N. Y., 53
Augusta, Ga., 52
Austerfield, Eng., 251

Bahama Islands, 11
Bangor, Me., 184, 249
Barbadoes, 13
Barley, Eng., 73
Barnstable, Mass., 110, 137, 182, 183, 236
Bluefish River, Duxbury, Mass., 214
Bolton, Conn., 101, 181
Boston, Mass., 1, 34, 39, 47, 50, 51, 63, 65, 67, 68, 69, 113-117, 124, 126, 128, 136, 140, 175, 176, 182-184, 240, 248-250
Bozrah, Conn., 41, 42
Brabant, Netherlands, 21
Braintree, Mass., 233, 236
Brewster, Mass., 249
Brewster Plain, Norwich, Conn., 8
Bridgeport, Conn., 122, 252
Bridgewater, Mass., 168
Bristol, R. I., 115
Brookhaven, L. I., 225, 227
Brookline, Mass., 50, 51, 115-117, 183, 184, 249
Brooklyn, N. Y., 52, 55, 122, 186
Buffalo, N. Y., 117
Burial Hill, Plymouth, Mass., 87

Cambridge, Mass., 89, 115, 183, 184, 220, 224, 249
Canaan, Conn., 101, 243
Canderhook, N. Y., 100
Canterbury, Conn., 104
Cape Cod, Mass., 78, 86, 87
Cape Cod Harbor, Mass., 86
Carver, Mass., 174
Cazenovia, N. Y., 116
Central Falls, R. I., 116
Charlestown, Mass., 25, 239
Chestnut Hill, Mass., 183
Chicago, Ill., 57-59, 187, 188, 252, 253
Cincinnati, O., 60, 123, 188, 189, 253
Clark's Island, Plymouth, Mass., 87
Claverick, N. Y., 243-245
Cleveland, O., 250
Clifton Heights, Penna., 56, 122, 187
Cohasset, Mass., 183
Colorado Springs, Colo., 124
Concord, Mass., 217, 218
Connecticut, 100, 243
Cornhill, Truro, Mass., 86
Cornwall, Conn., 101
Crown Point, N. Y., 38, 39
Cumberland, Me., 35

Danbury, Conn., 55
Darbyshire, Eng., 8, 73
Dartmouth, Mass., 147, 168
Davenport, Iowa, 51
Deering Centre, Me., 116
Delft, Netherlands, 19, 21
Delft Haven, Netherlands, 251
Denver, Colo., 251
Detroit, Mich., 50, 115, 188, 252

Dorking, Eng., 231, 232
Dort, Netherlands, 21
Duluth, Minn., 50
Duxbury, Mass., 6-8, 34, 64, 96, 97, 135, 163, 167, 183, 213, 214, 225, 234, 235, 245, 250

Eastham, Mass., 110, 111, 135, 215
East Hartford, Conn., 101
East Orange, N. J., 186
Edinburgh, Scot., 34
Elmhurst, Ill., 187
El Paso, Texas, 184
Enfield, Mass., 116
England, 2, 11-15, 19, 21, 61, 88, 89, 104, 216, 230, 231
Evanston, Ill., 58, 59, 116
Everett, Mass., 115, 116
Exeter, N. H., 89

Fairhaven, Mass., 184
Farmington, Conn., 101, 242
Flanders, Belgium, 21
Fort Edward, N. Y., 40, 102
Fort Hill, Conn., 41
Fort Sheridan, Ill., 186
Fort William Henry, N. Y., 179
Freetown, Mass., 110, 164
Friesland, Netherlands, 21

Goshen, Conn., 101
Grand Rapids, Mich., 53
Great Britain, 17
Green Bush, N. Y., 100
Groton, Conn., 39, 40, 103, 179
Gueldres, Netherlands, 21
Guilford, Conn., 140

Hague, The, Netherlands, 19
Hainault, Belgium, 21
Halifax, Mass., 174, 234
Hanover, Mass., 106-108, 166, 167, 234-237, 249
Harlaem, Netherlands, 19
Hartford, Conn., 55, 101, 122, 180, 181, 251, 252
Hartland, Wis., 253
Herndon, Va., 190
Harrington, Conn., 101
Hingham, Mass., 34, 106-109, 116, 164-168, 234-238, 249
Hobes Hole, Plymouth, Mass., 230
Holland, States of, 19, 21
Hornellsville, N. Y., 122
Hyde Park, Vt., 36

Irving-on-Hudson, N. Y., 52

Jamestown, Va., 2
Janesville, Wis., 53, 61
Jefferson, Wis., 58
Jones River, Plymouth, Mass., 7, 87, 216
Jones River Pond, Plymouth, Mass., 175

Kingston, Mass., 114, 174, 191

Lake George, N. Y., 39, 40
Lakenham, Plymouth, Mass., 64
Lansing, Mich., 117
Lawrence, Mass., 50
Lebanon, Conn., 101, 181, 193

Index of Places. 281

Leyden, Holland, 19, 29, 113, 251
Lime Rock, Conn., 122
Lisbon, Portugal, 40
Litchfield, Conn., 52, 101, 242
Little Rock, Ark., 186
Littleton, N. H., 50
Lockport, N. Y., 53, 186
London, Eng., 8, 219
Long Island, N. Y., 225
Low Countries, 21
Lynn, Mass., 184

Maidstone, Eng., 74
Malden, Mass., 117
Manchester, Ky., 50
Mass., 134
Maquoketa, Iowa, 51
Marietta, O., 253
Marinette, Wis., 53
Marshfield, Mass., 64, 108, 110, 129, 130, 164, 165-167, 213, 234, 237, 238, 256
Martha's Vineyard, Mass., 140
Massachusetts, 26, 28, 81, 89, 93, 160, 248
Medford, Mass., 50, 184, 249
Middleborough, Mass., 130, 192, 219, 221, 222, 239, 247, 256
Milwaukee, Wis., 184, 185, 253
Minneapolis, Minn., 52, 53, 61, 254
Mohegan (Norwich), Conn., 72, 74-76, 170, 171, 172, 193
Monongahela River, 39
Morrisville, Vt., 1, 50
Mystic, Conn., 103, 180

Netherlands, Protestant, 19
Newark, N. J., 52
Newburgh, N. Y., 53
New England, 2, 7, 9, 65, 68, 69, 78, 85, 91, 93, 96, 129, 133-135, 137, 200, 202, 213-215, 217, 230
Newent, Conn., 40, 101
New Haven, Conn., 50, 53, 187, 252
New London, Conn., 38, 53, 55, 71-73, 77, 170, 226
Newport, R. I., 250
Newton, Mass., 116
Newton Centre, Mass., 116, 184, 249
Newtonville, Mass., 116
New York, N. Y., 52, 53, 55, 116, 121, 186, 251
Noank, Conn., 41, 105
North Pembroke, Mass., 174
North River, Mass., 94, 213
North Yarmouth, Me., 34, 35
Norton, Mass., 167
Norwell, Mass., 106, 164, 192
Norwich, Conn. (see also Mohegan), 8, 36, 41, 42, 53, 101, 168, 173, 180
N. V., 55
Norwich Town, Conn., 39
Nottinghamshire, Eng., 7

Oakland, Cal., 115
Oak Park, Ill., 58, 188, 253
Oblong, N. Y., 243
Ohio, 39
Orange, N. J., 121

Painesville, O., 55
Pamet River, Truro, Mass., 86
Pembroke, Mass., 64, 106, 166, 168, 235, 236
Philadelphia, Penna., 56, 57, 122, 187
Pittsburg, Penna., 57
Plymouth } Mass., 5, 7, 23, 24, 26, 27, 29,
New Plymouth } 53, 64, 79, 87, 91-93, 95, 96, 98, 106, 129, 132-134, 139-141, 145, 148, 157, 158, 162, 174-176, 197, 200, 202, 203, 213-216, 219, 225, 226, 231, 239, 250, 254-256
Plymouth, Eng., 29, 86

Plympton, Mass., 128, 174, 175, 191, 192, 245, 246
Pocatanock, Conn., 38, 40, 41, 178, 244
Portland, Me., 64
Portsmouth, N. H., 115, 184
Preston, Conn., 42, 73, 101, 102, 104, 168-172, 193, 194, 196, 197, 255
Preston City, Conn., 255
Providence, R. I., 116, 117, 220, 250

Quincy, Mass., 50, 89

Redlands, Cal., 89
Rehoboth, Mass., 115
Rhode Island, 102
Rochester, Mass., 168
N. Y., 186
Rockford, Ill., 59
Rome, Italy, 19
Rotterdam, Netherlands, 19
Russia, 20
Ryegate, Eng., 218

Salem, Mass., 10, 12, 28, 192, 239
Salisbury, Conn., 243
Sandwich, Mass., 106, 137, 138, 215, 216
Saratoga, N. Y., 100
Saugus, Mass., 25
Saybrook, Conn., 39, 102
Scituate, Mass., 5, 8, 35, 39, 42, 64, 91-94, 106-110, 133, 164-168, 192, 233-238
Scrooby, Eng., 7, 251
Secunke, Mass., 216
Setauket, L. I., 225
Sewickley, Penna., 252
Sheffield, Mass., 243
Sistersville, W. Va., 61
Somerville, Mass., 115, 249, 250
Southampton, Eng., 11, 86
South Orange, N. J., 50
Southport, Conn., 55
South Scituate, Mass., 106, 164, 192
South Weymouth, Mass., 115
Sparkill, N. Y., 251
Springfield, Mass., 116
Squantum, Quincy, Mass., 89, 248, 249
Stillwater, N. Y., 100
Stonington, Conn., 39, 40, 105, 107
St. Paul, Minn., 53, 115, 186, 251, 254
Stoughton, Mass., 164
Suffield, Conn., 234
Syracuse, N. Y., 52

Taunton, Mass., 109, 116, 166
Troy, N. Y., 186, 251
Truro, Mass., 86

Utica, N. Y., 186
Utrecht, Netherlands, 21

Vineland, N. J., 50
Virginia, 2, 16, 78, 230-232
Voluntown, Conn., 37

Wales, Conn., 38
Waltham, Mass., 116, 183
Warsaw, N. Y., 53
Washington, D. C., 61, 124, 190, 253, 254
Watertown, Mass., 90
Wellingsley, Plymouth, Mass., 134, 136
Wells, Me., 166
Westerly, R. I., 40
West Indies, 11, 104
Weymouth, Mass., 93, 108
Willimantic, Conn., 55
Windham, Conn., 102, 114, 195
Windsor, Conn., 64
Woburn, Mass., 50, 108
Woodside, Md., 61

Ypsilanti, Mich., 249

www.ingramcontent.com/pod-product-compliance
Lightning Source LLC
Chambersburg PA
CBHW071422150426
43191CB00008B/1008